BORN UNDER A BAD SIGN

by TONY PALMER

Pictures by Ralph STEADMAN

FOREWORD by John LENNON

Typeset by Jonathan Downes, Ian Cramer and Jessica Taylor
Cover and Layout by SPiderKaT for CFZ Communications
Using Microsoft Word 2000, Microsoft Publisher 2000, Adobe Photoshop CS.

First published in 1970
This edition published in Great Britain by Gonzo Multimedia
c/o Brooks City,
6th Floor New Baltic House
65 Fenchurch Street,
London EC3M 4BE
Fax: +44 (0)191 5121104
Tel: +44 (0) 191 5849144
International Numbers:
Germany: Freephone 08000 825 699
USA: Freephone 18666 747 289

ISBN: 978-1-908728-49-4

BORN UNDER A BAD SIGN

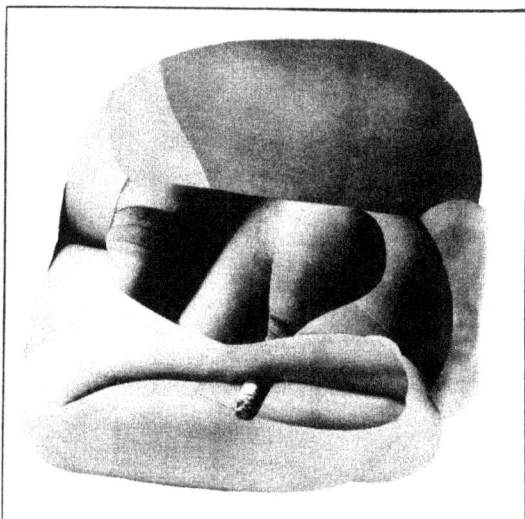

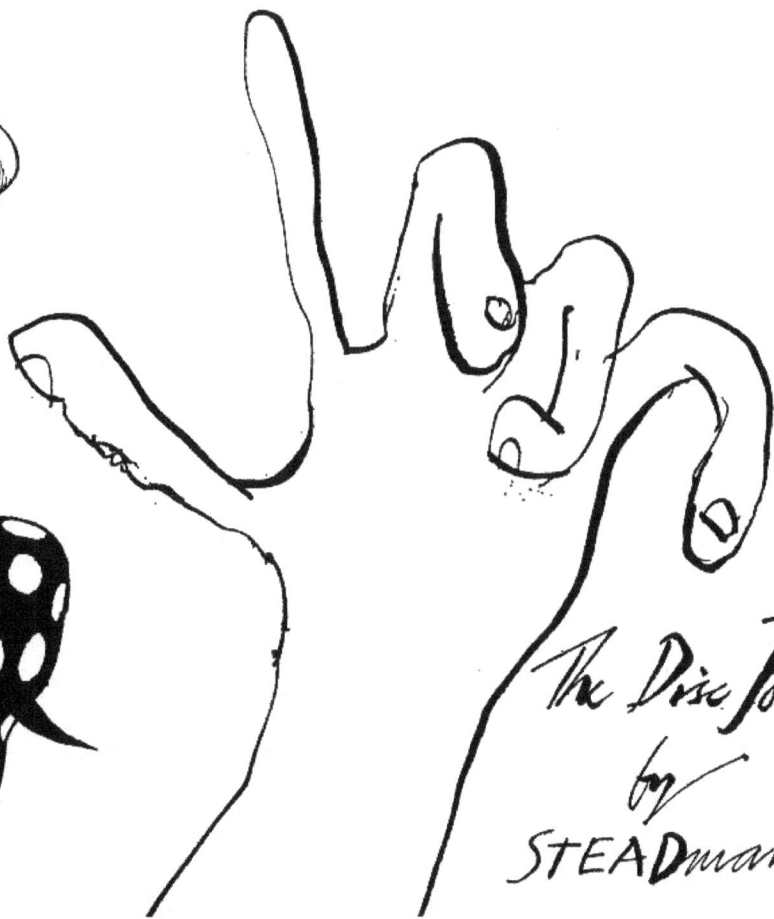

The Disc Jockey by STEADman

INTRODUCTION TO NEW EDITION

Reading this text after so long feels as if I had been transported back into another century. Which indeed I had, given that the events and feelings described belong to the 20th Century, and here we are in the 21st.

But it is almost as if the late sixties are as remote to us now as were the Napoleonic Wars to those of us who grew up after the Second World War. Part of history, curious, but not directly relevant to our problems today.

All generations imagine that theirs was a golden age, and it's hard to deny that those whose youth was spent in the 1960s and 70s will ever be convinced otherwise. Of course we were foolish, arrogant, naïve and filled with boundless energy. Such is the prerogative of youth. It's also hard to deny that many of our hopes and aspirations and revolutionary ideals have since been dashed upon the rocks of economic reality and political expediency. Very few of us, if any, have turned out as we would have hoped. Such is the penalty of maturity, or at least what passes for maturity.

Yet we have one undeniable witness to our true feelings of that time, unsullied by hindsight, uncensored by wishful thinking – the music and words of a galaxy of singer-songwriters, some stupid, some meaningless, some grotesque, but a surprising number eloquent, passionate, committed and prophetic, and even a few of genius, whose achievements I believe will stand for a considerable time to come. After all, it is by the poetry and sculpture and architecture and philosophy of the Athenians, for instance, that we remember them, rather than their wars against Sparta. Likewise, I am sure it is by the music of The Beatles and the songs of Bob Dylan that future generations will recall the 60s and 70s, rather than the absurd posturings of LBJ, Richard Nixon or Harold Wilson, posturings which now seem increasingly petty and squalid.

This book originally came about because I had made a film for the BBC entitled 'All My Loving', taking (at John Lennon's suggestion) The Beatles song of the same name as its cue. And that film had come about because an earlier film I had made (about the composer Benjamin Britten) had had the good fortune to be the first ever BBC colour film to be networked in the United States, by NBC on 'The Bell Telephone Hour'. Flushed with this apparent success, and knowing that I had many friends in the rock 'n' roll world, the BBC then asked me to make a film which 'explained' what was happening in 1967/8, which they could *hear* (they could hardly have avoided it) but could not see clearly for its significance.

Following Lennon's advice, I began to film those groups he reckoned were worthy of serious attention–Cream, Jimi Hendrix, Pete Townshend and The Who, Frank Zappa and The Mothers of Invention, Pink Floyd, Eric Burdon and The Animals and, of course, The Beatles. My first surprise was, that with marginal exceptions (the obvious one being The Beatles), none of these groups had at that time appeared on British or American television, and this in spite of being worshipped by countless fans across the globe. Not unexpectedly, for this reason alone the film caused a storm. An even bigger surprise, however, was the public reaction. Hostile would be a charitable description. Even those whom I admired, such as David Attenborough, subsequently world famous, and justifiably so, for his films about the natural world, but then Director of Programmes for BBC Television, wrote an internal memo stating that as long as he was in charge "this film would never be shown". Fortunately, he resigned soon after writing this memo, and the film was shown. I should add that since then he and I have become good friends.

Upon reflection, it was what these various musicians said, rather than the explosive nature of their performances which caused such offence, although film of Hendrix masturbating with his guitar and Townshend smashing his equipment to pieces was hardly likely to endear these performers to a wider audience. And yet what they said seems, to us now, harmless enough – we want to change the world, no more war, freedom of expression, relax the drug laws, particularly those related to cannabis. It's not as if they were advocating sexual permissiveness or violent revolution, although it should not be forgotten that in England at least homosexuality between consenting adults as a criminal offence, not to mention censorship of what could appear on the public stage, had only been abolished – I was going to say, within living memory – in fact, the year *after* 'Sergeant Pepper's Lonely Hearts Club Band' had appeared. In retrospect, therefore, I am amazed that what they said, some of which is recounted in this book, was and is so restrained.

My memory of the late 60s is that we were rather prudish, sexually unadventurous, somewhat ignorant of drugs and certainly disorganised when it came to organising *The* Revolution. Of course there were exceptions, firebrands who caught the headlines and demanded attention. There were also, as there always are, moments when the 'establishment' felt so threatened by what it perceived of as 'interference' in the natural order of things that it reacted with predictable silliness and often harm. To lock up Mick Jagger for possessing an insignificant amount of cannabis was absurd, although there were some who, for other reasons, wished they had thrown the key away. To send to prison three young editors of a juvenile comic called '*Oz*', about which I have written elsewhere, was more the consequence of a lazy and corrupt judiciary than a sensible reaction to the charge of pornography being levelled against them. Ironically, they were eventually 'saved' by the Lord Chief Justice himself who, at the Appeal hearing, asked his clerk during the luncheon break to go to nearby Soho and with £5 buy whatever 'pornography' he could find. When the clerk returned with his haul, the Chief Justice immediately and rightly dismissed the case against '*Oz*' because, by comparison, its questionable content was totally harmless.

Again, it's not as if we had a common agenda, a blue print for action. True, we were all against the Vietnam War; true, both in England and America we were all convinced that the police were corrupt; true, we all thought the Ku Klux Klan, for instance, was a monstrous outfit of hooligans that deserved to be dumped in the waste-bin of history; true, we all thought most politicians were venal, untrustworthy and deserved contempt. But in these beliefs, time has proved to be on our side, as The Rolling Stones unwittingly predicted.

'Talking about my generation', as The Who sang. That is really what this book is about. Don't expect coherence or The Ten Commandments. Don't expect explanation or apology. I wondered, as I was re-reading the text, whether I should try to up-date it or even, occasionally, knock some sense into parts of it. In the end, I resisted, and other than altering the tense of some of the factual reporting (it was daft, for instance, to describe something which happened over thirty years ago as 'recently') and removing my then fatuous habit of writing in the third person, I have changed very little. That is not to say that I don't regret some of what I wrote. Passages of wild fantasy, of indefensible hyperbole and of lurid prejudice, I have left unvarnished, probably more fool me. But it is what it is, and I think on balance properly reflects what we felt and were enriched by at the time. It was a limited time, perhaps a blinkered time, but I remain convinced it was a golden time, unmatched since. I believe we can learn from it, and above all take heart from it. Young people today have nothing comparable to offer.

I am grateful beyond words that Joe Petro III has chosen to rescue this book, long out of print. Walt Bartholomew has exercised enormous patience as I fiddled around with the text to his increasing distraction and, for all I know, irritation. John Lennon, sadly, can no longer answer for his influence on the book or on me. I had met him while I was still at Cambridge University. For some reason which remains a mystery to me, we found common cause, and friendship. I think he viewed my intellectual pretensions with suspicion; I certainly viewed some of his obsessions as wayward. I also think some of the latter-day claims for his 'genius' exaggerated, although he was a formidable talent. But together with Dylan, there are no better lyric poets in the English language in the last part of the 20th century. Dylan at least has as great a claim to the Nobel Prize for Literature as anyone else who has won it during his time.

And then there is Ralph Steadman. When I originally asked him to provide illustrations for my text, I knew only his scabrous cartoons, and it was not until the collages began to arrive that I realised here was a major satirist comparable with Hogarth and Doré. Looking now at his work, I appreciate its power and unnerving accuracy as never before. Beautifully reproduced here, these drawings truly are works of genius, and I am thankful to him for that and to his ongoing friendship and that of his wife, Anna.

So finally a personal note. The month the first invitation to reprint this book arrived, my daughter was born. She joined her brother, then just over a year old (later another brother), to bring unimaginable happiness to my first ever family. In years to come, I hope they will read this book and gain some insight into a time long, long ago, in another century, when their father first experienced the excitement and joy of what it is to be alive.

Tony Palmer, Pigniu, 2011

PEACE  TO

Tony Palmer
and his readers

GIVE PEACE A CHANCE!

love John Lennon & Yoko Ono
June 10. 1969.

ACKNOWLEDGEMENTS

I am indebted to a great number of people in the writing of this document. Particularly, my thanks to Horace Judson of *Time Magazine* and John Drummond of the BBC; to Helen Dawson, Richard Findlater and John Thompson of *The Observer* who encouraged me to write at all about this exceedingly complicated subject; to Richard Neville and to the musicians within who allowed me to talk to them, especially Paul McCartney, a conversation with whom made me begin to understand pop music; and to John and Yoko Lennon for their precise Introduction. I owe an obvious debt to Ralph Steadman who has complemented what I wrote perfectly. Thanks are due also to Mary Jackson and Pauline Swindells who typed it all out.

I need hardly say that any of the people quoted within are not responsible for the overall tone of the book. That is my fault.

I am also grateful to the following who allowed me to quote from material within their copyright: Chappell & Co. Ltd. for an extract from 'Call me Irresponsible', Mirage Music Ltd. for 'Street Fighting Man', Tip Top Tunes for Lulu's song 'Bet Cher'; to Frank Zappa Music, a subsidiary of Third Story Music, BMI, for the extract from 'Mr. Green Genes' by Frank Zappa; to Shroeder Music Publishing Company, Ltd., for the extract from the Jimi Hendrix recording 'Third Stone Under the Sun'; to Messrs. Lennon and McCartney for the extracts from lyrics of their composition; to Mr. Leslie Fiedler and Partisan Review for the extract from 'The New Mutants' (© Partisan Review 1965) included in *Innovations*; to Faber and Faber for the quotation from T. S. Eliot's 'The Hollow Men' included in his 'Collected Poems. 1909-1962'; to *The International Times* and to the *Record Mirror*.

Preface

This is not in any sense a history of pop music. Nor is it an explanation or analysis of pop music. It is merely a collection of observations concerning the phenomenon incorrectly described as 'pop music', with some indication as to how this phenomenon has influenced the thinking and social habits of young people at the beginning of the seventies. Some of the observations are mine, but most derive from the pop musicians themselves. I do not know whether pop music is good or bad and I'm not concerned with its musical stature or social significance. These things are for you to decide. Such conclusions as might become evident in the course of the book, therefore, are yours and not mine.

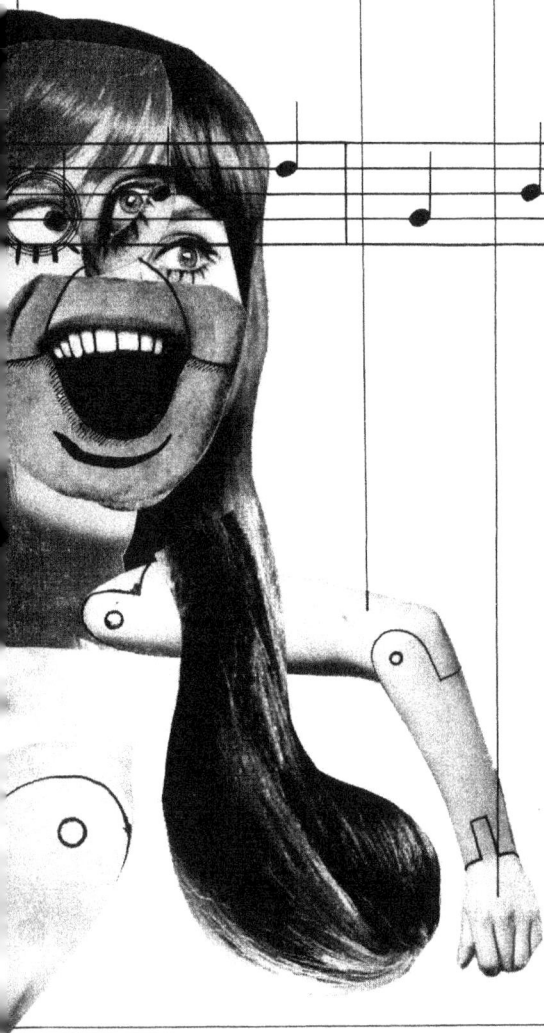

Eurovision Song Contest
by
Ralph STEADMAN

For Angelo, Apollonia & Gabriele

'Amongst thinking people,' said one,
'this will do you a great deal of harm.
That is because pop music and serious
music *cannot*, de facto, go together.'

Chapter One

On Thursday, May 29, 1969, at 7.45 pm, six or seven policemen burst into the London home of Mick Jagger in Cheyne Walk, Chelsea. Jagger told me: 'I didn't get the chance to say anything because one of them stuck his foot in the door. They kept me in the dining-room while they searched the place.' After about an hour, Jagger and his friend Marianne Faithfull were taken to Chelsea police station and accused of possessing cannabis. At the preliminary hearing the following morning, a large crowd had gathered outside Marlborough Street Magistrates' Court. 'We love you Mick!' one cried whilst Michael Philip Jagger and Marianne Evelyn Dunbar were being formally charged within. Television cameras peered at the front door of the Court awaiting their exit. The public must be told about these curious happenings. Jagger left by a rear exit, unseen. Later he told me: 'It was all very boring.'

To some, the re-arrest of Mick Jagger on a drugs offence seemed the proper reward for a young man who somehow had got off very lightly from his previous conviction. An opinion poll at the time had showed that over fifty per cent of the population thought that his three-month prison sentence for possessing four pep pills which he had bought legally was far too lenient. This was also the man who had since boasted of his illegitimate liaison with Miss Faithfull, who had consistently attacked or ignored the accepted moral and social values paid lip-service to by the rest of the community and who, because of his absurd profession, could never have done an honest day's work in his life.

To others, however, it seemed that Jagger's re-arrest was the action of a vengeful Law. Having been previously cheated of its rightful prey through a cunning lobby of leftists and deviationists, it had waited its chance to punish again those who defied it. But now the punishment no longer even remotely resembled the crime. It seemed the product of a righteous society seeking to demoralise its young in defence of elders and betters who had the power and who were determined to hang on to it. Jagger in particular must be put down. After all, he was a leader of youth, a pop star - and pop music, with its loudness, its vulgarity, its aggressiveness and its wealth, represented the greatest menace of all. It rarely occurred to anyone that, in fact, there was no such thing as 'pop music'.

Was one to believe, for example, that the technical virtuosity of a guitarist such as Jimi Hendrix and the musical illiteracy of a group like The Love Affair should both be described as 'pop music'? They were totally different not only in degree but in kind. Was one to say that a singer with the spine-chilling anger of Bob Dylan was in the same world, let alone the same league, as a singer with the raucous, tear-jerking tastelessness of Vikki Carr? Yet, for better or worse, all four were categorised as 'pop music'.

Pop is more misunderstood, misquoted, misrepresented and maligned than any other comparable phenomenon. Its products are often inflated out of existence through self-important and over-zealous praise, or else unnecessarily brought down by the adolescent and gossip-laden gruntings of many of those involved. The result has been that what is known as pop music has become confused and confusing. That some pop music may now have ceased to be popular and become music, is a possibility hardly given its proper chance to be heard. In the first place, neither this possibility nor a proper understanding of it has been encouraged by the communications media - radio, television, the news-papers; in second place, what is laughingly described as 'the enter-tainment industry' is, in England, at least, tightly controlled by a very small number of people who seem only to lust after those popularity polls called the Charts.

The Charts first took their name from a 1946 US sponsored radio show called 'Hit Parade'. In 1947 the *Melody Maker* started a column called 'Britain Top Tunes' calculated then on the sales not of discs but of sheet music. For years, the Charts were based upon an arbitrary and totally unscientific sampling of disc sales which reflect little except what is *already* being sponsored by radio, television and the newspapers. On radio, less than two per cent of air time already devoted to pop music is given over to non-chart sounds. Television, in the pursuit of a comprehensive understanding of pop music, devoted itself to spurious international bun-fights such as the Eurovision Song Contest, which even the Secretary of the Songwriters' Guild in 1969 dismissed as nothing but 'a useful publicity exercise for the industry and a pleasant outing for BBC officials'.

The official BBC entry for 1969, for instance, was titled 'Boom bang-a-bang', with a 'bang-a-bang, I love you' thrown in for good measure. 'It's an enriching experience,' one of the chief organisers told me. 'More than 200 million people watching the same thing at the same time - there's something wonderful about that.' It was almost as if someone had reported a major breakthrough in television, a totally new concept, which involved 200 million people sitting glued to a picture of a slice of bread. Said a spokesman: 'It was a moving moment'. One was never quite sure if one was listening to twenty-two songs being rendered by one singer or twenty-two singers rendering the same song.

The British 'entry' in 1969 was voted for by viewers watching a regular Light Entertainment Show during which six pre-selected songs were performed. That year it was the Lulu Show. What is not generally known, however, is that this same chief organiser, or one of his minions, had not only been responsible for the selection of the song-writers and the songs from which our entry was chosen (after the Music Publishers Association had submitted to the BBC a short list taken from its 400 members) but also had selected the singer who was to represent us; thus, viewers were only allowed to vote upon carefully selected material about which they had no say whatsoever.

In a previous year this carefully selected material had landed upon Cliff Richard. Said a spokesman: 'Cliff Richard can always show these Continentals a thing or two. He's very sexy - *and* he's religious.' He lost. So did Kenneth McKellar - described by our organiser as 'a straight singer' - who represented us in 1966. 'It wasn't fair,' said McKellar afterwords. 'The Swedes, the Norwegians, the Danes and the Finns all voted for one another.' The Spaniards, admittedly, were more equable. In 1968 they wouldn't let their first choice out of the country because he insisted on singing in his native Catalan. Instead, they sent the diminutive Massiel, who won. A grateful General Franco immediately made her a Dame of the Civil Order of Isabel the Catholic, and an English song-writer, Michael Julian, feeling the challenge of bigger things at last, translated the lyric into English. 'La, la, la' became, not surprisingly, 'She gives me love'. Mr. Julian was a Harley Street psychoanalyst.

Sandie Shaw presented Massiel with her crown, or prize as it's called, and was suddenly hit in the stomach - accidentally, it was reported - by a man dismantling the stage. Dismantling? Miss Shaw had to be helped from the arena.

The Eurovision Song Contest started in 1956 when TV was even more desperate than it is now to grab at anything which it thinks is International. Within a year, England was accusing other countries of rigging the voting and pulled out. England, of course, came back - to produce such memorable songs as 'Ring-a-Ding Girl' - remember that? And 'Looking High, High High'. Remember *that*? We did eventually win with 'Puppet on a String' - Miss Shaw again - which subsequently ran to 180 versions. And in 1969 we were allowed to choose from those six specially commissioned songs ranging from 'Boom bang-a-bang' (as above) to 'Bet cher, Bet cher'. Lulu gave them all equal verve and vigour. 'Get this understood, it's all for your good,' she sang, and concluded with a little ditty that had that specially international flavour - 'La la la la la la la la la la la la la, Come September, September, La la la la la la la la la la la la'.

According to its organisers, the Eurovision Song Contest *is* intended to represent all that is best in pop. The No. 1 song is tops in its field. But neither The Beatles nor the Stones, nor Donovan, nor Jimi Hendrix had ever entered or been entered. One particular song, 'Love is Blue', was a world-wide hit and topped the US charts for a month. In the Eurovision Song Contest, 'Love is Blue' had been placed next to last. There was a school of thought - headed again by such people as our chief organiser - that beat songs are less popular in continental Europe than ballads, a claim totally refuted by sales evidence. It was also claimed that many top artists refused to enter because of the fear of public defeat. A quick check revealed that most top artists have never been asked, and even those that have tended to refuse because of the appallingly low standard of most of the songs. 'A good song doesn't need a Festival,' Marcel Stellman, one-time head of the Continental branch of Decca Record Company, told me. 'The only people who can possibly benefit *are* the organisers.'

So the songs represented no-one and were representative of nothing except the Tin Pan Alley tradition of instant balladeering. Put in a boom-boom or two and a bit of hip swinging and you too can sing to 200 million. It seems that we were at the mercy of the taste, or lack of it, of the big boys who organised it all. One of these was telephoned by a colleague and asked if he would like Jimi Hendrix on one of his shows. 'No,' he said, 'Hendrix is not very popular.' (Hendrix was one of the five biggest money-spinners in Pop.) 'And anyway, we don't like the way he behaves on stage.' *That* was the view of most people, or so we were led to believe by the mass media.

Most people, it seems, think that pop music consists exclusively of songs that go 'la la, la la la' which were mostly created to satisfy recipe-crazed housewives. But the most cursory glance at all that is passing under the disguise of 'pop music' at the moment will reveal, even to the most prejudiced listener, that this is not so. But not only does much of what pop music has to offer never get on to radio or TV, it never gets anywhere else either.

Consider Bernard Delfont. Bernard Delfont, who started life as a tap-dancer, 'presented' the annual Royal Variety Performance which was supposed to include all that is best in the world of entertainment for that year. The 1968 show was remarkable for one thing in particular - it was totally lacking in pop groups. Delfont told me: 'No new British pop groups emerged in the past year, otherwise they would have been in the Royal Bill' - a statement which must have come as a surprise to Joe Cocker, Cream, the Crazy World of Arthur Brown and The Family, all rated as among the best of pop in 1968. However, it seemed that different standards existed in the choice of variety material, where Aimi MacDonald and Lionel Blair plodded through an extract from a *revival* of 'Lady Be Good' - about which the critics had raved. 'A heavily contrived plot of unrelieved mindlessness,' said one.

The Royal Variety Show took place in a theatre owned by Associated Television (ATV), which was run by Lew Grade - who just happened to be Bernard Delfont's brother. The proceeds from the show went to a charity - presided over by Bernard Delfont. Mr. Delfont was also a director of EMI, the largest record manufacturer in the world. In 1968, EMI absorbed one of England's two big cinema circuits - Associated British Pictures - of which Bernard Delfont was also a director. Bernard Delfont was also deputy chairman and joint managing director of the Grade Organisation, which was owned by EMI (of which Mr. Delfont is a director). Bernard Delfont thus owned himself - twice. So if, in England, you read the *TV Times*, buy Pye, Marble Arch, Regal, Columbia, Parlophone, HMV, Pathé, Music for Pleasure or Odeon Records; if you watched ATV or Thames Television, go to the Talk of the Town, the London Palladium, Victoria Palace, Hippodrome, Her Majesty's, Globe, Lyric, Apollo or Prince of Wales Theatres; if you went to one of ABC's 270 cinemas or twelve bowling alleys or one of Ambassador's ten bowling alleys, then Bernard Delfont had an interest in what you're doing. And this is the man who said that in 1968 there was no new good British pop.

One of the only outlets for pop on Independent Television used to be the Tony Blackburn Show. Blackburn's agent was Harold Davison. Also on Harold Davison's books was Mike Mansfield, Blackburn's TV producer. One show starred Barry Ryan. He is now Harold Davison's stepson. And Marion Ryan - remember her? - was on the same night. She was now Harold Davison's wife. And the Harold Davison agency is owned by the Grade Organisation, of which the joint managing director was Bernard Delfont.

It seemed that people like Bernard Delfont wanted to perpetuate the myth that 'pop music' was nothing but the harmless entertainment of adolescents. The more suspect stuff was either written off as nothing but the grotesque mumblings of a drug-sodden youth or else written up as being the most startling artistic upheaval since the Renaissance. Either way, it was best overlooked - and would have been, it appears, if people like Bernard Delfont had their way. And yet in view of the immense resources of pop, it seemed almost proper that so much of it should still have been controlled, directly or indirectly, by such a small number of big business tycoons.

In 1969, a hit song can earn more in twelve months than most people earn in a lifetime. The revenue of one publishing company during the previous five years exceeded the total famine relief sent to India during the last ten. Record sales in the United States in 1968 exceeded one billion dollars. Not surprisingly pop had thus become the most powerful selling medium of all time. The product will sell easily if the sound is right. Jingle executive Jim West, who was vice-president of the biggest jingle-factory in the world at Dallas, Texas, even told me that 'Music is a condiment. It's just a sensual pleasure. It's like looking at a pantry with a thousand different kinds of jams and jellies. With pop music, you could sell anything - including the Mona Lisa. With Mona, I'd use dignified instruments - like the French horn, which is a beautifully warm and colourful instrument. Then, maybe, I'd add a very light and subtle martial feel. In this way, we'd have no problem with Mona. All you'd have to do is package it properly with pop music - just as if it were a package of peas. This is what the whole ballgame is all about. Pop music is about selling and yet itself has to be sold - like any other commodity.'

If so, it seems reasonable that those who make the sound must be dressed and photographed and behave in a way that society which is sponsoring them, expects. Thus in newspapers, on television and on radio, pop is essentially the language of profit. Such, it might appear, is its price of acceptance.

But not necessarily its price of achievement. What it has achieved - which is perhaps very little as yet- it may have done so in spite of itself. 'Most pop people,' says Frank Zappa, leader of the now defunct Mothers of Invention, told me 'are stupid. They're concerned with "doing their thing" - whatever the fuck that's supposed to mean. Probably what they finally do is better than what they are.' But what they finally do represents a corpus of work which stares us boldly in the face and attacks our ears with a persistence that, despite its detractors, just *cannot* be ignored. The problem is quite simply how to evaluate it - either in social, musical, political or in aesthetic terms.

Fortunately any assertions as to the real nature of pop music are neither true nor untrue - because pop does not lend itself to grandiloquent theories and magnificent designs. Its ambition is no greater than to entertain and to make money. By chance, it has also made some remarkable music and some remarkable poetry. But this was not its intention and is not necessarily the standard by which it can be judged. There are no master musicians or master poets in the world of pop; but together, those who constitute the pop world have created an event whose very size and scope is probably its best claim to being given a reasonable hearing. As Dylan sings, *something* is happening; 'But you don't know what it is, do you, Mister Jones?' he asks.

What is happening is not necessarily intentional on the part of their creators - Shakespeare must surely have been completely unaware that he was the greatest dramatist and poet of all time. He wrote to order, for fun and for money. Paul McCartney told me that The Beatles were 'just happy little rockers' - as if to defy those who would weigh him down with sophisticated argument. He also says, however, that if everyone wants to say a certain thing at a certain time, it's lucky being a song-writer - you can put your finger on it. He *knows*, if only instinctively, that he is up to something *more* than just rocking and rolling back in the USSR. He *knows* that, however unwilling he may be, he has got himself involved in that nasty business called Art. As Brian Wilson of The Beach Boys (whom McCartney much admires) told me: 'The old idea of art was, for most Americans, unnatural. It's inevitable that *we* would create art which is natural to *us*.'

The old idea that Art has to do with longevity - if it lasts, then it must be OK - pop showed to be redundant. Pop is transitory, instant, disposable and derivative - and it knows it. Part of its value, therefore, has been that it attacked the musical establishment which had inflated the notion of 'culture' to provide an emotional replacement for the loss of Empire and the consequent passing of traditional and accepted nineteenth-century codes of moral and artistic behaviour. The Second World War had made Art into a national institution - factory concerts, 'good' music on Sunday afternoon radio after church. And then the musical establishment in England appeared to be desperately concerned with stemming the tide of Afro-American influence. It said its object was to preserve art from commercial pollution and popular appeal, whereas its accomplishment has been to secure a social sanction for a condition of non-competitiveness, for the renunciation of communicative responsibility.

It was against all this that the New Youth, with its cult of personal freedom and 'doing your thing', revolted. It was soon discovered that artistic 'values' had been sported quite often by a moribund cultural mafia who had used Art to inflate their ego and their class image. The social benefits of Art were seen as silly. If one could do without a suit and tie or a dress, went the feeling, one could do without Art as well. There was also a growing realisation that the emotional impact of Art does not have to be based upon redundant sentiments about Art being complex and obscure if it is to be worthwhile. And anyway, was there anything wrong with Art that is popular? Addison, writing in *The Spectator* of 1711, noted that 'music, architecture and painting, as well as poetry and oratory, are to deduce their laws and rules from the general sense and taste of mankind, and not from the principles of those Arts themselves.' So, meaningful and abstract questions like 'What does it represent?' were no longer of any interest. Frank Lloyd Wright, a hero of the New Youth, when asked to make suggestions for improving the sprawl of Los Angeles, just said: 'Abandon it.' And about Boston he said: 'What Boston needs is about two dozen good funerals.'

'If today's young people want to go to an opera there's nothing heretical about that, they just go', McCartney told me. 'But they will go without previous knowledge and without previous study. If the opera gets through to them, fine. If it doesn't, forget it'. After all, there's nothing as complicated as a simple response to a complicated work of Art - a dictum which the best of pop music knows very well. 'Basically, I like *any* music that remains simple,' Otis Redding told me. 'This is the formula that has made soul music successful. When *any* musical form becomes cluttered and/or complicated, you lose the average listener's ear. There's nothing more beautiful than a simple blues tune. But there is beauty in simplicity whether you are talking about painting, music or architecture.'

Unfortunately, the evaluation of pop in aesthethic terms is usually held derisively to be the 'intellectualisation of pop'. But by 'intellectualisation' critics tend to mean the use of nasty words like Schubert and Beethoven, forgetting thereby that pop music, if it is ever to achieve any respect at all, has to be made to stand on its own feet alongside such as Schubert and Beethoven. If it does not wish to, then it cannot expect to be taken seriously. It does not have to adopt a sophisticated pose, because no-one will insist that sophistication is any longer necessary to art.

I once compared The Beatles' songs with those of Schubert. Schubert? people cried. What blasphemy! What about Mahler and Wolf? All right, what about Mahler and Wolf? Many of those who attacked the idea in the popular press, would be hard put to name a single song by Schubert. And all of those who attacked the idea in the popular press, failed to notice that I had not said that The Beatles were the greatest *composers* since Schubert, but merely The Beatles were the greatest *song-writers* since Schubert. A personal view no doubt, but one which entailed the observation that since the songs of The Beatles and the songs of Schubert had certain things in common - they were both written at great speed, for entertainment and with no regard for any high 'artistic' content - a comparison might afford some useful study.

In any case, the comparison with Schubert doesn't demean Schubert. Even if one admits that Schubert was the inventor of Muzak (after all, much of his music *is* lunch-time Grand Hotel palm-court music), this is not necessarily doing a disservice to the great composer.

Others, of the 'Own Up' brigade, attacked me for admiring the rhythmic complexities of records like the 'Magic Bus' by The Who, and for comparing these rhythmic complexities with those of Stravinsky. I never said that they were as subtle or as organic as those of Stravinsky, but merely that within their different contexts, they were both 'cunning and devious'. I mentioned, by way of comparison, the rhythmic structure of the beginning of Stravinsky's 'Symphony in 3 Movements'. The 'Own Up' brigade dismissed the comparison out of hand, but conveniently forgot to notice that Stravinsky's Symphony, like The Who's 'Magic Bus', is in 4/4 time, and has exactly the same rhythmic structure. Others still, like Tim Souster in *The Listener*, leaped up and down in paroxysmic fury because one dared to mention The Beatles or The Who in the same breath as Schubert and Stravinsky. To have heard of Schubert and Stravinsky, apparently, is - according to Mr. Souster, an example of musical snobbery. 'What I really want to do,' Frank Zappa told me, 'is to produce some uncultured serious music that everybody could understand - if they worked at it a little bit.' 'Hail, hail, rock 'n' roll,' said Chuck Berry in the mid-50's; 'deliver me from the days of old.'

What is certain is that pop music cannot be evaluated only in terms of a teeny-bopper ravability quotient, nor just in terms of its placing in the charts, nor least of all in terms of a pop stars' diet, clothing, sex-life or hair-dos. It is true that certain developments in pop did coincide with certain social upheavals. The rise of rock 'n' roll, for example, happened more or less at the same time as the rise of the rocker. But it is difficult, if not impossible, to prove that one necessarily caused the other. Perhaps the one supplied the needs of the other, although each had developed separately. Perhaps the startling development of pop as an apparent social force was symptomatic of a profound unease about the role, if any, of the artist and his culture today.

There is the famous story which tells how the old cathedral of Chartres was struck by lightning and burned to the ground. Such was the distress throughout Europe that thousands of people came from all points, like a giant procession of ants, and together began to rebuild the cathedral on its old site. Master builders, labourers, stonemasons, wood-cutters, artists, priests, burghers, citizens, noblemen - all slaved together for 50 years to restore the cathedral to its former glory. In fact, it seems that they created a building far more magnificent than its predecessor, a work of art unparalleled even amongst cathedral buildings for hundreds of years. The irony is that with one or two minor exceptions, all those whose toil and sacrifice made possible this work of art, remain anonymous. To this day no-one knows for certain who made the cathedral at Chartres.

The artist in medieval times lived and died being no more nor less important than his fellow artisans. That he was tampering with 'eternal' values, or that being an artist concerned with Art, he was creating 'masterpieces' which would be 'immortal', were ideas totally foreign to him. He was a workman with particular skills and talents at the service of whoever employed him. His craft was learned, like any other. It had its function and its reward.

As a result of nineteenth-century romanticism however, the individual has hypnotised himself into believing that often he and he alone is of significance. Today, we have glorified the individual who is *also* an amateur. Paradoxically the development of electric circuitry has sponsored rather than diminished the cult of the individual through the growth of the all-seeing and all-knowing 'mass audience'. Consequently, the artist is actually *encouraged* to consider his isolation, his subjectivity and his individuality to be of sacrosanct importance. The tiniest, most fragmentary dent in his ego is rushed to the microscope for instant and prolonged self-examination. And so, thinking themselves a herd of individualists, many artists today stare into each other's eyes and yet deny the existence of each other. They huddle together in a vast encampment, bleating about their loneliness in a loud voice without paying the remotest attention to each other and without realising that through this indifference, they are mothering each other to death. Instead of searching out order from the chaos which surrounds them, their self-pitying anxieties allow them only to perpetuate the chaos.

It is the reaction to this chaos that has fractured - perhaps forever - the possibility of the artist ever returning to his former humility. Society, which sponsors and permits these peripheral and expensive activities called the Arts, has tried to determine the barriers and define the limits within which such activities can take place. Society has decided what Art is and should be in defiance or the artist, who seems, according to Society, not to know. And yet, at the same time, we have the misfortune to live in an age when the idea of an *ordered* society has been disturbed by violent and often bloody revolution. Whole continents have been awakening to a new political consciousness and thus the old accepted traditions of good government are seen to be not only repressive, but, more importantly, totally inadequate.

Psychological investigations are now getting into their proper stride and we are no longer sure of what exactly constitutes right and wrong - old Morality is now correctly understood as an unhealthy compound of old-wives' tales and monolithic, property-infested superstitions. World communications, and in particular television, remove ignorance and thereby fear by making the truth readily accessible to all, not just the prerogative of those in power who might wish to use or mis-use it in the furtherance of local, political needs. Peoples are being brought closer to peoples and so the need for prejudice and snobbery and intellectual arrogance, has less and less justification.

But despite all of this, the one realm of human activity where such barricades are most tenaciously upheld, is not political, nor social, nor psychological, but cultural. We cling, understandably yet ever more desperately, to sterile and tragically destructive notions of what Culture and Art are or could be.

At a time when the need to express oneself clearly and freely is paramount amongst all our activities, we find that we can only do so, safely and advisedly and discreetly, within the accepted framework of so-called cultural values. If you step only the hair's breadth of a heartbeat outside this framework, and do no more than suggest that perhaps, for example, there is *some* pop music that is worth our hearing, that perhaps there is some of it that can be favourably compared with the highest achievements of classical music, that perhaps the best of pop music has shown for the first time that the rigid, authoritarian categorisation of music into 'classical' and 'popular' - with the implication that the latter is somehow inferior - is just no longer good enough, and that it is perhaps pop music rather than any other form of artistic realisation which has caught the aspirations and imaginations of the young, then you are likely to be chastised as a cultural sensationalist.

But if you do want to observe how the outrage and self-pity and bitterness and anger and love of an entire generation were, in the late sixties, seeking a new language and a new hope, you are forced to look not to painting nor to sculpture, nor theatre, nor even cinema, but to a musical discipline mockingly called 'pop' music. 'When people are asked to re-create the mood of the sixties,' Aaron Copland, the great American composer, told me, 'they will play Beatle music.'

Ultimately, there can be only three kinds of music - whether it is composed by The Beatles or Brahms - good music, bad music and non-music. All sound which we describe as music can be reckoned in these terms. So if one is to say that a certain song by The Beatles is a good song, and if one is also to say that a certain song by Schubert is a good song, then one is saying about both these songs that they are good rather than bad. Further, one is making an *aesthetic* evaluation. The rights or wrongs of the evaluation and the whole question of aesthetics - who is to say? etc. - are here irrelevant. The fact remains that both are described as good songs; they can thus be compared because they are comparable. The qualities that a good song must exhibit - perfect interplay between words and music, internal balance and freedom from cliché and so forth - these qualities can be discussed and disputed. But such discussion and disputation does not prevent comparison; nor does it prevent such comparison being informative and instructive.

An Australian emigré organ called, with admirable simple-mindedness, *Oz*, once quoted an interview with a group called The Soft Machine who, some think, were mostly distinguished by a great degree of bombast and a little degree of talent. The spokesman, referring to a film which perhaps over-extravagantly praised another group called Cream, said that the film ascribed qualities to Cream which Cream, for all their virtues, clearly did not possess. These qualities included instrumental virtuosity, mastery of improvisation, subtlety of rhythmic intensity, bass-playing whose audacity demonstrated the influence of Bach (an influence which the player readily admitted) and a collective musical boldness which was somewhat stronger than that of their fellows. For a group whose musicianship had earned the praise of Leonard Bernstein and Stravinsky, these claims seemed modest enough. But not so. The Soft Machine spokesman was apparently so outraged that pop had qualities which could loosely be described as musical that he could only react with precisely the kind of introspective leave-us-alone-we're-alright protectiveness which has often successfully managed to stifle a proper understanding of pop.

We have a simple choice. We can go on considering pop music and those involved at the lowest possible level, without critical evaluation or intelligent response, like our Eurovision Chief-Organiser and his colleagues in the same media and like those who sneered at Mick Jagger. In that case, pop music deserves remarks like those of Corina Adam in the London Diary of *The New Statesman*: 'Anyway,' she wrote, 'being within a few yards of a pop group was a new experience for me, and an absolutely exhilarating one. I see now why teenagers scream, the noise is quite extraordinary; it really *does* make one's bones shake. It was nice to be on the right side of the generation gap, in spirit at least, for once.' Never a truer word, as they say.

Or we can hold up the belief that some pop music is good music - by any standards. We can suggest that Art is not the privilege of a social and intellectual élite. We can hope that if treated with a little intelligence and some respect, the best of it will survive all the bitchery and unthinking sarcasm of its witless and gutless attackers and be seen in years to come as the true voice of a generation whose eloquence could find no other satisfactory outlet. Considerations such as Art and

Culture are in a sense as totally incidental to Pop as they were to those unnumbered and unnamed builders of Chartres Cathedral. But together they share that same sense of purpose and of ambition - inarticulate and ill-defined though it might be - to express in a language they can understand the energy and wonder they feel.

There is no real sense in which Pop has a history in which one event can be said to have caused or even influenced the next, just as the guiding hand for the building of Chartres - if there was such a person - is unknown. There is also no sense in which any grand theory about the development of pop music will either be relevant or even interesting, just as no amount of theorising about Chartres will uncover the author of any master plan. The sculptured figure of the devil or of an angel or of a nobleman may have been by completely different artists, for all we know. They are not related except that they stand side by side in the finished work, individual reminders of a corporate enterprise. It is the whole that counts. The individual parts are not aspects of a hypothetical grand design. They are just the individual parts. So in pop music; the most we can do is consider a highly selective group of practitioners in the hope that together they will serve as indications of a particular mood and a particular set of ambitions. Pop has no master plan, only the collective aspirations of those involved.

But however dissimilar the pop people whom we shall linger over may seem at first sight, they share the ability to evoke abuse from Mr. Always Right about Art from Surbiton. On average, I used to get in 1969 about 50 letters a week complaining about my modest plea for an open-minded listen to pop music. One such I received after Cream - a not undistinguished group - had appeared in the same TV programme as the great concert pianist, Julius Katchen. It gave a specific address in Hampshire and was signed by 'a gentleman'. It read: 'do you *really* think those ghastly young vomit-fart-and-piss-kids whispering into the microphone (almost swallowing it in fact) are a "good group"? Either you are mentally deficient or else a living lie. Only *completely* mixed-up kids could be seen applauding the art of Julius Katchen one minute, and screaming themselves silly over The Beatles, The Rolling Stones or whoever they were, or something even *more* primitive the next.'

Pop music must indeed have been born under a bad sign.

Chapter Two

If pop music has any specific place of birth, it must be located somewhere in the Deep South of the United States. It has since had many foster-parents and many wet-nurses who have succoured it, influenced it and moulded it. The so-called Mersey Beat, the ham-fisted balladeering of Tin Pan Alley, the demands of American money making, country and western music, jazz, all played their part in stamping the lurid child with its present image. But these were environmental rather than genetic influences.

Its most important hereditary factor is what is now loosely and often mistakenly called Soul music. Like all the bland categorisations which pop takes unto itself, 'Soul' is both meaningless and misleading. Yet within its history, it contains the seed that was to bring forth pop; for Soul is more than the description of a type of sound. It is an attitude towards life, an assertion of life, a feeling about life - and from this feeling, contradictory and confusing though it is, comes the feelings that dominate and excite and energise what is called 'pop music'.

But for as many feelings as there are people, so are there meanings for the adjective 'Soul'. For some, Soul is swagger. Soul is uninhibited self. Soul is being true to your heart. 'I can tell from the way you walk, you got Soul,' sings Johnny Nash. 'I can tell from the way you talk.' 'It comes from life,' Ray Charles, who *is* Soul, told me. 'The way you have lived. It's not just a bad feeling, but I believe you have to have known hard times, ups and downs, you know. It's the voice of experience.' 'Soul is feeling,' says Aretha Franklin, who's hung up on playing the white man's black woman. She's got her technical thing together, but still has butterfly soul. 'It's the emotion you feel,' she told me, 'and the way it affects other people. It's being able to bring to the surface what's happening deep down inside.'

England's answer to Soul is Tom Jones. If Soul could be studied and learned, he'd study and learn it. But it can't. With amazing Welsh perspicacity, Jones observed to me that 'Soul is different from other music in that you let it come out the way you feel it. If you feel two or

three extra words, you sing them. If you feel a groan, you sing one.' He
does.

Soul is a way of life, usually the hard way. It's ingrained in those
who suffer and endure to laugh about it later. So it's what has made
black people hip forever. Soul is being natural, telling it like it is. Telling
it how it really is. At first, that just meant telling it in music - in the
plantation fields, and later the church. It was the only form of self-
expression that black people were allowed. Now, for the black man it's
a source of power. It's a pulsating assertion, emotionally, sexually, and
intellectually. Now, soul is everywhere - in politics, in food and in
haberdashery. It has its own language - for haberdashery, read clothes; its
own history, its own shorthand, its own hierarchy. Its members are
called the 'Soul brothers and sisters'. *Time* and *Esquire* both did surveys
of who they thought were the Soul brothers. Bonnie has soul, Clyde
doesn't. Captain Hook does, Peter Pan doesn't. Fagin does, Oliver
Twist doesn't. Charlie Chan does, Sherlock Holmes doesn't. Kwame
Nkrumah, then President of Nigeria, does - why shouldn't a black man
have flashy Cadillacs? Sure he's soulful. Norman Mailer doesn't. To be
soulful is to be at peace with yourself. Norman's been at war since 1945.
Nor has Picasso - a plagiarist of African art. He took out the life and left
the mumbo-jumbo. Nor has LSD advocate Timothy Leary. Soul is close
to home, baby. And you don't have to take a trip to get there. Nor had
Presidential contender Hubert Humphrey - at least, not since 1964 when
he sold his soul to LBJ, and has been ugly ever since. Nor had Marlon
Brando. He hung out in the right places. But with him, it was all effort
and no ease. Nor had Richard Nixon, the Great Pretender. Would the
real Dick Nixon please stand? Not on a bet.

In other words, soul is a life-style. It has no colour and no creed -
although it has black origins. The only rule is that a soulful person must
be at harmony with himself and that everything but everything that he
or she does must be an honest form of self-expression. You don't need
to put it on; it just comes right out. It sounds like the newest thing, but
it ain't. It's got roots. Like the brothers.

The brothers made the Language three hundred years ago. Before
the Civil War in America, there were numerous restrictions placed on
the speech of slaves. Newly arrived Africans first had the problem of
learning to speak a new language. They also had to learn that there were
many topics of conversation forbidden by slave masters. So they made
up songs to inform one another of, for example, the underground

railroad's activity. When they sang 'Steal Away', it wasn't to dear Jesus that they were planning to go, but to the North. Since slaves could be severely punished if they were caught using the words 'freedom' or 'rebellion', a semi-clandestine vernacular grew up and wrote itself into Negro spirituals, songs which were often nothing more than coded cotton-field lyrics. So for the black man, to hear these songs sung today by a talented soul brother or sister, is to be reminded of a unique historical spiritual bond that cannot be satisfactorily described by the mere spoken word.

Now since the American Negro, like the black man throughout the world, has constituted a vastly disproportionate number of any country's illiterates, and since illiteracy has a way of showing itself through in all attempts at coherent vocal expression, Coloured English - the sound of soul - has, with the aid of slang, battered and fractured grammar, malapropisms and verbal diarrhoea, evolved. To the soulless ear, this sound is dismissed as an incorrect usage of the English language. 'My' is pronounced 'Mah'; 'going to' is 'gonna'; 'baby' is 'bay-buh'; 'Bread' is 'Bray-ud'. Borrowings from spoken soul by white men's slang are frequent - most people know spoken soul by this method. Expressions such as 'groovy', meaning 'the best' or 'tops'; 'up-tight', meaning originally 'in financial straits' and later 'having taken offence' or 'closed-off'; 'cool' meaning relaxed and co-ordinated; 'outta sight' meaning 'way out'. Soul language changes fast. Since it's hip to be soul, it's necessary for the whites to steal the words; but whenever a soul term becomes popular with whites, it's common practice for the soul folks to relinquish it. If white people can use it, it isn't hip enough for me, says the black brother. Nonetheless, in-talk abounds with soul sounds. Swinging, freaky, larceny, busted, square, lay, joint, blow, shot, thing, heat - all used as slang, all derive from soul.

There's an eating house off 116th Street in Harlem called, appropriately, Victory Restaurant. You'll get a plate of pig's knuckles, black-eyed peas, and rice, a thick slice of corn-bread, a glass of lemonade and a small homemade sweet potato pie, and you'll be eating soul-food. Again, it has roots. The plantocracy would have starved the black man to death. The plantation owner had plenty of pigs, but *he* ate all the bacon, the ham, the spare-ribs and the chops, and left the carcass. So out of that carcass, the slaves came up with pig tails, pig knuckles, ham hocks, hog maws, pig ears, snout, neckbones, chitlins, tripe and sow belly. Soon came the Gospel Bird, or smothered chicken, candied yams and fruit cobblers - all raised from little patches called the back garden. It was improvised but delicious. Whilst the white man is buried beneath his canned fresh frozens, the soul brothers are still eating that sweet potato-pie. Nearest thing we had in England was Blooms in London's Whitechapel. Gedempte meat balls *was* Jewish soul.

But it's the music and its bastardisation that occupies most attention. Once upon a time there was Ray Charles, Aretha Franklin, Johnny Nash, above all James Brown. And suddenly there was also Elvis the King Presley, strumming his flash guitar and wagging his tail across the American continent, raping fame and fortune. As Eldridge Cleaver in his magnificent book 'Soul on Ice' recalls, Presley sowed the seed of a new rhythm and style in the white souls of the white youth of America, whose gut hunger was no longer satisfied with the antiseptic white shoes and whiter songs of Pat Boone. 'You can do anything,' sang Elvis to Pat Boone's white shoes, 'but don't you step on my Blue Suede Shoes!'

Then came the beatniks, all shouting and screaming and twisting. 'Howl,' howled Allen Ginsberg - the 'suzuki rhythm boy' as James Baldwin called him, 'tired of white ambitions and . . . dragging himself through the Negro street at dawn, looking for an angry fix.' Bing Crosbyism, Perry Comoism and Dinah Shoreism - not to mention Eisenhowerism - had led to a throbbing cancer, and the vanguard of the white youth and their music knew it. The Twist was a guided nuclear missle, launched from the ghetto into the heart of suburbia. Its fallout, the Hully Gully, the Mashed Potato, the Dog, the Smashed Banana, the Watusi, the Frug, the Swim, the Bicycle, were increasingly desperate attempts to capture the spirit of Soul in dance. Some reacted violently. Beverley Nichols wrote in 1962: 'I'm not easily shocked but the twist shocked me . . . half negroid, half Manhattan and, when you see it on its native heath, wholly frightening . . . I can't believe that London will ever go to quite these extremes.' But suddenly the bourgeois, the middle class, those who *had* the power, were suddenly dancing alongside those who wanted it. They were swinging and gyrating and shaking their dead little asses like petrified, frightened zombies trying to regain the warmth of life, to revitalise their rotten limbs, the stone heart, the stiff, mechanical, lip-yaking joints with the spark of life called Soul that they knew and could see their black brothers had, and that they, the purveyors of white man's bullshit, wanted.

So recognising this white need, black business men invented Motown in Detroit, a school for deodorising black performers and making them suitable for the white night clubs. The cellophane sound of the Supremes.

'Our relationship was like a marriage', their leader Diana Ross told me. Her voice was smooth-sexy and came crackling out of her spiky, spindly, mannequin-beautiful, predatory body. On stage, with their neat little trouser suits, the Supremes looked like three tiger-limbed ritual priestesses oooing and aahing with such immaculate togetherness that one became convinced that one was seeing double - or treble. They recorded 12 best-selling albums and earned 7 gold discs in 1967 alone. They began singing as a hobby, taking part in church gospel meetings. Overtones of race-music dominate their sound - Miss Ross offered a line and the other two echoed it. Call and response was the basic ingredient for all their songs. They made 10 flops but the eleventh - 'Baby Love' - became a world wide hit and they set off to conquer the world; ten months touring, one month recording and one month off was the pattern to come. Florence Ballard, an original Supreme, couldn't stand the pace, so left. An enormous entourage, including three artistic co-ordinators, travelled with them wherever they went ensuring that they would be powered, pampered and protected. They became the star product of the Tamla Motown label whose studio address was, or course, Hitsville, USA. Like The Miracles, The Marvellettes, The Temptations and Martha and The Vandellas, they were streamlined, thoroughly packaged and black. They were the white man's black music.

Berry Gordy, a Negro ex-production line worker in a local car factory in Detroit, began the process in 1959. By taking a simple repetitive tune, a simple-minded lyric boxed in by a rigid, impersonal and unswinging background, and by adding it to the instant coyness of socially-acceptable sexy black singers, he had a formula for instant success. His label soon became the largest record producer of singles in the world. He understood that packaging didn't stop at choosing the OK performers for the OK songs. He would need to control his employees' accommodation, private lives, hair-styles, make-up and clothes. The Supremes referred to these as their 'uniforms'. As if they were a packet of peas, Gordy meticulously preened them for international love. He propelled them into the tranquillizer-sodden, coke-soaked, suck-assing, status-seeking undercover world of white man's show-biz. He understood that to make money you had to escape the black ghetto and get in amongst the white man to take his bread and steal his affection. But as Baldwin carefully observed in 'The Fire Next

Time', 'white people cannot, in the generality, be taken as models of how to live. Rather, the white man is himself in sore need of new standards, which will release him from his confusion and place him once again in fruitful communion with the depths of his own being'. As Baldwin's dream was slowly realised in the United States, so Berry Gordy's factory slowly became redundant and his products were seen at last as fabrications. Gordy's performers became incapable of distinguishing between the glamour of singing and its soul. 'But', Miss Ross added rather pathetically, 'you can only live one dream at a time'.

So listen again to Diana Ross and her Supremes; those whining, wheezing, rasping, choking voices; those platinum lacquered wigs and blasted smiles; those mechanical, flaxen-waxen inch-long silver fingernails scratching castles in the sky; those super-lifted breasts pouting and seducing the white man into believing he's hitting the high spots on the darker side of the Negro mind where it's really at. Eldridge Cleaver recalls a conversation between two Negros watching two whites doing the Twist (which is a Negro dance).

'It ain't nothing', said one. 'They just trying to get back, that's all.'

'Get back?' said the other. 'Get back from where?'

'From wherever they've been. Where else?'

But getting back was to prove mighty difficult. In the first place, Soul was bigger, grander and not related to the trends and fashions that pop seemed to demand. It spoke of hope and not of chart-topping success. It spoke of the disappointments of the race and not just of the inarticulate frustrations of untidy kids. As such, it could not be readily absorbed into the grotesqueries of pop. Pop wanted the pride, the respect that came with soul. It didn't have the guts or the know-how. It didn't have the strength, and so couldn't - like Claude Brown says - walk down that street like the nigger whore comin' along . . . ja . . . ja . . . ja like she's sayin', 'here it is baby. Come an' git it.' Pop sucked off the hot juices alright, but didn't know what to do with them once it had got them. If you hear a plunky piano, a screeching, moaning voice, a few stuttered out 'yeahs' and 'come on, baby's' and 'sock it to 'em', a touch of the bongos and the odd brassy fanfare, you're probably listening to soul music. Or at least, what passes as soul music in the pilfering gloom of pop.

But the absorption had to be made if only because of the appalling condition of white 'popular music.' Previously, white 'popular music' had been effectively owned by big business. Since 80 per cent of the population of the United States went to the cinema every week during the 30's, it was thought necessary by those who had invested heavily in the cinema, that every film should have its title song. After all, these same people also had a controlling interest in The Radio which, as it played the latest film music over the air, was thereby also promoting the film. Inevitably, the financiers demanded a say in the final product. It is surely no coincidence that the first commercial talkie motion picture was a musical - 'The Jazz Singer'. Nor was it just a curiosity that NBC radio, in 1928, blacklisted the words of over 200 songs. None of these, or course, had been used in films.

Pop music in the late 40's and early 50's was dominated by the American Musical - in which those same financiers *also* had an interest. Carousel, Finian's Rainbow, Can-Can, South Pacific and Pyjama Game - this was the stuff of carefully packaged sentimentality that rock 'n' roll sought to break loose from. To escape from the big business hangover, rock went for its inspiration to anything that owed nothing to that. Jazz, country and western music, skiffle, rhythm and blues and above all Soul music - being itself a fusion of the blues and gospel songs - thus became the feeding house. In other words, pop turned primarily for its stimulus to the voice of Black America and to the voice of the poor farmers of the mid-West.

Jazz (American slang for fuck) thus contributed to pop a sense of style. It was the coming together of the strict tonal system of the West with the free rhythmic patterns of Africa. Since the end of the swing era, Jazz had become almost exclusively instrumental. So it desperately needed the melodic innocence of pop if it was to develop rather than stultify, just as pop today needs the jazz musicians' instrumental experience if it is to develop likewise. Skiffle or Do-it-yourself Music - which first happened in Ken Colyer's New Orleans style Jazz band in the early 50's - contributed a sense of fun, and country and western music provided much of the early raw material.

Country and Western music - as the name implies - involved three separate influences. First, it involved so-called country music which came from the area East of the Mississippi and had been born of the isolation suffered by generations of rural Americans cut off from the modernisation going on everywhere else. It was essentially hill-billy music - the simple music of informal country dances. With its high nasal tenor vocals and its prominent display of the five string banjo, it had a straight-forward, uncomplicated, earthy appeal. Lester Flatt and Earl

Scruggs were among the most famous exponents and were later to provide the musical soundtrack for 'Bonnie and Clyde'. Country music thus became one of the few authentic touches to that supposedly authentic film.

Its immediate and vast popularity has not diminished to this day. Jimmie Rodgers, 'The Singing Brakeman', sold more than 20 million 'country and western' records before his death by tuberculosis in 1933. The Carters, Woody Guthrie (whose influence first reached England through Lonnie Donnegan) in the 40's, Hank Williams in the 50's, and Roy Orbison and the Everly Brothers in the 60's, kept alive and vigorous the influence of country and western, as did Arthur Crudup's 'Grand Old Opry' radio show, begun on November 28, 1925 by WSM Radio and still going strong.

Second, there was rhythm and blues which owed *its* distinctive sound to a bizarre and inexplicable combination of other sounds - folk and jazz chord progressions, baroque instrumentation, English madrigal themes, and the rhythms and atonality of Indian ragas and near-Eastern folk dances. It first gained popularity in Chicago in the late 40's under the leadership of Muddy Waters. Bo Diddley and Chuck Berry - and, much later, The Rolling Stones - perpetuated this particular influence.

Third there was 'western swing' which had developed in the early 30's in the South-West of the United States. Its important characteristic was that it was rhythmically very infectious. It used a heavy, insistent beat with jazz-like improvisations on the steel guitar and a heavily bowed fiddle. Bob Wills founded the first swing band in 1932 and called it 'The Light Crust Doughboys'. The Honky-Tonk band, whose very bouncy style was very similar to swing, grew up independently.

Together, these three elements joined together to make country and western music.

But in spite of all these influences, there was also a growing realisation that it was primarily the black man who was where it was happening, because he was constantly in motion, constantly about to change. So Ivory Joe Hunter, Ruth Brown, The Drifters, The Clovers and The Coasters became the main influence for Haley, Presley and others. White singers began to imitate black music because it was the most clearly identifiable music in America. The white Negro is, in a sense, a prelude to the hippie. Since, in black culture, the singers are the physical embodiment of the emotions and experience of the community, the new white singers copied not only their aggressive sense of style, but more importantly, their sense of purpose. Soul music thus provided the reason for pop music. 'Because it is capable of and willing to assimilate everything,' Frank Zappa told me, 'pop music has made *everything* possible.'

Incidentally, the immediate commercial success of rock 'n' roll in the mid-50's had been helped very considerably by the coincidental communications explosion - the rise of the electric media such as television, radio and the mass-production of long-playing plastic discs. Indeed, radio and the disc had *justified* the black performer, because no-one had to look at him. Even so a singer such as Chuck Berry, to whom Elvis and later The Beatles owed a great deal, was never as internationally popular as either - because he was black. So it was whites - crude though they were by comparison - who first reaped the benefit.

One of the first to benefit had been Bill Haley.

In 1954, he claimed he was 24. In 1969, Haley was reported to be 46, so draw your own conclusions: perhaps he's rocked around the clock faster than the rest of us. Like many other super-duper stars, he was constantly being revived. His last instant revival was in 1968, when he was between 38 and 45.

Kiss curl and all, he told me: 'We never sold no sex or sideburns. If we'd wanted to sell sex or sideburns, we'd have dressed differently.' Alas, gone were the days when trousers would split simultaneously revealing lots of lovely white underwear - by chance, of course. 'We wear ordinary trousers now,' he said, a little sadly. It's hard to believe that he too was once described as 'the most significant musical achievement of a generation'. Haley, a disc-jockey by trade, had been around since 1951 and was already in decline by the time his song 'Rock Around the Clock' was released in 1954. His subsequent film of the same name focused the paranoia of the first post-Second War generation. The Rocker became the symbol of adolescent defiance. Haley's immediate success was also partly an internal music-business reaction to the intellectualisation of jazz. It coincided with the rise of the super-intellectual Modern Jazz Quartet and the death of Charlie Parker. It was another disc-jockey, Alan Freed of WHB Radio in Kansas City, who had actually 'invented' rock 'n' roll. He merely chose the two words - rock and roll - most frequently used in rhythm and blues lyrics, and then put them together. They described a sound which had nothing particularly original about it but which with its new name might avoid the racial stigma associated with that kind of 'popular music'.

Carl Perkins - him or the 1956 million-seller 'Blue Suede Shoes',
Eddie Cochran, Conway Twitty, Duane Eddy, Terry Dene - remember
all those lovely people? Some of them recorded superb songs like
Cochran's 'Summer Time Blues', but most didn't. Even Buddy Holly -
the Texas clod with the seductive voice, the broken teeth and the
wire-glasses, put his name to some turgid stuff. Well, even if you don't
remember, the vulgar bangings and inarticulate screeches of some of
them were thrust down our ears once every two years in an attempt by
the publicists to convince us that if the beat is big, then so is the music.
The revival in 1968, for instance, happened essentially because The
Beatles wrote a harmless little number, 'Lady Madonna', which
sounded vaguely Boogie cum rock 'n' roll cum anything you like.
Fetish-crazed publicists, operating totally parasitically upon the pop
world, decided that the pop audience, or what the publicists conceived
of as the pop audience, needed a shot in the arm (or mind) or adolescent
pow-pow in order to remain truly virulent and aware. The only thing
one had to be mildly grateful for in the 1968 Revival, was that the
publicists didn't this time bring Bill Haley, a singer, into the political
realm. On a previous Revival in 1958, East German Defence Minister
Willi Stoph, had thought that a visit of Bill Haley and the Comets
to West Germany constituted a devious and sneaky NATO plot.
Presumably on the 1968 Revival Haley was in the pay of 'rivers-of-
blood' British politician Enoch Powell - stirring up the youth as he does.
    'Ever since we arrived here,' Haley told a packed Albert Hall (1968
Revival) audience, 'people ask us - is Rock 'n' Roll coming back? - Wait
until the Albert Hall. If there's anybody there, it's come back.' The
leather rag-trade had obviously been working overtime because there
they *all* were - thousands of them. They waved studded leather belts, hit
Duane Eddy's drummer on the head with a bottle, attacked dancing girls
and threw compère Rick Dane off the stage. Meanwhile, bass player Al
Rappa climbed all over the amplification equipment - seven feet high -
still clutching his instrument and his smile, whilst big Bill Haley, a
singer, having rendered 'See You Later, Alligator' (from the Latin 'to sing
tunefully') fled - pursued by a bear and several Rockers. It must have
sent shivers down the memories of many a vicar who in previous years
had lain down many an unfinished sermon to pen articles for the Press
on 'Terror in the Suburbs' (1958) or 'Edwardian gangs repair church
they wrecked' (1954) or 'Teddy Boy turns to God' (1968).

Such excesses soon multiplied, among them Janis Joplin. In 1969, she seemed the ultimate in vocal overkill; black power come to life. She screams, groans and prowls in a high-pitched witch's giggle, I wrote at the time. Her bourbon-sodden voice tears and curses as if she were being continuously strangled. Her parchment arms flail about like a berserk windmill and she frequently chews her long, frizzy hair as if in defiance of those who might want to comb it - a bit. On stage, she slinks about like tar, wearing clothes that look as if they have come from a Woman's Institute Jumble Sale.

She is aggressively and arrogantly sexual; 'I live for happiness,' she told me. 'I suppose you could call me promiscuous because I like men day *and* night' - and with that she licks her lips. Her language is the epitome of overshock - a relentless stream of four-letter words spewed out like some irrational diatribe against those who have the nerve to dislike her. She used to boast that she could drink a whole bottle of 100 per cent proof 'Southern Comfort' bourbon during her act. Now, it's gin or champagne. She fingers her thighs and frequently hitches up her black pants. Like the best of soul singers, she is also desperately trying to tell us how it really is; but unlike the best of soul singers, she is grotesque ugly and grisly with that special quality of brassy burlesque which kills off any real feelings.

This 28-year-old King Kong in drag from Port Arthur, Texas, first startled the 1967 Monterey Pop Festival by fronting a group called 'Big Brother and the Holding Company'. She swaggered around like some nigger-loving whore; 'nigger-lover' was precisely the description given to this heap of raging ego-mania by her Puritanical home town. However, the LP that she and Big Brother released together, sold a million copies on the first day and her subsequent single 'Down On Me' propelled her into the front-line where she's been ever since. She wanted star-billing which the group wouldn't give her, so she left. She ostentatiously painted a blood-stained American flag on the side of her Porsche, and remained stubbornly conscientious about her 'Art'. 'Tell me I'm good, tell me I'm good,' she cries out. Her one ambition was to be on the same stage as the 'Soulsinger', Otis Redding. It was all arranged - and then he was killed. 'He was my idol,' she told me. 'I wanted *him* to tell me I was good.'

She wrecks almost every song she performs with a kind of mindless determination to be meaningful. With her bottle of booze placed proudly on the top of her amplifier like some religious symbol, she struts around like a debauched carnival queen, wiping the floor with her songs. 'Hey, I've never sung so great,' she shouts. 'Jesus Christ, I'm *really* fucking better. You've got to believe me.' Thus she lacks that self-protective distancing from her work that any great artist seems to need. It's not modesty that is required but just an uncomfortable awareness of what you are about. Janis Joplin, as she fingers her thighs and hitches up her pants for the 53rd time, doesn't know or seem to care.

At the end, she sang with a six or seven-man band, at first unnamed. They wanted to call themselves by the same title as that million-seller LP, but the record company wouldn't let them. It was called of course, 'Cheap Thrills'. Not surprisingly, she died before long from a heroin overdose.

For a long-time the soul brothers didn't react much to this wholesale sterilisation of their birthright, their race music. But when they did, they reacted violently; *they* had produced the music, but the white man had cashed in on it. Soul on stage began to revert to its gospel origins. Singers appeared to have been seized by God; they tore off their clothes, called for witnesses, collapsed and rose again. Some thought that the bejewelled James Brown's whirling convulsive nightmare performances were re-enactments of the Crucifixion. Ray Charles' 'devil songs' fused forever the old Negro distinction between gospel and blues - the sacred and the profane - and called it soul.

He also reminded everyone of the cause of soul:

Oh listen to the blues, to the blues and what they're sayin'
Oh they tell me; they tell me that life's just an empty scene,
Older than the oldest broken hearts, newer than the newest
    broken dream.

'Before it got the name of soul,' Mahalia Jackson, at 56, the high priestess of soul, told me, 'men were sellin' watermelons and vegetables on a wagon drawn by a mule, hollerin' "Waterme*llll*on!" with a cry in their voices. And the men on the railroad track layin' crossties - every time they hit the hammer it was a sad feelin', but with a beat. And the Baptist preacher - he was the one who had the soul - he give out the metre, a long and short metre, and the old mothers of the church would reply. This musical thing has been here since America been here. This is trial-and-tribulation music.' As James Baldwin - a onetime Harlem storefront preacher - noticed in 'The Fire Next Time': 'to be sensual, I think, is to respect and rejoice in the force of life, of life itself, and to be *present* in all that one does, from the effort of living to the breaking of bread.' *That* is soul. And it became the heartbeat for the best of pop.

'Soul is like electricity,' Ray Charles told me. 'We don't really know what it is or where it is. But it's a force that can light a room.' As a word, like the word 'pop', it's abused and misused. As a feeling, it's often the excuse rather than the real thing. Hubert Humphrey told college students just after he'd announced he'd run for the Presidency that he was a soul brother - which was all wrong. Soul is letting *others* say you're a soul brother. Soul is not needing others to say it. 'Soul is getting kicked in the ass until you don't know what it's for,' Godfrey Cambridge the Negro comedian told me. 'It's being broke and down and out, and people telling you you're no good. It's the language of the subculture; but you can't learn it, because no-one can give you the black lessons.' Just as the best pop music embodies the frustrations of youth, so the energy of soul music embodies the bitterness and violence of the oppressed Negro. But the energy has spilled out across the white lands. For some, the soul concept remains a mystique, a glorification of all that is black. 'The only thing that white people got that black would want is, power,' James Baldwin told me. The black man shows this want in the loose, cocky way he struts down the street. After all, the white man - with the exception of the Jews - has got no centuries of hurt to work off. 'Soul music *is* music coming out of the black spirit,' playwright LeRoi Jones reminds us. But its compound of raw emotion, pulsing rhythm and spare, earthy lyrics, although remaining soaked in the melancholy vibrations of the Negro idiom, has now penetrated to the core of white popular music. The tone and beat of the Negro has conquered. Whereas Tin Pan Alley might have written:

> You're still near my darling, though we're apart
> I'll hold you always in my heart.

Soul would sing:

> Baby, since you split the scene the rent come due
> Without you or your money it's hard, yeah, hard to be true.

Soul has power, and truth.

Mahalia Jackson, Ray Charles, B. B. King, Nina Simone, Billie Holiday, Sam and Dave, Aretha Franklin - these are the soul brothers and sisters. They sing of their hopes and of their sufferings. We listen and are moved. We cannot feel what they feel, for such is the nature of feeling. Their message to us is simple. They bear witness to their feeling in the hope that we will throw off all our sugar coating and pretence. This is what pop music also wants us to do, but this is just what we find difficult. We lust for fashion, read the Sundays, get designed for living, work in television, get groovy and tell everybody. We're sluiced and raped by the *Vogue* set. We believe in football, ice-cream and so-called reality television. Instead of looking quietly into our own hearts, we look noisily into others. That's how it is - amongst the white men. Complicated. Soul is simple. And full of courage. 'Feelin' takes courage,' Aretha Franklin told me. 'I am singing "Dig me; if you dare".

Not surprisingly, there had been no such challenge from Bill Haley as he had banged his way around the Albert Hall (1958 and 1968 Revivals). During the latter visit, great emphasis had been put on the amazing revelation that his amplification equipment was British. Ironically by then, it was not British amplification equipment but British manpower which had dared, and which had thus translated the life force of soul into a contemporary language which in its turn had revitalised the tradition from which it had come. But to have made such a claim in the mid 50s when Bill Haley had first arrived, would have seemed totally preposterous, as there emerged at that time one colossus who seemed to bestride popular music on both sides of the Atlantic. The colossus was Elvis Presley.

Elvis Presley personified the fusion of all the influences that went to make up rock 'n' roll. His parents were a popular local revivalist duo - the blues and gospel music. Presley himself began his career touring local country and western areas, billed as the 'Hilly Billy Cat' - country and western music. His loud sexuality soon earned him the description as 'the pelvic oracle', and as if to accentuate this, his music was dominated by a large and relentless beat - skiffle plus rhythm and blues - and that very special slightly off-key slightly behind the beat quality reminiscent of the best blues-influenced Jazz. When all these elements combined in the person of a white male, Elvis' popularity contributed open respect for black music - which was to have far-reaching effects.

Elvis Presley always walked as if he was sneering with his legs. When he's on stage, he bounces like a Jeep driver crossing a ploughed field. His blue eyes and dark brown hair are lacquered and glazed; his six-feet two inches have developed a stoop. His lopsided grin told us that the Elvis factory has grossed in excess of 200 million dollars. Fifty-one of his records sold more than a million copies each and the total number of discs bearing the Presley imprimatur is around 300 million. He made four films a year for which his fee was a million dollars a picture - plus a large percentage of the profits. His twenty-nine films cost an estimated 30 million dollars to produce but grossed over 200 million. Merchandising alone of Elvis products - hats, T-shirts, stuffed hound-dogs, dolls, bookends, skirts, blouses, sandals, handkerchiefs, hair-cream, heartbreak-pink and tutti-fruiti lipstick, charm bracelets and lavatory paper - brought an annual 3 million dollars in pocket money. He thought he needed a yacht for vacations, so he bought one. Not any old yacht, but the Presidential Yacht *Potomac* on which Churchill and Roosevelt had drawn up the Atlantic Charter. But then he didn't use it much, so he gave it away - to a children's home in Los Angeles. The London Palladium thought it would invite Elvis to star in a week's spectacular. The management rang up Colonel Tom Parker, Elvis' guardian. 'Come to The Palladium,' said the management, 'and we can get you 28,000 dollars for the week.' 'That's fine for me,' said Parker; 'Now how much can you get for Elvis.' Said Presley's mother, 'Elvis lays it to no one but the Lord. More than once he's told me: "Hasn't the Lord blessed us, Mother?" '

Presley is the most remarkable figure in all of pop. In a sense, he *is* pop, not only because he brought together all the different elements that went into pop, but also because he was the first teenage symbol that grown-ups couldn't possibly share in. When he first smashed into the scene in 1955, he was young and arrogant and outrageously loud. Besides epitomising all that was rock 'n' roll, he also - co-incidentally - epitomised everything that a new generation of post-war adolescence wanted - their own jargon, their own fashions and above all their own music. Chronologically he was slightly pre-dated by Bill Haley, but Haley was already 30 when rock 'n' roll began and had none of the aggressive sexuality that the greasy teenage Presley could provoke. Presley was exploited in a way that has been a model for every super-star since; his entire life is the blueprint for the original showbiz rags to riches saga which in this case out-fabled even Hollywood. Almost alone, he secured the domination of American popular music for a decade. He was the medium through which the gospel rhythm-and-blues soul

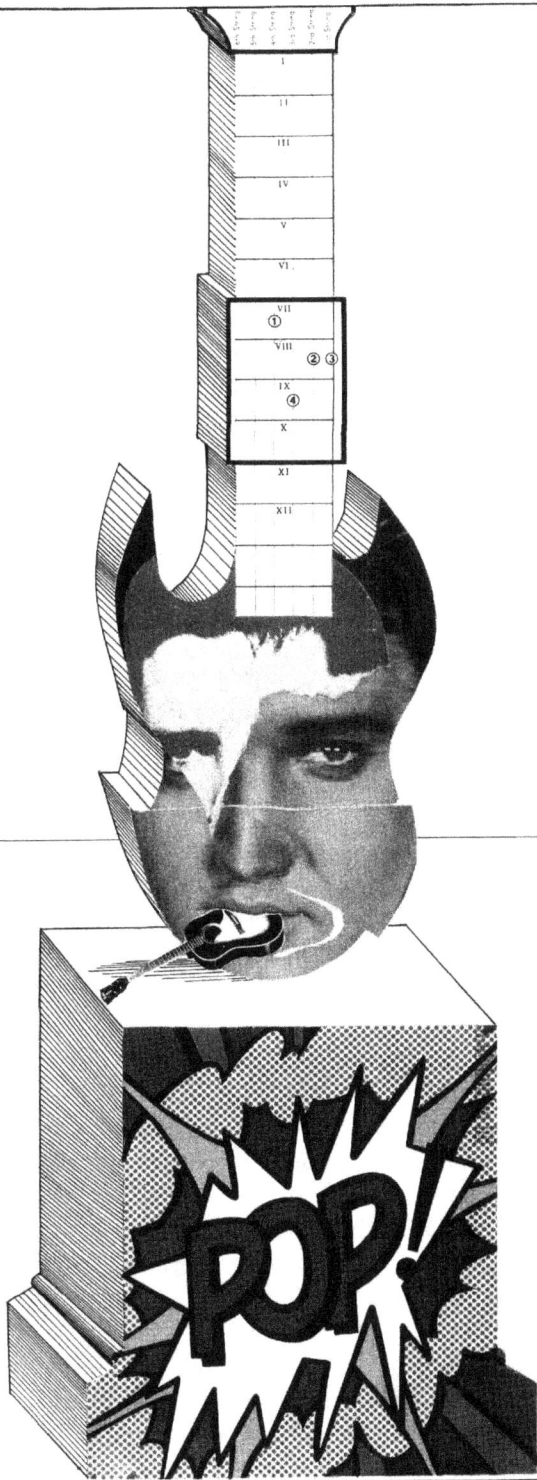

Elvis,
by
Ralph STEADman

big-beat country-and-western sounds passed into Western folk-lore. Everyone who followed him owed something of their style to his influence. He was a giant, and he knew it.

Elvis Aaron Presley was born in 1935 in a two-room insanitary shack in Tupelo, a shanty town in Mississippi. The surviving town of a hobo, he was brought up in - of course, Memphis, Tennessee. His career had a classic beginning. An out-of-work truck driver, he stopped off one day at a local recording studio. 'How d'ya make a disc?' he asked the pokey girl behind the pokey desk. 'You pay four bucks and you do your stuff into a mike,' she snarled back. 'You do anythin' in particular?' 'I'd kinda like to hear my own voice,' said the eighteen-year-old Presley; 'With this,' he added indicating a battered guitar, 'Okay,' said the girl. 'Name?'

'Elvis Presley,' came the reply. Within a year, the same girl offered her entire life savings for a single hair of Presley's head. A Cincinnati ironworker shot his wife for being overfond of Elvis records. A street in Brighouse, Yorkshire, was renamed Presley Drive. He bought six Cadillacs - in pink, canary blue, pale green, gold and black, pale yellow and chrome. He appeared in a gold-leaf suit complete with gold-leaf shoes. One teenage girl admitted that she could no longer undress in her bedroom with the light on because the walls were covered with a thousand photos of Elvis, all of which seemed to be staring at her naked body. Others carved Elvis' name on their forearm leaving scars that are still boasted of to this day, and a single leaf from his garden would sell for ten dollars. The East German Communist paper, *Young World*, declared that Presley was a weapon in the 'American psychological war aimed at infecting a part of the population with a new philosophical outlook of inhumanity . . . to destroy everything that is beautiful, in order to prepare for war.' On the Ed Sullivan Show, the sponsor would only let Presley be seen from the waist up. In Miami, he was prosecuted for obscenity; in San Diego the city fathers threatened to outlaw him unless he omitted from his act his 'vulgar movements'; and in Jacksonville he was threatened with jail after a Baptist preacher said that Presley had hit a new low in spiritual degeneracy. Said Presley a little hurt: 'God gave me my voice. If I turned against God, I'd be finished.'

And so he sang, and sang. 'Hi wa-wa-haunt you-hoo, hi need-hee you-hoo-hoo, hi-luh-huh-huv-you-hewww.' Spasms racked his body as if it were he and not his guitar that was plugged into the electricity. A TV network offered Presley 50,000 dollars for an appearance. 'OK,' agreed the ubiquitous Colonel Parker, 'but I won't let him sing.' Within his first two years, he'd sold 30 million records. He couldn't read or write a single note of music; he didn't drink or smoke, but he did admit to a passion for kissing girls. One of his 1957 girl friends, Penney Banner, attained the right to kiss Elvis by defeating four other girls in a wrestling contest. Appropriately, Penney Banner was a member of the Memphis Girl Grapplers.

He was conscripted into the US Army; his acceptance without demur was perhaps the shrewdest move that even Colonel Parker could have devised. Because of the King-and-Country bit, the wild and evil Presley was transformed - at least in the public's eye - into every mother's goddammit son. The Pentagon issued an order of the day: 'make as few statements as possible - and keep them dignified!' The head of the draft board, Millyon (he just had to be called Millyon) Bowyers was not so pleased. Distraught fans rang him to demand Presley's release. After all, they said, the Army hadn't conscripted Beethoven. Replied Bowyers: 'That's because Beethoven wasn't an American.' The army issued a three-page brochure about Presley's army career, whilst Colonel Parker issued carefully stockpiled recordings so that no one would forget. He needn't have worried for whilst US53310761 was actually costing the Treasury 2 million dollars in lost tax, fans were selling all their possessions to afford just a teaspoon of dust collected from Presley's combat boots. 'I shall consider it,' said Parker, 'my patriotic duty to keep him in the ninety per cent tax bracket.' 'I'm very proud,' said Elvis.

Upon his release, the resultant publicity put the money-machine into top gear. For an appearance in Las Vegas, the Colonel demanded cash in advance. 'They've got an atom bomb testing place out there in the desert,' he said. 'What happens if someone pushes the wrong button?' For a single performance at the Seattle World Fair, the Colonel settled for a quarter million dollars - but insisted on adding into the contract a 'rain clause'. In the event of rain, said the contract, Presley and associates reserve the right to sell their dollar plastic umbrellas. He went on making films - 'Blue Hawaii', 'GI Blues', 'Follow That Dream', 'Fun at Acapulco', 'Roustabout' - all of increasing triviality and slush. He got fifty per cent of the gross takings - besides his million dollar fee. Surprisingly, perhaps, he went on making records. 'Have you ever had singing lessons?' someone asked him. 'No,' he said. 'Can't you tell?' Of his first recording he says: 'Sounds like someone beatin' on a bucket lid' - grinning, as he remembers, with his sparkling-white teeth - most of them capped. He can't tell you who influenced him, although he admits liking the old cowboy singers like Roy Acuff, Hank Snow and above all Gene Austin. Eventually, he didn't appear live anymore, although he did record a memorable 'live' TV Special. He turned down an invitation to visit England because, he said, he wouldn't come unless he felt the Queen would want to meet him. His songs like 'Heartbreak Hotel', 'Blue Suede Shoes', 'All Shook Up', 'Hound Dog' and 'Are You Lonesome Tonight', are being re-released so that they will become the Gospel for this decade of pop as they were for the last. An International Elvis Presley Appreciation Society was formed. It had its own international anthem, called 'Steadfast, Loyal and True'.

And Presley himself? He lived in total seclusion in a 100,000 dollar colonial mansion called Graceland near Memphis, and was 'protected' by twelve beautiful male bodyguards with whom he practised Karate and marksmanship - with water pistols. The house is still painted luminous blue and gold and glows at night. It's filled with stuffed pandas, elephants, monkeys, dogs and hundreds of teddy-bears. He never went anywhere without them - the teddy-bears, that is. He called everybody who was older than him, including me, 'Sir' - 'cause his Mama said he should. Purity remained an essential attribute - no-one ever goes to bed in *his* movies, although he did once seduce a nun (Mary Tyler Moore).

'I don't aim to let this fame business get me,' he said. His only proud possession, he said, is a double piano - a piano with two key-boards. It is, or course, made in solid gold. He rarely ventured out himself, except to the film studios; to keep his fans appeased he occasionally sent his solid gold Cadillac on a coast-to-coast tour, so that his fans could touch it. In 1967, to the horror of every pubescent teenager in the land, and to the annoyance of those who had accused him of being homosexual, he married a long-time sweetheart, Priscilla Beaulieu. Elvis and Priscilla chose to be married in a hotel. It was called, of course, the Aladdin Hotel.

And the music? Well, who cared about that. Increasingly, the suspicion grew that someone should care, that the music could express something more than love is blue. Increasingly, there was the realisation that the 'star-system' - beloved of the financiers and their movies - still dominated the pop scene and thus still subordinated the music to extra-musical activities. The rise of the composer/performer reversed this. So it was not Bill Haley nor even Elvis Presley which set the youth of England and subsequently the youth of the world on fire. It was The Beatles.

Chapter Three

'I declare,' wrote Timothy Leary, 'that The Beatles are mutants. Prototypes of evolutionary agents sent by God, endowed with a mysterious power to create a new human species - a young race of laughing freemen.'

The Beatles tore the hackneyed pants off pop music like frenzied lovers. They completely squashed the Coke-soaked, chocolate-sundae bunch of singers which had dominated the scene since Elvis and The Everly Brothers had gone off into the army. In the late 50's, Jerry Lee Lewis and Chuck Berry had been almost driven off stage for performing 'distasteful nasties'. Buddy Holly had been killed in an air crash and Fats Domino and Little Richard were in retirement. Everyone else who was anyone was black - which for the communications media such as television meant instant depth. In response to this vacuum, The Beatles grew large. The hysteria with which they were greeted was nothing new. Heine's description of the effect that the composer-pianist Liszt had had upon women sounds as if it might have been written of The Beatles. 'Women shrieked, fainted and fought,' wrote Heine, 'when the great pianist arrived because of magnetism, galvanism and the electricity of histrionic epilepsy, tickling musical cantharides and other unmentionable matters.' The Beatles were used by those who would make The Beatles part of their own romantic fantasies. They looked like being heroes who would promise never to rock the boat. They 'did their thing' and it just happened to co-incide with one of society's needs. So their record 'Sergeant Pepper' was the great success it was, partly because we wanted it to be. It tidied up the drug scene and made psychedelia as mind-blowing as 'Late Night Line-Up'. That has always been one of The Beatles' functions - to make pop and the pop scene socially acceptable.

The Beatles were the great democratic principle at work in pop, reducing everything to the ordinary. They wanted to outwit the media who didn't want to know about the things that hurt. As Nat Hentoff told me, The Beatles 'turned on millions of American adolescents to what had been hurting all the time . . . but the young never did want it raw; consequently they absorbed it through The Beatle filter.' So The Beatles performed an essentially middle-class function - they filtered out the 'hurting'. They served as the introduction to and the popularisers of a whole new world of creative adventure. They travelled only a few miles beyond the avant-garde, consolidating gains and making acceptable new ideas. In this way they cleaned-up the lyrics of rock 'n' roll, and used the most obvious aspects of black music - the big-beat amplification (picked up from Chuck Berry), ensemble singing and a vague hint of blueness - as the foundation of their wrongly labelled 'new' music. 'Yeah' thus became the bridge word from black to white music. *The Times Educational Supplement* noted that 'Lennon and McCartney's lyrics represent an important barometer to our society - sentiments which are shared by pupils in every classroom in Britain . . . . If (Sergeant Pepper's) understanding were to be reflected in Britain's teachers, our schools might be more sympathetic institutions than some are now.' Richard Goldstein in the *New York Times* noted that 'their jester's approach to "serious" music and "deep" thought clamours for interpretation, and their intentional embrace of ambiguity sets a tempting critical trap; how hard it is to resist when Ideas are the part.'

Wilfred Mellers, Professor of Music at York University, declared that the essential quality of The Beatles - which they had in common with Boulez, John Cage and Bob Dylan - was 'an attempt to return to magic, possibly as a substitute for belief.' McCartney himself admitted - in an interview with Miles in *The International Times*: 'With any kind of thing, my aim seems to be to distort it, distort it from what we know it as, even with music and visual things and change it from what it *is* to see what it *could* be. To see the potential in it all. To take a note and wreck it and see in that note what else there is in it, that a simple act like distorting it has caused. It's all trying to create magic; it's all trying to make things happen so that you don't know why they've happened.'

'Their story,' Derek Taylor, their close friend and publicist, told me, 'is the biggest running story in history. Longer than the Second World War. But nobody died.' 'They've got enormous momentum,' said one of their legal advisers. '*Whatever* they do has a measure of popular support. If they were to start an Undertaker firm tomorrow, teenagers would be making provisions in their wills that they should be buried by The Beatles.' 'The Beatles,' says Derek Taylor, 'have the capacity of very attractive children for really getting away with it. They've said, "we are more popular than Jesus," tried LSD and admitted it, signed the Legalise

Marijuana petition and two of them have been heavily fined for smoking it, and followed the Maharishi. They've survived all that and still people smile when they see them. They no longer feel they have to be anything but themselves, but they're still a continuously big event and *you* don't want to miss it.'

En route, almost by accident it seems - these four likely lads from Liverpool who were only one of 350 groups to suddenly emerge from that city, removed what felt like the sterile martyrdom from Art, and revived its sensual qualities. In a very short time, they composed over 200 songs, some worthy of any comparison, and amassed a fortune. In a sense, therefore, Liverpool's poor were to make England rich, in song, in fashion, in youthful energy and in foreign currency.

Between 1963 and 1969, The Beatles' records grossed at least £100 million - much of it in dollars. Sales of their 230 songs topped the 200 million mark some while back - and that's not including the 10,000 or so cover versions. 'Yesterday' alone had 119 different recordings. Each Beatle earned enough old £1 notes in that period to make a pile 1 1/2 miles high; it would take you five months of solid counting at the rate of two £1 notes per second to get through their total earnings. John and Paul, for example, used to be paid 4 3/4d. per single and 1/8d. per LP, by way of publishing royalties. This revenue was assigned to a small private company called Northern Songs Ltd., over which they only recently lost control. The two Beatles originally owned twenty per cent each of its shares. In its first eighteen months, the company earned £289,292. The company then went public, offering its shares at an initial 7/9d., thus making it worth £1,937,500. Within a week, both John and Paul sold a quarter of their holdings, netting £96,875 each, tax free - the capital gains tax was not yet in force. For a group whose first record sold all of five copies, whose early fee for a gig could be as much as £4, whose first public appearance was as a rather indifferent supporting act for 'Wump and the Werbles', and whose career is even now only eight years old, that's a considerable achievement.

Although their personal fortunes (after tax) were probably far less than is popularly imagined, there was little doubt that if they had continued at anything like the same rate - and in 1968 alone they wrote 40 new pieces, one of them called, ironically, 'Northern Song' - they would *earn* in their lifetime more than the total present national debt of the country whose mood and temperament they so accurately embody. Their financial problem used to be quite simply what to do with such resources; and the answer seemed to be an apple, for they sank their fortunes into a multi-million pound entertainment, electronics and merchandising enterprise called Apple Corps Ltd. 'It's a pun,' Paul told me - helpfully.

'The aim of the company,' John told me, 'wasn't a stack of gold teeth in the bank. We'd done that bit. It's more of a trick to see if we could get artistic freedom within a business structure, and to see if we could create things and sell them without charging three times our cost.' Apple Corps was conceived primarily by Harry Pinsker, then one of The Beatles' chief financial advisers, though he declines responsibility for the name. It was effectively a re-incarnation of the old Beatles Ltd., the company into which The Beatles' vast income from years of Beatlemania had been poured. 'I suggested to the boys,' said Pinsker, 'that they bought freehold property and went into retail trading.' The Beatles responded with that infectious enthusiasm which they had - until then - reserved for Indian mysticism and jam butties. 'We want to be like Marks and Spencer', they told Pinsker.

The organisation needed to achieve this extraordinary ambition set itself up in eight countries. Its permanent administrative staff of thirty-six were housed in a £500,000 office block at 3, Savile Row - premises previously occupied by the impresario Jack Hylton.

The Apple offices were designed conventionally. The atmosphere, according to one report, was one of 'casual efficiency enlivened by surrealistic incident.' Occasionally, a Beatle drifted by clothed in yellow satin frills and white bell-bottomed trousers. Almost everyone looked aggressively young and extravagantly hirsute in the current manner. A thin girl behind a reception desk would say, 'I'm sorry, we're not equipped to handle poetry at present.' It all liked to give off the impression of a respectable firm which had been seized during a hippy sit-in and was now being run in the cause of revolution.

In the basement was to be a recording studio described by Paul at the time as the most technically sophisticated in the world; but plans for four feature films, a couple of mod clothing stores and for the development of some eighteen patented inventions by a tame Greek colleague nicknamed 'Magic Alex', went slightly astray. These inventions included, apparently, a 2-inch square, 1/8th inch thick metal plate which - when attached to an ordinary battery, became red-hot within twenty seconds. If the positive and negative attachments were reversed, it became ice-cold - also within twenty seconds. With this invention, it was hoped to revolutionise refrigerators and all manner of heating appliances. Another tit-bit was an audio-visual memory-bank for a telephone. You tell the telephone the name of the person you wish to call, and the telephone automatically connects you to the person wherever he may be.The nation-wide A T and T Telephone Corporation of America was reported to have offered The Beatles one million dollars for the invention.

John and Paul became worried about the falling sales of discs in the United States. With the development of the mini tape-recorder, or casette, record-buyers found it cheaper to tape the songs off the radio than to buy the disc. Under The Beatles' sponsorship, an electronic device was developed to prevent this happening, and the grateful record companies were reported to be desperate to buy this world-patented invention. It seemed quite possible that within a few years, every single record sold anywhere in the world would carry this device, and thus pay to The Beatles a royalty. With the number of records being manufactured annually throughout the world exceeding 100 million, it seemed like a good scheme.

As their various contracts with recording companies, distribution agents, publishing houses and film producers expired (the last ran out in 1976), The Beatles intended their affairs to be solely administered and accounted by Apple and its subsidiaries. They offered £20,000 as a starting salary for anyone who thought they could cope with the financial management for their affairs, but for a long time no one whom they interviewed impressed them as being serious enough in their commitment to the cause. Paul intended to start a staff insurance scheme and would have like to have had a works brass band. He had no intention, however, of becoming a white-collar businessman. 'This *is* a business,' he told me. 'But we want to have fun doing it.'

To that end, they held their first U.S. board meeting aboard a hired Chinese junk, which sailed - appropriately - up and around the Statue of Liberty in New York harbour. For Liberty was precisely what they aimed to have within their new organisation. Liberty - not only to run their own affairs - but to offer to others the kinds of opportunity they themselves felt had been closed to them. 'We *wanted* to help other people,' Paul told me. 'But without doing it like charity and without seeming like patrons of the arts.' Even Stravinsky had noted that the two biggest patrons of the arts in America - the Ford and Rockefeller Foundations, were buying up surplus symphonies as the government bought up surplus corn. 'If you came to see me and said, "I've had such-and-such a dream",' Paul added, 'I would say, "Here's so much money. Go away and do it." We'd already bought all *our* dreams. We wanted to share that possibility with others. When we were touring, and when the adoration and hysteria were at a peak, if we'd been the shrewd operators we were often made out to be, we might have thought - *that's* nice! Aha. Click. Let's use this for our own evil ends. But there's no desire in any of our heads to take over the world. That was Hitler. That's what he wanted to do. There is, however, a desire to get power in order to use it for good.'

Could the Rev. David Noebel have imagined such a statement when, shocked by initial American reaction to The Beatles, he told his Baptist audience in Claremont, California: 'You listen to this, Christians. These Beatles are completely anti-Christ. They are preparing our teenagers for riot and ultimate revolution against our Christian Republic.' It's all part of a 'Communist Master Music Plan.' The Communists are recording songs with a beat 'synchronised' to the 82 per minute beat of an infant's heart, thus inducing a hypnotic state. 'Those sneaky Beatles step up the beat and add Marxist lyrics which could mass hypnotise the American youth.' The first Beatles LP released in the United States was aptly titled, 'This Is The Savage Young Beatles'.

'You meet a lot of people,' continued Paul, 'who think we planned a lot of this. This power thing. But we haven't, you know. We've never planned anything. I *still* don't know what Sergeant Pepper is all about. We only think of ourselves as just happy little songwriters, just playing in a rock group. But - alas - it gets more important than that after you've been over to America, and got knighted.'

Certainly, if it *was* planned, it all got off to a terrible start. John's last school report noted that 'he is on the road to failure'. Ringo's knowledge of music theory was poor. John's father left home when he was eighteen months old and his mother died when he was young. George was nearly thrown out by his parents for being an 'out-and-out teddy boy'. Paul failed in all his academic ambitions. Ringo, an only child ('they gave up after me'), was just 'educated at Butlins'. A career, if such you could describe it, in the tatty world of rock 'n' roll was for them the equivalent of becoming a boxer at the turn of the century. It was the only quick way to escape poverty and to acquire an OK ticket to wealth and fame. But even in their chosen career, they were a disaster. The story of how they trouped around Liverpool and Hamburg, first as The Quarrymen, then as The Rainbows, then as John and the Moondogs, then as The Silver Beatles and finally as The Beatles, is well documented in all their fan books and assorted hagiography. For nearly five years, they had neither luck nor recognition. A founder member, Stu Sutcliffe, died of a brain haemorrhage; the original drummer, Pete Best, was sacrificed for a recording contract, although John now says that they never really liked him anyway. Recording manager George Martin had suggested he wasn't up to scratch. Brian Epstein just seemed like a good bet for a manager. To four working class layabouts, Brian - with his big car, his proper accent, his education, his apparent knowledge of the business - seemed okay.

What is less well documented, and in a way more to the point, was their persistent rudeness and aggressiveness to all whom they encountered. Nowadays we like to call this quality a 'sophisticated detachment' or 'an endearing honesty'. Whatever euphemism we give it, however, it is undoubtedly the quality that caused them to survive, both as people and as artists. For it is not their musical ability nor their minor talent for poetry nor the accidental expression in their songs of the deep feelings of a whole new generation, that carried them to their present authority. It was this abrasiveness, this mockery, this gentle rudeness, inherent in them and their work, that brought them to success. More than anything else, it prevented them from being swept away in the deluge of adulation that was to come hurtling their way, and it enabled a quick and readily acceptable identification between us, who wanted to cock a snoop, and them, who were so obviously willing and able to do so. Their triumph against musical snobbery and social prejudice was our triumph also. And their success against authority and demagogy and pedantry was our success also.

What is peculiarly twentieth century, moreover, is that success has always been as necessary to The Beatles as failure was to Mozart. For theirs is the story of how a whole society - not otherwise noted for its generosity to poets - managed to subsidise its revolutionary subconscious to the tune of around £25 million per year. If that society once became aware that its revolutionary subconscious was no longer being satisfied, then hey presto, the bubble would explode. Thus, as The Beatles committed themselves more and more exclusively to Apple, and not just to its financial advantages and rewards but more importantly to its philosophies and idealism, so the success or failure of that particular enterprise embodied the success or failure of their ability to keep pace with the insistent demands of this revolutionary subconscious. It seemed as if *we* were asking The Beatles to do for us in business organisation and in artistic sponsorship and patronage, what they had already done for us in song, namely to revitalise the language in which we choose to express the way we are, and the way we live.

'It's all right if people don't like us,' George told me. 'As long as they don't deny us.' From the start, partly because of this persistent rudeness, denying The Beatles had been hard to do. After their first recording audition, The Beatles were asked by George Martin to tell them what they didn't like. 'As a starter,' said George Harrison, 'I don't like your necktie.' During their first visit to America, they were invited to a reception by the British Ambassador in Washington, Sir David Ormsby-Gore, now Lord Harlech. Confused about their names, the Ambassador asked John if *he* was John. 'No,' said John. He was Fred. Then, pointing to George he said, '*He's* John.' Sir David started to address George as John. 'No,' said George. 'I'm Charlie,' and pointing to Ringo, 'He's John.' As The Beatles left, Ringo turned to the unsettled said: Ambassador and inquired: 'And what do you do?' 'People in the cheaper seats, please clap,' said John to a West End audience that included, according to the famous story, the Queen Mother, 'The rest of you, just rattle your jewellery.' At earlier performances, John used to appear in bathing trunks, wearing a toilet seat around his neck. 'We're unassuming,' Ringo told me, 'unaffected and British to the core. Someone asked me once why I wore four rings on my fingers, and when I told him it was because I couldn't get them on my nose, he didn't believe me.' 'We're rather crummy musicians,' George told me; 'we can't really sing.' 'We can't really do anything,' Paul added, 'but we're having a great laugh.' 'Don't you think the joker laughs at you?' sang John in his song 'I am the Walrus'.

This extraordinary lack of self-consciousness and innate aggressiveness also protected them from the massive dose of intellectualisation that was to follow their sensational debut as public property. No-one could quite understand how four rough rug-headed kerns whose apparent intelligence was nil and whose apparent musical inclination was crude and worthless, could seize the imagination of so many in so short a time. Even Billy Graham broke one of his strictest rules never to watch TV on the Sabbath to observe the lads. Richard Buckle called them the greatest composers since Beethoven. William Mann, music critic of the London *Times*, spoke in awed tones of 'pandiatonic clusters' and 'flat-submediant key-switches'. Ned Rorem, an American musicologist and noted commentator, said that 'She's Leaving Home' is equal to any song of Schubert, and Leonard Bernstein cited Schumann.   Glenn Gould explained away the success of Lennon and McCartney by pointing to 'our need of the common chord as purgative.' This analytical game reached absurd heights, or depths, in 1968.   Derryck Cooke, writing in *The Listener*, said of 'Strawberry Fields': 'it has a first 9-bar section divided into 1 1/2, 2, 2, 1 1/2 and 2, the penultimate bar being in 6/8 instead of 4/4, quaver equalling quaver. After a delaying 6-beat major phrase harmonised by the tonic chord ('Let me take you down, 'cos I'm going'), the tune plunges fiercely on to the flat 7th, harmonised by the minor 7th on the dominant, for a solidly rhythmic beat phrase (*to* 'Strawberry Fields').' Musicologically, Mr. Cooke was absolutely correct - whether The Beatles liked it or not. But it's as well to remember that he was actually referring to four happy little rockers who could neither read nor write a note of music. Similarly, Jack Kroll of Newsweek described 'Day in the Life' as The Beatles' 'Waste Land'.   Cyril Connolly thought John's books much influenced by Joyce.

John had never read Joyce.   He did buy 'Finnegan's Wake' subsequently but couldn't manage more than the first page. He framed William Mann's 'pandiatonic clusters' review, but thought the rest mostly laughable. To the psychiatric pedantry which reckoned that The Beatles 'are speaking in an existential way about the meaningless actuality', and to the hip-religious fervour which suddenly descended upon them when, for example, a Rev. Ronald Gibbons wanted The Beatles to make a tape-recording of 'O Come all ye Faithful, Yeah, Yeah, Yeah' because, he said 'The Beatles cult can be the very shot in the arm that the Church needs today', and to the semi-political band-wagonning which gave them the M.B.E. and caused a Mr. K. Amirvdham, an Indian Communist M.P., to refer to their sojourn with the Maharishi as evidence that they were 'not only Western Imperialist war-mongering lackeys, but spies' - to all this, John replied, for example, by drawing anti-religious cartoons depicting among other things Christ hanging on the Cross with a pair of bedroom slippers at the foot. His M.B.E. used to dangle idly from a dummy inside his front door. It then sat on his Aunt Mimi's television. In the days when he lived in Weybridge, his private telephone at one time had an answering device which said 'This is an answering machine that will not answer you'. And then laughed.

This is not to say that they were ignorant of what it is they are up to, both socially and musically. Indeed, it was because their awareness was often too acute to be comfortable, that their careers took their two most far-reaching twists; firstly, to give up public performance altogether, and secondly to live artistically almost entirely in their electronic playroom, the recording studio. Both decisions were accelerated by the intolerable pressures of Beatlemania touring, but Derek Taylor recounted to me what seemed to him to have enforced the first decision. 'We were in Australia. In a hotel. Suddenly, the manager came to me and said: "The cripples are ready". I said, "What are they ready for? For The Beatles?" He said "yes." "What do they want?" I said. He said, "Well, they can't move that much, so maybe if The Beatles patted them that would be enough." I said, "You mean, lay their hand on them. Faith-heal them!" He said "yes". So I went into the boy's rooms and said "There's a dozen paraplegics waiting for you in wheel-chairs". So good enough, they trooped out, touched them, grinned and said "See you again". But it left its mark. And when it happened over and over and over again, they treated it like a joke. But they never forgot.'

The second decision came with a growing realisation - shared by others - that pop as it existed then, could no longer contain what they themselves wanted to express through the *medium* called pop music. To effect this second decision, it became clear that the full resources of the recording studio would have to be utilised. Thus, although Pop was already more varied in its sources than Jazz had been 40 years earlier, and although the young white Pop musician was less shackled by the diatonic-harmonic tradition which had dominated and finally suffocated the Jazz and Swing eras, the deus ex machina of recording techniques gave pop its ultimate advantage and its ultimate newness. Phil Spector had been the first to understand this, but in George Martin, The Beatles found an equally sympathetic record-producer. 'Recording', he told me, 'gave us the advantage of being able to make up music as we went along.'

What had started as the Sound of Soul in America's Deep South and had since absorbed everything from Memphis Rock to British Music Hall, suddenly took on the full paraphernalia of sophisticated music-making. Their first LP was recorded in a day. Sergeant Pepper - described by a lecturer at New York's Free University as 'the great contemporary Bible' - took 3 months and 700 hours of studio time to create. Their next LP, called 'The Beatles', took longer. The orchestration for Sergeant Pepper included combs and paper over a string octet and harp for 'Lovely Rita'; multiple-tracked percussion and strings, into which tambouras and swormandels are embedded for 'Within You, Without You' whose rhythm alternates continually between 4/4 and 5/4; 3 tambouras, a dilruba, a tabla, an Indian table-harp, a sitar, 3 cellos and eight violins for 'She's Leaving Home', John on Hammond organ, recorded at different speeds and then overlaid with electronic echo and 4 harmonicas for 'Mr. Kite', and a 41-piece orchestra for 'A Day in the Life' which provided the song-cycle with a final crescendo reminiscent for some of a giant, crippled turbine, struggling to spin new power into a floundering civilisation. By chance perhaps, this desire to spin new power into a floundering civilisation also became the artistic ambition of Apple.

Apple existed for only three years - following the death of Brian Epstein. Its list of products read like the handout for some none too prosperous cottage industry rather than the export list of the dynamic liberator of artistic and business freedom it was cracked up to be. Less than eighteen months after it had been set up, John Lennon publicly announced that if things carried on the way they were going, The Beatles would be broke within the year. 'I'm down to my last £50,000,' John told me. 'My bank balance is really scratching the desk. It would do it good to get back to work.'

Apple's first adventure into retailing - the 'Apple Shop', in London's Baker Street, was in trouble from the start. Its gaudily painted exterior survived for only 6 months before local residents objected and it was painted out. The shop changed management twice, its staff designers went, it made a loss, and then closed. The Beatles gave away the remaining £20,000 worth of stock. Apple Shop had been run by Terry Doran, 'the man in the motor trade' from 'She's Leaving Home'. He also managed a group called Grapefruit, another Apple off-shoot which failed to make any hit records. A second shop in which, Paul told me, 'We shall sell clothes, radios, records and books. If somebody wants to sell something, they can just bring the things in.' 'Apple will be like a bazaar,' he said. It actually turned out to be a smart King's Road boutique called Apple Tailoring (Civil and Theatrical), with an exclusive gents' hairdressing salon in the basement. Apple Films did do a bit better, for a while, with a world-wide financial disappointment - 'Magical Mystery Tour', a cartoon it bought - 'Yellow Submarine', which at first couldn't get any general release in the United Kingdom, 3 tiny

CENSORED

The Beatles(s)
by
Ralph STEADman

promotional films and a rag-bag of plans to its credit. Headed by 42-year-old Denis O'Dell, an associate of Richard Lester, plans included such startling epics as 'The Jam', officially described as 'the story of a traffic jam and the love-hate selfishness and greed it can cause.' Apple Merchandising was run by John Lyndon, a one-time Portobello Road store-keeper. He planned to start up a mail-order catalogue, but...... nothing. Peter Asher, brother of Jane, ran the new artists who included Mary Hopkin and James Taylor, and then left. In management, there was 26-year-old Peter Shotton, John's schoolboy chum and a former member of the former Beatles' group, The Quarrymen. Eventually, he was made John's personal assistant, at £30 per week. He had previously been a skilled washboard player. Managing director was Neil Aspinall, one-time road manager, bouncer, and all-purpose hefty. Actually, he was quite small, and had 8 GCEs. He was, therefore, an intelligent member of the group. He still survives, in 2004, as Managing Director of what remains of Apple.

The electronics division - whose devices, it was claimed, would cause a revolution or two in the refrigeration and recording business especially when headed by Alexis Mardas, also produced almost nothing. Mardas is said to have arrived in Britain knowing only two people here: the Duke of Edinburgh and Lord Snowdon. It seemed natural enough that he should have soon met The Beatles, who asked him what he did with that direct curiosity they share with Alice. 'I invent things,' quipped Mardas. Within the turning of an eye, they promptly set him up on a workshop in Marylebone with four research assistants.

Another key figure used to be John's private astrologer. He made his calculations daily before John arrived at the office. On these, John planned his day. So if an important business trip to America had been planned and the astrologer predicted that long journeys over water were unwise, the trip would be cancelled and that was that, or so the rumour went.

It's ironic that the word 'béatilles' used to be defined in 16th century cook-books as 'all kinds of ingredients that may be fancied put together into a pie, viz.: Cock's combs and bottoms of Hartichokes', for that's about the mixture that went into Apple. There was no regularity of purpose or of planning. In their former office accommodation in Wigmore Street, no-one was ever quite sure who lived in what office because from time to time (often twice a day) people would change round - just for fun. 'It wasn't being *run* like a business,' John told me.

'It was more like a fun-fair.' An American businessman called Allen Klein, previously associated with The Rolling Stones, was brought in to try and sort things out. For these services he was awarded twenty per cent of The Beatles' income.

When The Beatles had first moved to their new offices in London's Savile Row, the four leaders would come in daily to oversee the operation. Klein or no Klein, they drank tea and listened to records. Ringo thought it would be fun to go into the building industry, but that didn't come to much because, as he told me, 'No-one wanted to buy the houses we put up.' John would say that he suddenly needed a £1,500 cine-camera with all available attachments to film a tit-bit he had decided was memorable. A minion would be dispatched to bring back the goodies. No-one thought twice or even once about the expense involved.

'At EMI' (their parent recording company), Paul told me, 'we said we wanted to spend £5,000 on a cover and we think it'll be worth it, and they reel back and take Disprin and say, *we only spend £75.*' EMI, of course, had recently taken over ATV, and ATV suddenly tried to take over Northern Songs Ltd., - the company which handled many of The Beatles' songs. ATV was part of the Grade Organisation, the joint managing director of which was none other that Bernard Delfont. 'Once again,' Paul told me, 'we found ourselves fighting the men in white overalls and big machines and corporate bodies. We're adults now, we're not kiddies any more. Leave us alone, and we'll give in the product and come home with our tails wagging behind us.'

One of the most bizarre aspects of this new adulthood occurred when George and John became co-directors of Hayling Supermarkets Ltd. Someone suggested accordingly - perhaps a little unkindly - that it was the *supermarket* that would prove to be the forum in which the power that The Beatles had won so ferociously, would be displayed. What dreams would they buy there and whom they sponsor? They'd have endless fun no doubt, but to what end? and for whose good? Can Savile Row really be the apotheosis of all that they have dared? Elgar had his chemical shed, Sir William Walton his villas. Beethoven had his nephew, Mozart his wife. The Beatles had Apple. It was like a congenital, occupational hazard - this need of artists to dote upon the worthless and irrelevant. It was also the ultimate self-indulgence, and for The Beatles it surely diminished their ability to capture that revolutionary subconscious which was the source of their power. Being businessmen also transformed their relations with those whom they need. To sell, and continue selling successfully, you require good PR - quiet, efficient and regular. Out must go the rudeness and aggressiveness, once essential to their survival. And in its place? The myth of the omni- powerful Beatles carried them along for a time. And then? The tragedy would be if their new vocation stifled their priceless gift of song.

The tension that this playing at businessmen provoked, was not without its toll. George Harrison had a terrible row and threatened to leave The Beatles for ever. Again, John and Paul seemed to be aware of what was happening to them. Hence their escape to India, not so much to pursue the Maharishi - by then a failing interest, but just to get enough peace and quiet to write some more songs. Even that seemed at first sight impossible. According to one of those apocryphal Ringo stories, a day with the Maharishi began with piped music throughout the camp, and a broadcast request to 'wakey, wakey'. Nonetheless, John, Paul and George managed 32 new songs. But after their return, the creative pace slackened. Their LP called 'The Beatles' got further and further behind schedule and recording sessions were sandwiched in between, or even interrupted by business meetings.

Most pop-stars recorded intensively, and at night. A session could start around six p.m. and not finish till five or six the following morning. Such was the schedule of The Rolling Stones, for example. Of late, The Beatles preferred more normal working hours, two until ten p.m., but this very normality, lacking as it did the solitude of the night, also conspired against their freedom. In their desire to free themselves from what they correctly perceived to be outmoded, restrictive business and sponsorship practices - like Brian Epstein's old organisation, NEMS Enterprises, they gradually enchained themselves more securely than ever before to an ideology whose very liberality looked as if it might bring about its own destruction.

One reaction to this sense of impending doom and also to the increasing boredom of being constantly required to play The Beatles, was that each of them began to pursue their own separate interests. 'This was the big thing,' Paul told me. 'This great self-realisation thing. We started talking about ourselves as a third person.' (John looks round and asks 'Would The Beatles like to do that?' Then he turns to George Martin - their record producer - and says, 'Yes, I think they might want to.') Ringo went off to co-star in Peter Sellers' film of 'The Magic

Christian'. George Harrison, having already anointed the nineteen sitar strings with the oil of newness, became completely absorbed in things Indian and wrote the soundtrack for the film 'Wonderwall'. Paul got lost in running Apple and John married the Japanese artist, Yoko Ono.

To John and Yoko's credit, they appeared to survive all kinds of private and public bitchery and to be living happily ever after. Together, they took to film making. Her art exhibition - 'To Yoko from John', John had filmed by candid camera. At one time, Yoko had had a camera crew follow her about with her previous husband so that every time they had a fight, it could be filmed for posterity. John and Yoko made a film called 'Rape' which won critical acclaim and was concerned with ridiculing the documentary technique of ciné-verité. The film told of how this technique could only be honestly truthful at terrible cost to the subject matter. The subject matter was, in effect, raped. An earlier film had just shown John smiling. In a sense it was the apotheosis of The Beatles who for a long time had drawn us into a fantasy world of their own creation, and thus produced entertainment without involvement. Now we were faced with the prospect of John, the vanishing Lancashire cat, with nothing left but the smile.

'John and I are very shy people, very vulnerable,' Yoko told me at the time. 'Really quite naïve. People have sent us *such* strange letters. "If you (John) have anything to do with that Jap (me), don't forget that we were fighting the Japs only twenty years ago, and if you're not careful she'll slit your throat." My film No. 5 is in Technicolor and stars John and is directed by me. It consists of John smiling. Just that. At one time I wanted every government in the world to send me their smile shots and so build up a big library of smiles. But eventually I just took John's face as sort of representative. It's a very polite film. And we hoped that the smile would send vibrations all around the world. But not just for now. The vibrations should keep on going for people to get a thousand years from now. After all, the love vibrations that were sent by some people *two* thousand years ago, I can still feel, can't you? John and I are fighters. We don't compromise. There wasn't any point in just making love, secretly, and everything. We had to make a film which had the same vibrations as making love. By being together, John and I are making good vibrations which we hope other people will catch.'

Just in case they didn't, John and Yoko sent Acorns for Peace to the heads of every government throughout the world, and made a record called 'Two Virgins' on the sleeve of which they appeared holding hands and stark naked, front and rear view. When asked whether he was just laughing at our desperate and pathetic attempts to interpret his meaning and get his message, Lennon told me: 'No more nor less than *you* are laughing at us.' As Richard Goldstein noted, 'The Beatles became the clown-gurus of the 60's, mocking us as we had mocked them'.

Had John Lennon gone mad? It was a question that everyone seemed to want to ask. He spent his honeymoon in bed and then invited all peace-lovers throughout the world to join him and his wife in their bed-in for peace. 'If everyone stayed in bed for a week,' John told me, 'there would be no killings.' Everyone thought that was such a groovy joke that no-one did anything about it. John and Yoko then went to Montreal where they checked in at the Hotel Reine Elisabeth for another seven-day stint. They sent a telegram to Prime Minister Trudeau inviting him to join them or to plant his acorn for peace. Trudeau was too busy for peace-talk and sent an apology telegram 'with regrets'. It was in room 1742 of the hotel that John and Yoko and forty friends calling themselves the Plastic-Ono Band, recorded the Hawaiian love-chant later called 'Give Peace a Chance'. It was like a football crowd shout-a-long, instantly memorable and endlessly repetitive.

John had begun to promote peace as if it were washing powder. 'Think Peace today, and keep Nixon away,' ran the slogan. In a consumer society, believed Lennon, Peace had to be sold like any other commodity. As a result, all his massive talent and all his declining resources were being sunk into that one aim. 'We will keep going until peace comes, until we've got them all indoctrinated with peace. Including the students. I'd like the militant students to show me one militant revolution that worked. We all have Hitler in us,' John told me, 'but we also have love and peace. So why not give *peace* a chance for once?' John had once said he was more popular than Jesus. By a tragic twist, he had become, for many young people, Jesus himself and so was treated in the same way. As a result, he was perceived as mad.

John held a press reception for his new record at Chelsea Town Hall. Somehow it had to be Chelsea Town Hall. How many electioneering speeches must that hall have heard? How many tin-pot self-important Aldermen have cuckooed banalities on its stage? Across the balcony hung an enormous banner proclaiming, 'Give Peace a Chance', and across the stage another saying, 'Think Peace'. If it hadn't been a private gathering, those slogans would have been ripped down as anarchist trash by some local church-going do-gooder who would probably then have got the OBE for services to the community.

In peace-loving Australia, meanwhile, another new Beatles disc 'The Ballad of John and Yoko' had been banned because of the chorus which said: 'Christ, you know it ain't easy.'

It remained a miracle, however, that in spite of having become some of the most famous people in the entire world, and in spite of the gradual enchainment entailed in their pursuit of business freedoms, they still managed to go on making music and writing songs with an effortless ease and apparent simpleness that can only be described as miraculous. In a sense, the whole tradition of song-writing which is at the centre of all musical expression descended upon The Beatles. Great opera stars such as Maria Callas were, often for economic reasons, no longer primarily concerned with miniature forms such as The Song. 'Serious' composers like Stockhausen were, for scientific reasons, no longer primarily concerned with human utterances - of which singing is the most primitive and hence the most expressive. And since a master like Stravinsky had never been famous for his solo vocal writing, all our expectations of good song-writing tended to shift towards The Beatles. Two LP's at least seemed to fulfil these expectations - 'Sergeant Pepper's Lonely Hearts Club Band', and 'The Beatles'. A single copy of one of their sleeves came to be almost as valuable as any holy relic ever was.

The idea of making Sergeant Pepper into a coherent and continuous song cycle - thought by some to be the result of a brilliant master plan, in fact occurred only halfway through the project, which would account for the apparent 'irrelevance' of the mystical 'Lucy in the Sky With Diamonds', the ludicrously banal 'Within You, Without You', and the early seventies sound of 'A Day in the Life' - this last appropriately banned by the BBC. The record contained thirteen songs altogether - all of them, with one exception, by Lennon and McCartney. It took about three months to record (Mozart wrote 'Don Giovanni' in less) and was plugged more assiduously than any recent Beatle record in recent Beatle history.

Its Pop-art cover 'staged' by Peter Blake and Jann Haworth, set the uniformed, pop art Beatles *and* their wax doubles (?), firmly amongst photo cut-outs of some all time greats - Diana Dors, Peter O'Toole, Tony Curtis, Dylan Thomas and other worthies. The 62 faces and figures - and especially those wax doubles - clearly indicated that The Beatles felt themselves to be living not only in the shadows of those whom they admire, but also of themselves. As the song says:

> And the time will come
> When you will see we're all one
> And life flows on within you and without you.

It was like some victory photograph gleaned from the archives of a gratefully absurd Spanish American revolution. Like the music recorded therein, it had a ritual cynicism that passed for intelligence, an irrepressible lust for fun that passed for a desire to please, and a sarcasm that masqueraded as hip.

Serious criticisms of The Beatles and their music became an almost forgotten privilege. The *New Statesman,* a left organ, plastered itself so richly with clichés, that its all purpose do-it-yourself review made one gasp for Cliff Richard - sing us one of the old songs, Cliff. 'The Beatles,' groaned the organ, 'despite their priceless simplicity, aren't as simple as all that.' The record, 'though it starts from the conventions of pop, it becomes "art" - and art of an increasingly subtle kind.' 'The triumph (of The Beatles) is equivocal, though not double-faced.' According to the *New Statesman,* The Beatles had cunningly devised a song cycle which depicted the transformation of old-style camaraderie into new-style aloneness, the aloneness of God's little children who are left only 'with the things that make us simple, social creatures' (greed, violence, bitterness, anger, dreams?).

The august Mr. William Mann of *The Times* (the first serious-minded Beatle advocate) preferred to think in terms of the mixolydian and pentatonic. Shapely bass-lines and hurricane glissandi appealed to him greatly. A pity he did not mention the mumbo-jumbo recorded on the inside track of side two which owners of automatic disc-players luckily escaped, or the high-pitched dog-whistle singing away simultaneously with the last chord of the last song just so that the doggies weren't forgotten.

It was ironic that most of the songs were now so electronically complicated, so manifestly the product of a recording studio, that very few could ever be performed in public sounding as they do when they had been devised in private. As if wishing to be *nothing* but moustachioed and clapped-out dandies, The Beatles discovered the *need* for this monster playroom to keep themselves collectively amused. In this way, they were able to go on gaining energy from one another, to go on regenerating themselves and equipping themselves for survival.

All this is not to deny that when the record first appeared, The Beatles actually resurrected the hope that 'light-music' just might be as interesting and worthy of attention as is what is nervously referred to as 'serious music'. Undoubtedly, they were a standard which other groups were forced to emulate in order to stay fashionable: an aloof and insistent reminder of the woeful ordinariness of much popular culture; an affront to the sentimental and mealy-mouthed: for some, The Beatles were an uncomfortable even forbidding gesture towards the hordes of the respectable and the coach parties from Luton. Surprisingly, they never protested nor marched. They were not Left wing, nor Empire Loyalist. Yet they were political in a way that Harold Wilson, then Prime Minister, was not, for they and not he were the mentors of the age, the spokesmen - artistically - for all colours.

The most eloquent and also the most frightening of these spokesmen was undoubtedly John Lennon, whose fine gift for pun and under-statement disarmed many a high-minded critic. But on The Beatles' own testimony, Lennon withdrew more and more, even from them. His white Rolls-Royce - once painted all over in yellowy flower-patterns, now had darkened one-way windows through which he viewed the world but through which the world could not view him. His house in Weybridge had a room full of halfs - half a chair, half a radio, half an ironing-board, half a bookcase, half a kettle and half a shoe - all of them painted white. Four white hammers hung on a piece of string above the fireplace and he used a chess set, the members of which were *all* white. His conversation was often elliptical and visionary. He was scornful of critics - favourable or hostile. His music was harsh and brittle and his poetry a bleak and terrifying outburst. The Walrus, the voice of corporate society, wears 'corporation tea-shirts', weeps crocodile tears and is a raving maniac. Society itself was depicted as a sordid madhouse. Another song - 'Day in the Life', used at the funeral service of the murdered British playwright, Joe Orton, begins:

> I read the news today oh boy
> About a lucky man who made the grade
> And though the news was rather sad
> Well, I just had to laugh
> I saw the photograph.
> He blew his mind out in a car.

Whether this is a dirge for a friend of John's killed in a car crash, or whether (as some claimed) it was a lament for the assassination of President Kennedy, it didn't matter. Like Joyce, it works on all levels.

But there remains a dazzling simplicity about the image, and a pitiful grimness about its use. There is cynicism about the occasion described, and a hopeless despair about its implication. 'Within you' ends the cruellest of laughs, giving all the songs a strange double-edge. For Lennon, the society into which - through no choice of his own - he had been born, had for him deliberately enervated the souls of men and thus noiselessly unwound the springs of action. Such choice as he had, must surely be the freedom to choose how he would exercise his mind, and how he would stimulate his imagination - provided he did not thereby restrict the freedom of others.

> And so we live, a life of ease -
> Everyone of us, that's all we need
> Sky of blue, sea of green -
> In our yellow submarine.

That simple verse from a song dismissed as trite, says much about the aspirations of a man like John Lennon. They are the aspirations of Locke, of Hume, of Mill, of Plato, of Aristotle. They neither worship false gods, nor praise famous men. They are not concerned with power or pomp, with sex or sin, with violence or with victory. They are not words of wisdom or even of authority. These were merely a personal statement of a dream more real than the fabric of any dogma that society would wish to impose upon it.

> Always, no sometimes, think it's me
> But you know I know when it's a dream
> I think I know I mean a 'Yes'
> But it's all wrong
> That is I think I disagree.

A work of art is, after all, nothing more than a reflection of man's image as he imagines it in a mirror. But the mirror has no reality of its own, only the reality of what it reflects. So even 'Yellow Submarine' has its bitter laugh before the final chorus. Our freedom was a freedom to give The Beatles theirs.

Perhaps we cannot forget the image of unruly little rockers that it once suited The Beatles to promote; perhaps we find it hard to overcome the suspicion that wealth and popularity can mean anything but vulgar success and cunning promotion. Perhaps the cheapness of their public sycophants and the arbitrariness of their imitators who must number millions, destroy the uniqueness which alone gave them their freedom. But Lennon eventually seemed to escape into a kaleidoscope world all his own. Whilst he mocked the semi-detached conventions that crowd our public behaviour -

> She (we gave her most of our lives)
> is leaving (sacrificed most of our lives)
> home (we gave her everything money could buy)

he offered also the hope of a better life than was our father's:

> Picture yourself in a boat on a river
> with tangerine trees and marmalade skies . . .
> Lucy in the sky with diamonds.

It is a hopeless vision, unworldly and unreal; but whether it was expressed in Love-Ins or Be-Ins, or whether it was sought through drugs or stimulants, it was not deserving of prison or even handcuffs. And it was infinitely preferable to talk of war and hatred, of racial discrimination and snobbery of all kinds. However muddled its message, it was at least worth our sympathetic attention. Just as its urban poetry was worth our reading, and its haunted music worth our hearing.

In spite of the *New Statesman*, and all of them.

A year later, came an even more extraordinary record called simply, 'The Beatles'. It was wrapped in a plain white cover adorned by the song titles and those four faces alone, faces which for some still represented the menace and illogicality of long-haired youth, for others the beginnings of a profound cultural Renaissance, and for others the desperate, apparently endless struggle against cynical defunct so-called betters. In their eyes, as in their songs, we saw again the fragile fragmentary mirror of the society which sponsored them, which interpreted and made demands of them and which punished them when they did what others reckon to be evil; Paul, ever hopeful, wistful; Ringo, every mother's son; George, local lad made good; John, withdrawn, sad, but with a fierce intelligence clearly undimmed by all that organised morality could throw at him. They were all our best hope - heroes for all of us, and better than we deserved.

It's not as if The Beatles ever sought such adulation. The extraordinary quality of the thirty songs on the double-album remains one of simple happiness. The lyrics overflow with a sparkling radiance and sense of fun that it is impossible to resist. Almost every track is a send-up of a send-up of a send-up, rollicking, reckless, gentle, magical. Like their subsequent LP 'Get Back', they seemed to have become obsessed by parody and self-parody. This obsession had always been clear in their public statements thus making many of their utterances (including the ones quoted in this chapter), untrue, misquoted, irrelevant or all three. But it never seemed to matter. Nor did it when the subject matter of the songs ranged from piggies ('have you seen the bigger piggies/In their starched white shirts') to Bungalow Bill of Saturday morning film-show fame ('He went out tiger hunting with his elephant gun/In case of accidents he always took his mom'), from 'Why Don't We Do It In The Road?' to 'Savoy Truffle'. The skill at orchestration had matured with finite precision. Full orchestra, brass, solo violin, glockenspiel, saxophone, organ, piano, harpsichord, all manner of percussion, flute, sound effects, were used sparingly and thus with deftness. Electronic gimmickry had been suppressed or ignored in favour of musicianship. References to or quotations from Elvis Presley, Donovan, Little Richard, The Beach Boys, Blind Lemon Jefferson were woven into an aural fabric that had become the Bayeux Tapestry of popular music. It was all there if you listened. Aristophanes had lengthily misquoted Sophocles and Euripides. Shakespeare had re-written Holinshed. The Beatles had copied and absorbed everybody - including themselves. Even a line from 'King Lear' Act IV, Scene 6, had got into 'I Am the Walrus'. Possibly, this willingness to accept anything and everything that they absorbed, had - like Janis Joplin - caused a lack of critical distance between them and their art which lead to self-indulgence. But with The Beatles, the questioning always remained. Lennon sings, 'I told you about strawberry fields' and 'I told you about the fool on the hill'. And now?

The Beatles were competent rather than virtuoso instrumentalists - but their ensemble playing was intuitive and astonishing. They bent and twisted rhythms and phrases with a unanimous freedom that gave their harmonic adventures the frenzy of anticipation and unpredictability. The voice - particularly that of Lennon - became just another instrument, wailing, screeching, mocking, weeping. Like the best composers, their music thrived on the unexpected. They always managed to make the words go against the music. Beneath the words was a harmonic shiftiness which gave them a continuous uneasiness. The introduction to 'Michelle' actually changes key in the second bar. This element of suspense enabled The Beatles to be the generous masters but never the creatures of their audience.

There was also in 'The Beatles' a quiet determination to be finally rid of the bogus categorisation that often had surrounded them and their music. The words were almost deliberately simple-minded - one song was just called 'Birthday' and included lines like 'Happy Birthday to You'; another just went on repeating 'Goodnight'; another said 'I'm so tired, I haven't slept a wink'. The music was likewise stripped of all but the simplest of harmonies and beat - so what was left was prolific outpouring of melody, music-making of unmistakable clarity and foot-tapping beauty. The sarcasm and hostility that had always given their music its edginess still bubbled out - 'Lady Madonna trying to make ends meet - yeah/Looking through a glass onion'. The harshness of the imagery was, if anything, ever harsher; 'The eagle picks my eye/The worm he licks my bone,' black birds, black clouds, broken wings, lizards, destruction. And most grotesque of all, was a terrifying track just called 'Revolution 9', which comprised sound effects, overheard gossip, backwards-tapes, janglings from the subconscious memories of the floundering civilisation, cruel, paranoiac, burning, agonised, hopeless - given shape by an anonymous bingo voice which just went on repeating 'Number nine, number nine, number nine' - until you wanted to scream. McCartney's drifting melancholy overhung the entire proceedings like a veil of shadowy optimism - glistening, inaccessible, loving.

At the end, all one could do was stand and applaud. Whatever your taste in popular music, you could find it satisfied here. If you thought that pop music was Engelbert Humperdinck, then The Beatles had done it better - without sentimentality but with passion; if you thought that pop was just rock 'n' roll, then The Beatles had done it better - but infinitely more vengefully; if you thought that pop was just mind-blowing noise, then The Beatles had done it better - on distant shores of the imagination that others had not even sighted. It is, perhaps, a curious quirk of our psychological vulnerability that everybody demands the existence of heroes, whether they be lone yachtsmen, generals, God, TV personalities, cultural leaders, or pop stars. Being semi-myth, moreover, these heroes seem increasingly neither to feel nor care in a way that we were able to understand. But the best of pop heroes, and in particular The Beatles, did care and cared with increasing desperation about the way we organised our lives and the way we expressed what we believed in.   They expressed with indefinable accuracy the sense of outrage felt by most civilised people against all human indignity, whether in Vietnam, in Alabama, or in London.

If nothing else, pop music - with The Beatles undeniably to the fore, was now describing this sense of outrage with a great tenderness. And if The Beatles could overcome their present preoccupations, it ws hoped, we might look to them again for the fulfilment of that revolutionary subconscious. But if Apple went broke, then so might they - both as businessmen and as artists. Are The Beatles only in it for the money? The interesting thing about *that* question is that *we* keep on asking it and never get a satisfactory reply.

John gave a hint as to his real intentions. He gave back his M.B.E. in protest against Britain's involvement in the Biafran war.   He indicated also that The Beatles were dead and that he wished to begin the seventies not as John Lennon, M.B.E., not as Beatle John Lennon, but as plain Mr. Lennon. One newspaper described the M.B.E. event as the irrelevancy of the decade. Bertrand Russell wrote to congratulate John.

But perhaps the best hope, we thought, lay in John's first unpublished book which was called, *Sport, Speed and Illustrated, Edited and Illustrated by J. W. Lennon.* It had a serial story which ended: 'If you like this, come again next week. It'll be even better.' John was seven at the time.

Chapter Four

If The Rolling Stones had not existed some friendly demon would surely have had to invent them. They were the fire to The Beatles' ice. They are as necessary to a proper understanding of pop music as Bob Dylan was to a proper understanding of fashionable social protest movements. They epitomise the best in pop - its aggression, its uninhibited violence and its resolution; and the worst - its banality, its repetitiousness and its self-pity. In Mick Jagger, they have one of the most electric stage performer to have emerged from the entertainment world during the last fifty years - narcissistic, ugly, magnetic. But after the departure of their eminence grise and manager Andrew Loog Oldham, they have wandered in the doldrums - aloof, persecuted, incoherent, still active in an insolent kind of way but nonetheless lost in some paranoiac musical wilderness, rebels totally without cause, anarchists totally without self-justification.

Whereas The Beatles seemed to personify all that had promise, seemed to hold a delicate balance between being scornful of society and yet obedient children of that society, The Rolling Stones were outlaws from the start. Destructive in tone, arrogant in style, apocalyptic in performance, they raped the easy conscience of a public which still clung to the desperate hope that if only the young would listen to adult advice, all would still be well with the world. But all was not well, and the Stones more than any other pop group, upended the notion of order being essential to art and proclaimed - very loudly - that art was chaos and chaos art. As their colleague Jim Morrison, lead singer with The Doors, told me: 'erotic politicians, that's what we are. We're interested in everything about revolt, disorder, chaos and *all* activity that appears to have no meaning.' On an early Rolling Stone LP, manager Andrew Oldham wrote: 'If you don't have enough bread (money) to buy this disc, get that blind man, knock him on the head, steal his wallet and lo, behold, you have the loot. If you put the boot in, good. Another sold.' Not surprisingly, Decca Record Company refused to print Oldham's sleeve notes.

The Rolling Stones
by
Ralph Steadman

When the Stones had first visited the West Coast of America, a group of young radicals issued the following proclamation of welcome:

'Greeting and welcome Rolling Stones, our comrades in the desperate battle against the maniacs who hold power . . . They call *us* dropouts and delinquents and draft-dodgers and punks and hopheads and heap tons of shit on our heads . . . But we will play your music in rock 'n' roll marching bands as we tear down the jails and free the prisoners, as we tear down the state schools and free the prisoners, as we tear down the military bases and arm the poor, as we tattoo "Burn, baby, burn" on the bellies of the wardens and generals, and create a new society from the ashes of our fires.

'Comrades - you, The Rolling Stones will return to this country when it is free from the tyranny of the State, and you will play your splendid music in factories run by workers, in the domes of emptied city halls, on the rubble of the police stations, under the hanging corpses of the priests and under a million red flags waving over a million anarchist communities.'

Mick Jagger told me; 'I believe there can be no evolution without revolution. Why *should* we try and "fit in"? Our generation is growing up and they believe in the same things as we do. I *know* I earn too much, but I'm still young and there's something spiteful inside me which makes me want to hold on to what I've got.'

In view of this revolutionary fever, it was not surprising that almost none of The Rolling Stones compositions were concerned with the traditional middle-class moralities such as Love, self-pity, jealousy, sadness or happiness. In an age that worshipped nostalgia and whimsy, the Stones seemed determined to proclaim physical excitement, mental chaos, sexual exploitation, and a barbaric hedonism. They consistently offered Pop an access to the sordid and the grotesque and the evil - in contrast to that which was normally admitted as Culturally healthy, attributes such as goodness and truth. Consequently the Stones' ethic was usually thought to be unacceptable to a complex, industrialised society whose foundations were hard-work and Protestant righteousness. And it was this very unacceptability that encouraged the Stones to develop a message (if such it was) which, being essentially primitive and sensual, was probably more universal than that of those middle-class, middle-aged capitalist businessmen called The Beatles.

But society is not slow to effect a devastating vengeance on those who preferred to ignore it. One by one, it seemed, the Stones and The

Beatles were rounded up on petty offences, and scolded publicly like naughty children. One Detective Sergeant of the Police Force, or Violence as it's sometimes called, seemed to have devoted his life-work to nabbing the bastards. He was reported to have said: 'My ambition is to get The Beatles.' Two down and two to go, was the tally so far, he said. 'Oz' described him as 'London's deadliest male groupie'. And the first to be 'got' had of course been Mick Jagger.

When Jagger was first found guilty in March 1967 of being in possession of drugs, the tragedy was not in the ludicrous jail sentence imposed, disproportionate to the crime and self-defeating as it was, nor in the hasty righteousness of the top people's newspaper and the corresponding and long overdue discredit of the rest, nor even in the succès de scandale which the trial gave to each and every participant, thus obscuring the delicate problems therein. Society in its more proper and legal manifestations showed itself yet again totally incapable of understanding not the fact of what it patronisingly calls 'the new hedonism', but the causes. The absurdity of the whole affair was caught perfectly when the presiding Judge declared that Brian Jones should now 'buckle down to some honest-to-goodness work'. Brian Jones didn't and died.

What was lacking at the various trials was the imagination to see that the need to take drugs such as pot or LSD, is not out of perversity or out of a lust for evil, but out of a demand to explore, to open the windows of experience. The assumption that such an exploration is necessarily bad was a conclusion based upon insufficient medical evidence, insufficient psychoanalytical evidence, and no *philosophical* evidence whatsoever.

But in spite of this persecution, and eventually partly *because* of it, the Stones, like the Negro-blues soul tradition from which they sprang, touched off a deeper protest than The Beatles could fathom - inarticulate and guttural though it might have been.

Technically, they were way behind their more sophisticated rivals, The Beatles. The quality of their recordings was poor and their lyrics invariably inaudible. They relied on four-square rhythms, harmonic drones and negligible chord progressions. Their instrumentation was primitive and has hardly developed since they first appeared. 'Jumpin' Jack Flash' could have been made 2000 light years away. Their attempts at Hi-fi dexterity were confused and wasteful. But somehow when confronted with the Stones and all that therein is, any musicological analysis is tedious and irrelevant.

What they achieved, if indeed it was an achievement, was to celebrate the abnormal as if it were normal. Mental disintegration, sexual deviation and intellectual dishonesty were proclaimed not as exceptional circumstances but as prevalent conditions. Dubious psychoanalytical evaluations such as 'persecution' or 'paranoia' or 'the individual' whilst seeming to have direct relevance to the social status of the Stones, were, in fact, of no consequence at all since the Stones *were* the precise embodiment of those conditions. Their significance lay in their ability to communicate those conditions to a society which preferred not to know about them, except when the demands of a liberal education made such knowledge imperative. And somehow, this magic, this black magic, compensated for and balanced out the almost too good to be true, and certainly too good to be real, Beatles. It may just have been an extraordinary chance that whilst The Beatles were releasing their double-album, 'The Beatles', The Rolling Stones brought out a stranger and more savage record - within a few days. A coincidence, perhaps, but not without its irony. While The Beatles sang of 'Dear Prudence', and 'Martha My Dear' and 'Goodnight Sleep Tight', the Stones sang of a Street Fighting Man itching for bloody Revolution. Mick Jagger introduced himself on the record as the Devil, craving for bloody sympathy.

> I'll shout and scream, I killed the King.
> I was around when Jesus Christ had his moment of doubt and
>   pain.

> Killed the Tzar and his ministers . . . pleased to meet you, hope
>   you guessed my name.

Interspersed with grunts and screams, the effect was one of cold horror at the self-destructive jubilation in which we - through *their* relentless, pounding, mocking beat - were being forcibly urged to take part. The aura of decadent moaning gave even the most angular of tunes that special smell of whisky wallowing.

> For the girl I'm to marry, is a four-legged sow -
> I've been soaking up drink like a sponge.

Whether the public agonising of those who self-consciously consider themselves outcasts is of interest to anyone except those who feel likewise spurned, and whether that agonising when dressed up with the musical footnotes of enfeebled and paralysed imaginations is of merit to anyone except those whose own agonising also lacks intelligent expression, is primarily a matter of psychoanalysis and not musical understanding. The music itself did seem only to drone and bang and rattle in some kind of purposive determination to keep going. It had the monotony supposedly characteristic of good, meaningful blues music; it had the hypnotic fascination of a skewered beetle writhing and throbbing as life drains out from that scaly, filthy body; it had the guilty throb of lust, with the expectation of pleasure and the hope of satisfaction. It was irresistible certainly, but also gloating and secret. It communicated nothing but the closedness of the adolescent nightmares which were paraded before us by way of truth, and nothing but the debauchery and gluttony of indiscipline. No wonder Stanley Kubrick used 'Paint It Black' as the coda for his great anti-war film, 'Full Metal Jacket'.

The cover of one record sleeve captured their seedy self-congratulation perfectly. The Rolling Stones were depicted at the aftermath of some squalid feast set in a decaying baronial hall. Jagger, in battered trilby, sneers at the camera, his mouth stuffed with an apple. Drummer Charlie Watts is slumped, feet on the head of the table. The others are splayed morosely amongst the remnants of an orgy that might have been. The whole scene, like the record, was accurately titled, 'Beggars Banquet.'

It seems odd that the tradition of popular music which was a tradition involving simple-minded self-expression and enjoyment, should have come to this. But one only has to take a quick glance at those who still upheld the supposedly noble tradition of so-called 'popular music', to realise the bankruptcy of those involved and the consequent vacuum which pop, unwittingly perhaps, was beginning to fill. The old-timers still paraded the halls, legendary but defunct, loved but for no good reason. Take, for example, Donald Peers.

Back in the good old days of sound radio, when music was music, there was one particular voice which used to sing out across the air waves in Britain bringing comfort and succour to the critically ill and the dying. One lady after hearing the voice, wrote to the BBC saying: 'Tell him, tell him, I shall now die happy.' 'I'm a pro,' he said. 'People in show-biz are a commodity - like detergent.' Donald Peers had been making records since 1930; eye-witness accounts report that he had more dimples per square inch than the average pock-marked out-of-work Chinese waiter. Three times a grandfather, estimates put him (in 1969) at least aged 60. Truly, he is the Ancient Briton of Song. Just before his birth, his mother had had a throat operation which had left her almost voiceless. 'Never mind,' she said, 'Donald Bach will sing for me.'

He began life as a housepainter at 9d. an hour. The peripatetic son of a Welsh colliery worker, Donald Rhys Hubert Keith Peers turned up in Lowestoft where - inspired by an end-of-the-pier minstrel show, he learnt to play the ukulele. He cut his first 78 r.p.m. single on his 21st birthday. It only cost 6d. but it flopped. During the War, his powerful voice was beamed to France - presumably to sustain among others the French. Another 78 r.p.m. single 'By a Babbling Brook', was recorded in 1941. It hit the charts - eight years later, and for Peers, it hit the jackpot. Success had taken him 20 years to achieve, but most of those years had been usefully spent like a tram (his own description) - going round and round the same old route and eventually back to the same old depot. The 'Babbling Brook' changed all that. In 1949, he became the first singer to give a solo recital at the Royal Albert Hall, the first, that is, who couldn't read a note of music. Women tore off their clothes (as well as his) at the merest sight of him. He was the first of the ravers and he actually topped the bill at the London Palladium, the only British star to do so since Gracie Fields.

Alas, a year later, he ruptured his larynx and a world tour to Australia had to be postponed because his favourite poodle bit his lip. The adulation, however, continued - elderly ladies wrote in their hundreds to say that because of him, they were at peace with the world, although one critic did venture to say that Peers was just 'a very good second act, good enough, that is, to put the audience in the right mood for the star'.

Eventually young Donald, now 43, set off for Australia for a six week tour. He stayed for nearly four years. When he finally returned, 'Powder Your Face With Sunshine' and 'Daddy's Little Girl' were forgotten songs. The raving mums had grown old and some even had difficulty in remembering who Donald Peers was. Undeterred, he set off to discover the Northern Circuit of Working Men's Clubs, a circuit then the bread and butter of many an old timer and many a young hopeful. 'After all,' said Donald, 'I was never really a West End entertainer.'

For ten years, he appeared between the fire-eater and the stripper until, as the ever young hopeful that he was, launched himself once more into the pop market. Two Tin Pan Alley arrangers lifted Offenbach's 'Barcarolle' from 'The Tales of Hoffmann' and called it, 'Please Don't Go'. "I beg you, don't go,' sang the aging Romeo. 'The words are me,' he said. 'I'm not at all embarrassed by them.' The record got to No. 3 in those charts, to the consternation and astonishment of everyone except Peers. Like some kindly dinosaur, it seemed, he had deliberately chosen to wander amongst the debris of show-biz's mythological golden era - the good old days which were only good in that they were now mostly forgotten. Recently, he was driving past the site of the old Finsbury Park Empire: 'I was top of the bill in that particular theatre,' he told me, 'six times in eighteen months. Now it's a block of flats.' 'Please Don't Go' ached for a nostalgia that was never really there except in the memory. It sobbed with tears of acid and it pleaded for self-pity. Peers had never really escaped from the whimsy that caused him.

Such was his belief in his own professionalism, that the sugar world which once gave him such female adulation, had now swallowed him up completely. Not only did he seem unable to express any private sorrow in his so-called Art, but 'Please Don't Go' was the clear admission that he was now trapped for ever in the shabby ideals and glamour which inhabit that professionalism. He really did believe that he was just a commodity - like detergent. Someone suggested recently that he retire. 'Retire to what?' he said.

Those who sought to follow Peers in the tradition of popular ballad singing, got sucked into the cabaret circuit. It was only there that they could now be assured of a sympathetic audience. The Savoy Hotel in London, for example, maintained an excellent tradition for cabaret. Amongst their star performers used to be the all-purpose French entertainer, Sacha Distel - or, as the jovial Savoy MC used to describe him, Sashel Destelle. Distel was a sweet little man with suntan and freckles. His crême-de-menthe eyes and cupid dimples gave him that kind of ageless appeal that you wouldn't mind letting your daughter go out with. He was every mother's answer to a jet-set son-in-law. He drove a Porsche and flew a plane, was once engaged to Brigitte Bardot, had an affair with Annette Stroyberg, once married to Roger Vadim (an ex-*M*. Bardot), had three homes - a skiing chalet in Mégève for December until March, a Paris home for March 'til June, and a villa in St. Tropez for the rest.

'I take love seriously,' Distel told me, 'but I would not go and kill myself for a girl.' He rarely drank and never smoked and although he was once the doyen of the French pop scene - Les Yé Yés, as it was called - he successfully matured or graduated into that select band of saccharine entrepreneurs, the champagne set, the cabaret worthies. With nonchalant modesty, he confessed to me - in a French accent - that 'Nobody can teach old monkeys how to make new faces'. He was, as they say, a good egg.

He couldn't really sing, but that didn't seem to matter. His perfectly tailored act had a sophisticated correctness that Rex Harrison would have found difficult to fault. Most of his songs went luba duba doob or froyba dooba doob or booby wooby booby. He was a groaner without the groans, the original cuddly toy. He wasn't too hot on the guitar either, in spite of having played for Juliette Greco, taught Miss Bardot the rudiments and been voted No. 1 guitarist in France for 15 years on the trot. He impersonated - a bit, and the ghost of Maurice Chevalier used to be dragged out fairly frequently. But that didn't seem to matter either, because in the first place he apologised in advance like all good troupers should for his lack of practice, and in the second place there can have been few entertainers who played wrong notes with such style and such heart-throbbing tenderness. He had jokes - at which he laughed - and a nice little song which mentioned 'Hair', the balance of payments and The Beatles and Wow, man, this cat's hip.

The audience weren't too sure when to rattle *their* jewellery but they *did* wave their hands and gurgle contentedly as he mentioned Frank Sinatra (who recorded some of his songs), Petula Clark and some of the other all-time greats. And as he murmured, with his lips pouting, 'Although I'm no Brigitte Bardot, I hope you'll spend the night with me,' many a 45-year-old sequined heart did flutter.

He was and is 100 per cent goodness - polished, desirable and lovely. He was also totally professional - no fuss, no hard sell, no gymnastics. This was never more apparent than when his act would close with one of those carefully rehearsed routines by the professionally smiling Savoy Dancers who - according to that redoubtable MC - gave us 'Latin with a fruity flavour'. There was a lot of leg, but the seduction had gone.

Perhaps it was M. Vadim who had taught him the gentle art of seduction. When Vadim had finished his film 'Seven Deadly Sins' he wanted seven different composers to write the music for each episode. For his friend Sacha Distel, Vadim had chosen the one entitled 'Vanity'.

But undoubtedly, the mother figure for all these great old-timers was Judy Garland.

Judy Garland had been coming back ever since she was invented. She appeared for the last time in 1969 on what must have seemed like her ninety-third comeback at London's Talk of the Town. Spencer Tracy used to say that 'Garland audiences don't just listen - they feel'. They also feared - and in some cases hoped - that they were about to witness a nervous breakdown, which was one of the insistent qualities of this 47-year-old disaster-prone star.

She didn't really give a concert - she conducted a seance. She evoked pity and sorrow like no other super-star. 'Audiences,' she told me, 'have kept me alive.' They also fed on her agonised and well publicised past - her teenage stardom, her tantrums, her alcoholic voice with its frequent crack-ups, her broken contracts and her four busted marriages each to increasingly younger men, her suicide attempts and her aches and pains. The audience *knew* that life had beaten her up but not destroyed her. Her survival gave her power and sex-appeal. Her inevitable death gave her immortality.

She was curiously bi-sexual and generated the hysteria that homosexuals found it easy to identify with, and necessary to idolise. She was greedy for applause - 'We love you, Judy,' shouted the audience. 'I love you too,' came the response. 'I've been through a lot. People ask, "Is she going to appear? Is she dead?" Well, I'm hear and you couldn't keep me away.' Even the cynical were sucked in.

Frances Gumm had been born in a trunk in the Princes Theatre at Grand Rapids, Minnesota. 'Little leather lungs' started at MGM when she was thirteen. MGM put her into twelve starring pictures whilst she was still in her teens. She grew fat and was told by a studio executive, 'You look like a hunchback. We love you but you're so fat you look like a monster.' She took psychiatric treatment from the age of eighteen and was kept alive on pills - sleeping pills, tranquillisers, stimulators and waking pills. Psychologists were her parents and the camera was her lover. By twenty-three, she was already once divorced.

> Call me unreliable

she sang,

> But it's undeniably true
> I'm irrevocably signed with you.

With whom it was none too clear.

She became very thin, almost haggard; her hair flicked back like a boy's. The orange-sequined suit that she liked to wear made her jaunty - a pantomime principal boy got lost in the East End. Her performance remained stunningly alive although she herself is dead. With hand on hip, she tottered and stomped and prowled - tigerish and restless, her great brown eyes darting amongst the audience for a friendly face. 'I haven't been taught anything new since silent movies,' she croaked. She kissed the musical director, Burt Rhodes. He smiled. He indicated the band. They smiled. She smiled. We all smiled. She pretended to listen to requests from the audience, her ear cocked like a cheeky schoolboy expecting a wallop. 'What do you want? OK darling - we'll come to that.' She wrestled with the microphone lead, wandering round the stage as if in search of a place to put it. She offered the microphone to the audience and invited them to join in. At one of her last performances, a woman actually seized it and sang 'Over the Rainbow' herself, whereupon the audience jeered and hooted that the woman continue in place of Miss Garland. 'I love you all,' she cried. She drank and toasted herself. Her words became more and more slurred. Her hands appealed, shouted, implored: 'I'd like to hate myself, but I can't.' Her new husband was dragged on and kissed while she sang: 'For once in my life, I have someone who needs *me*.' The audience heckled and interrupted, between the crème brulée and the liqueur. She smoked, borrowed a handkerchief, looked amazed and embarrassed by the applause. Her little finger went to her mouth in a well-rehearsed sob of joy.

It was all immaculate and meaningless. The shoddy tarnished world that had created her had also emasculated her. In her we could see the broken remnant of the whole gaudy age of show-biz which believed that glamour was a good enough substitute for genius. Her raucous masculinity for all its fashionable and legendary attraction, had given her away at last.

And then, to close each show, she would sing that song - 'Somewhere, over the rainbow, blue birds fly. Birds fly over the rainbow - why then, oh why can't I?' She would sit cross-legged, lit by a single spotlight, alone in a great emptiness. No more gimmicks, no more show. Just a little girl who has been putdown but who has refused to give in. Her voice croaked a little, sighed a little. No more smiles, no more noise. It was pathetic and lonely and dignified - but the audience could only carry on burping and gossiping:

You made me love you;
I didn't want to do it . . .

she would sing. Precisely.

There were many who followed Judy Garland and all that she involved. They aped her eccentricities and tried to emulate her star quality. None of them could do either.

Dusty Springfield, for example, appeared at one point to fall from popularity altogether. She was replaced by Julie Driscoll as Britain's best female singer in the 1968 *Melody Maker* poll and a contemporary press report began with those memorable words, 'Whatever happened to Dusty Springfield?' Her songs continued to have passion and power. But they no longer got into those charts like once they did. Her song, 'I Will Come to You', was, none-the-less, as delicate a thing as ever she made - dignified and poised, with that aching, lyrical wistfulness which characterised her best work. It demonstrated that in only six years she had matured from a giggly, cocky, teenybopper Springfield into what she called a star.

The lady whom Cliff Richard once described as, 'a singing white negress' was christened Mary Isobel Catherine Bernadette O'Brien. Of London-Irish parents, this Catholic red-head was sent to a Convent in High Wycombe where she nearly had her first show-biz experience at an end-of-term concert. She had wanted to sing a somewhat erotic version of the 'St. Louis Blues', but the geography mistress interceded. She worked as a dustbin saleswoman and as a laundry assistant before joining the Lana Sisters in 1958. Her first professional appearance was at the Savoy Cinema, Lincoln - a performance made notable by the stunning first entrance of Miss Springfield; she fell headlong down a flight of stone steps. But when in 1960 she joined her brother Tom and their friend Tim Field to form the Springfields, success was assured. Her subsequent solo career brought her fifteen hits out of sixteen records. She could command £1,000 a night; her dresses - from Darnelle's of Baker Street - cost her £150 a time; she bought a £20,000 house in Campden Hill, Kensington and once happily admitted that her simple everyday spendings often amounted to £500 a week, probably £50,000 in 2004 values.

But the strain of the pop world's grotesqueries took a terrible toll. Her one ambition became to get out. She felt herself to be an 'article which has to be sold'. Meeting some old school chums of hers recently she told me: 'How I envy them. They seem so content.' She became obsessed by her unbeauty. She took to wearing dark stockings to cover up varicose veins and lumpy legs. She retreated behind neon-sign make-up and innumerable blond wigs - lacquered into immobility. She was hopelessly short-sighted, but too vain or proud to wear spectacles. Her Catholic upbringing had brought a certain moral high-mindedness - she refused to perform before segregated audiences in South Africa. She detested loneliness, but after an unhappy series of lesbian relationships, she preferred for a while to live alone - alone, that is, except for her constant companion called Einstein whom she discovered one day sitting sadly in a junk-shop. Einstein is a teddy bear. She had wanted to quit but admitted to me: 'Just what *do* you do when you stop being a pop singer?'

Her songs and their unusual sting, tell you a lot of this - if you forget that they are called Pop songs. In miniature, they have a world of sadness - caught forever in a shaft of Irish sunlight.

The lady who had replaced her in that popularity poll had no such quality.

One promotional photo-spread of her was titled: 'These pictures of Jools in action prove the value of carrot.' Carrot - along with wheat germ and fruit juices - appeared to be the main diet of twenty-four-your-old Julie Driscoll, a cockney singer who with her group, the Brian Auger Trinity, seemed at one point intent on single-handedly proving the absolute fashionability of Pop. No wonder her hit single, 'This Wheels On Fire', became the title song for the TV series 'Absolutely Fabulous', the absolutely sine qua non of the fashion industry.

We were told that Miss Driscoll's clothes came - predictably - from the Chelsea Antique Market. Her hair used to look like an electrified loofah, all crinkly and short as if shocked into frizziness by a massive dose of voltage. But the fashion changed, so it became close-cropped. Her face was pale, her lips paler. She made her eyes up with little vertical lines running up from the lids. She recently discovered Michelangelo after reading the paperback of the film which starred Charlton Heston and Rex Harrison and was called, 'The Agony and the Ecstacy'. Harrison once said of the film, 'I play the Ecstacy.' 'Nobody turned me on to this before,' Julie told me. Presumably Michelangelo helped her in her ambition to write songs - 'I usually write when I'm emotionally disturbed.' For the actual writing, she kept a bass drum by her bed, on which she also noted down telephone messages, whilst a toilet roll holder in the lavatory played Strauss waltzes on request. Her other ambition was to own a Health Food Store which would keep her supplied with her non-animal fat make-up.

For the French - who claim to have discovered her - she became the symbol of the swinging London chick. With her drooling, tuneless vibrato, the French - with predictable 'accuracy' - acclaimed this self-indulgent wheezing as the true voice of English music. Her fruity, stabbing lyrics might have been the death chortles of a soul-hot red-hot Mississippi mama - except that they lacked the fire, the authority and the ultimate arrogance of such music. 'What comes out is very me,' Julie told me. 'I'm sort of groping.'

This groping presumably found fulfilment in a record called 'Jools and Brian'. Brian - voted the 'Brightest Hope' in the *Melody Maker* poll of 1964 - was an organist who, on his own admission, 'just steams and steams.'

Their 'new' record - released in October '68 - had one amazing distinction. Most of it had been recorded in 1965.

Two other English singers in particular followed in Judy Garland's wake - Lulu and Sandie Shaw.

Sandie Shaw, an ex-punch card operator from Dagenham, Essex, was very tall. Or at least, she *looked* very tall. In 1968, to celebrate her 21st birthday, she hired the Chamber of Horrors at Madame Tussaud's and was there presented with a multi-tiered cake topped with a plaster-cast of her feet sculptured in ice-cream. The same year, she married dress-designer Jeff Banks - 'I market her', he told me. 'After all', said Sandie, 'songs *are* a bit like dresses. They wear out and you get tired of them. And anyway, most of us so-called stars are amateurs.'

She was originally discovered by either Adam Faith or Quentin Crewe, according to which handout you read. She looked alternately like a mournful spaniel or a clothes horse. She was squeaky, short-sighted and breathless. She had blue eyes and a squashed nose and frequently got laryngitis. When her second record - 'Always Something There To Remind Me' - got to No. 1 in those charts, Sandie got laryngitis. She was, of course, photographed having laryngitis. When she won the Eurovision Song Contest with 'Puppet on a String', she again got laryngitis. She was, of course, again photographed having laryngitis. She was photographed getting a parking ticket, having bunions and going through customs with a bottle of codeine tablets. She was once invited to a party at which Princess Margaret was also to be a guest.

Her manager telephoned the hostess and asked if Sandie could be accompanied by a photographer.

'When Sandie said she was going into show business', her Mum, Mrs. Rose Goodrich, told me, 'we spent a few sleepless nights'. When she sang at the Paris Olympia, she used to sit on the edge of the stage waggling her bare feet at the middle-aged men in the front row. They responded by taking off their shoes and socks and waggling their bare tootsies back. At the London Savoy, she was not quite so successful. When she broke down in the middle of one number, she blamed the audience. 'If you're nervous,' she told them, 'you make me nervous.' No-one was nervous in the audience. They were just waiting patiently for the singing and the performance to begin.

Miss Shaw had that unique ability to make all her songs sound alike and all sound equally indistinct. She bit her lower lip and stared meaningfully into the middle distance in a cocky expectancy that the audience would burst into hysterical applause at her every mechanical, puppet-like gesture. When the audience did not burst into hysterical applause, she told them to. She was all flash and no gut. It seemed that for all she cared she might have been singing the telephone directory. She waggled her hips and looked as if she thought it was sexy. In fact she never escaped looking like a gawky schoolgirl waggling her hips. Occasionally the audience of her cabaret shows clapped in a rather desultory gin-and-tonic way, not so much out of ecstasy, as out of boredom. Occasionally they shouted abuse. 'No, let's be serious' said Sandie. "Yes, please," said the audience.

To some she was graceless and cold, beseeching the audience but not talking to them in a language they could understand. At one performance, she wore what we were told was the most expensive trouser suit in London. She stood with her legs apart, pouting. A vamp. Even her £2,000 outfit of sequin embroidered lilac chiffon, she managed to make look like the left-overs of the Christmas crepe wrapping paper. When she had first put it on Sandie was too stunned to speak, although not - alas - to sing. She went on to reduce Harry Nillson's delicate, wistful lullaby 'Without Him' to a prattling, mumbling dirge. She robbed Judy Garland's standby 'Someone Who Needs Me' of all its natural poise, and left behind only its self-pity. She was a great leveller, number 419 of the pop assembly line. Tinselled and toothy.

'The most difficult thing of being a Pop Star,' she told me, 'is living up to the success image.' That was partly because she was a product of

the great Light Entertainment Factory which devoured its progeny with
Mephistophelean glee. The Factory demanded pre-packaged soft-sell
gloss. It could not understand that songs had to be about something if
they were to have any power. Sandie was instant success, ready mixed.
Somebody poured in the water and found she only went fizz. But they
forgot to tell Sandie, which is hardly her fault. After all, she was only
that puppet on a string.

Lulu had had the same instant success. She, like Sandie, tried
desperately to sing with guts, to sing *about* something, to sing with soul.
But from the start, this had never really been possible.

When she was 5, Marie McDonald McLaughlin Lawrie, a butcher's
daughter from Glasgow, had staggered onto an enormous stage to take
part in one of those awesome children's singing competitions. Others
had attempted such classics as 'Ba Ba Black Sheep' and 'Auld Lang Syne',
but when No. 13 was called, tiny Miss Lawrie, microscopic Miss Lawrie,
hitched up her frilly dress and climbed onto a chair so that she could
reach the microphone. She took a deep, careful breath and suddenly,
with a voice twice as magnificent but just as strident as that of a Glasgow
foghorn, she powered her way into an unbeatable version of 'Your
Cheatin' Heart'. The adjudicator fell off his chair and there was uproar
in the house. The mischievous, Enid Blyton pixie, later known as
Lulu, had arrived.

Lovely Lulu, the bounciest, jolliest, cuddliest, most gossipy,
garrulous, loveliest little girl in the land. With her standard fee at £2,000
per performance, with her £20,000 house in West Hampstead, with her
first starring role in only her second movie - 'On The Subject of Jennie'
- with the prospect of further tours to Miami, Los Angeles and Las Vegas,
with her joke victory in the Eurovision Song Contest, with her true-love
marriage to Maurice Bee Gee, she could truly be thought to have arrived
and been.

This green-eyed, marmalade-haired explosion who told the appoint-
ments man at her school, 'I wanna be a disc star, sir', stumbled headlong
from success to success. After her spectacular public debut in Glasgow,
she practised - loudly - in Dennistoun public baths. 'I had a voice like a
coalman,' she told me. Or a cheese-grater; or a klaxon-horn; or a stuck
pig. Her first record, 'Shout', she recorded at 14, but it wasn't released
until she was 15 - just after she'd left school. Her next four flopped. She
left her backing group - The Luvvers - and moved into cabaret. And TV
comedy. And films. Her film debut was with Sidney Poitier - she had

Judy Garland by Ralph STEADman

a cameo role in 'To Sir With Love'. But the title song from the film became an American No. 1. And so, in the States, she became famous, and rich, and loved. She moved into fashion. And cosmetics. And hair-styles - lending her name to various looks.

Everywhere, there was Lulu. And everywhere the image was perfect - no smut, no scandal, no intrigue. 'But I've got nerve,' she told me. Except in morality. She publicly opposed drug-taking, extra-marital sex, hedonism, anti-religion, and screen-debauchery. Her first screen-kiss with Dave Clark in his TV show, she found embarrassing. 'I hope you didn't kiss him, if you didn't like him,' said her mother. 'I'm learning what life is all about,' Lulu told me. 'And anyway, I'm old-fashioned.'

The girl next door, called Lulu, swung her hips and tapped her feet. Her songs were repetitious but happy. When she'd toured the world eighteen times, made fifty-three films, opened ninety-one boutiques, bought sixteen houses, had five children, she admitted that she would be ready to settle down. Maturity would come for her with the acquisition of such possessions; the re-assurance of acclaim; the feeling of having arrived; the knowledge that one was a star. But if Judy Garland was her spiritual mother, then Judy Garland must surely have demonstrated to her that real stars are people who are most unsure of their stardom, most unsure of their having arrived, most disturbed by acclaim and most scornful of possessions. To be a star is to have a death-wish. Lulu's songs, however, had only the punch of adolescence, and its harmlessness. They had the enthusiasm of youth, and its emptiness. As one of her own songs said:

> I look like a little girl
> Living in a big man's world
> But the ribbons that you see
> Hide the real me.

The real me had shouted from the first, and was still shouting. And the energy that had launched her onto that chair, was endlessly dissipated. In success, she found success and not stature. So her music had the tingling freshness of a toothpaste ad - just as attractive and just as pointless.

But she was and is lovely - Daddy's little girl from Bridgetown, Glasgow.

Amongst male singers there were many who raved and crawled, who copied directly or indirectly the mannerisms and vocal gymnastics of the Negro Soul brothers. From Elvis Presley came fourth ex-Caveman Tommy Steele and Cliff Richard. Steele went off to be a lovable film star and Richard to be a lovable Son of God. The tradition, such as it was, lapsed almost by default onto a new generation of crooners. The new generation often owed more to such as Donald Peers than to the soul tradition which they themselves claimed to be the paramount influence. One such crooner was the Welshman, Tom Jones.

When Tom Jones had first appeared at the London Palladium in 1967, he was on the same bill as some performing elephants. It's not clear who stole the show or for what reason. Green-eyed Tiger Tom, as he was described, appealed to the maturer woman. What with his George Raft sideburns and Sicilian Sunday suit, this self-confessed ex-drunkard, ex-Teddy-boy and ex-mini gangster who used to wear a ring in the shape of a skull and cross-bones, groaned around the stage like some bubbling Quatermass monster, seizing every song by the scruff of the neck, rattling it about and eventually choking it to death.

A one-time £15 a week labourer, he was soon earning an estimated £500,000 a year. His 1969 TV show cost £3,000 a minute and was sold to the States for 20 million dollars. The TV show, 'Robin Hood', it was noted, could only manage a measly 12 million. When he opened at New York's Cocacabana Club in May 1969, he outgrossed Frank Sinatra and Andy Williams. For a lad whose mother used to take him to the local grocer shop, stand him on an orange box and make him sing for 3d., that's some progress. 'Mr. Emotion - the song and sex symbol from Pontypridd,' as he was described in Miami, sold 26 million records in his first four years; said one American lady after watching his cabaret act in Las Vegas - 'No man should bring his wife to see that. At least I'm thankful we didn't bring our daughter.' 'How do I see his future?' his manager Gordon Mills told me. 'Bigger and bigger'. Before a recent performance in Brisbane, Australia, a copper came barging into Tom Jones' dressing room. 'Listen son,' he said. 'This is a clean town and it's gonna stay clean. Any trouble from you and we'll shove you inside, OK?' 'Thank the Lord, we're a musical nation,' said Dylan Thomas.

Tom Jones or Thomas John Woodward as he was born, or Tommy Scott the Twisting Vocalist as he was christened professionally, is a big man with big hands. Vocally, he is a rabble rouser. He performs rather than sings. In days when nice little pop singers were still mods, he was unashamedly a rocker. He was the mums' Mick Jagger, the performing bear of the middle-classes. And for those who couldn't understand or didn't want to know about the more subtle happenings of pop, the no-nonsense corn of Jones the miner's son had an immediate - and obvious - appeal. He was the first pop idol whom the mums could feel safe with. When asked about his contemporaries who appeared less satisfied with the scene, he told me: 'When I see them squatting with their banners and their sandals, I feel like telling them to get off their backs and do something. They do *nothing*. They're bums.' At this, loud cheers could be heard from the middle-aged women in his audience, gaping at the time like fourteen-year-olds. 'I'm not tempted,' Jones told me with a grin.

A few years ago he wanted to record 'Yesterday'. McCartney had got it all wrong, he said. What the song needed was a singer with soul. For most people, he is soul. Or feeling, as it's sometimes called. Or singing with conviction as it's always called. Jones, officially, described as 'the most successful solo singer Britain has ever produced,' seemed to fit the bill. But with him, it really was all effort and no ease. He grunted about like a lumbering Mafia King. The suspicion of underworld masculinity made three-dimensional his Roman coin profile. At home, his drawing-room fireplace used to be draped with a black stetson, spurs, stirrups and a holster containing a dead revolver. Upstairs, he had 50 or 60 knives and a dozen guns and swords. He collected them.

Ironically, his first break as a singer had come in 1963 when he was booked for a date which another artiste was suddenly unable to fulfil. The other artiste was Mandy Rice-Davies, then appearing at the Old Bailey criminal court in a sex-scandal trial that was soon to bring down the government of Prime Minister Harold MacMillan.

The Mums' prayers were also answered by the appearance of a super-duper group of lovey-dovies called the Bee Gees, one of whom eventually married Lulu.

Totally devoid of harmonic or melodic or rhythmic invention, their songs sounded like several hundred cows in pain - self-pitying garglings delivered in a tone of unremitting mumble.

As two of the group were said to be Australian, the Home Secretary in his infinite wisdom tried to send them home after their visitors' permits had first expired. A national outcry - led by a baby elephant in procession down Whitehall - caused the Home Secretary to reverse his decision. They were, he said, 'A social and national asset.' Actually, they had been born in Britain, so were quite entitled to stay.

They were given to performing grand concerts at the Albert Hall. At one, the compere gloated: 'No other orchestra can be playing in London tonight, 'cause *we've* got every string player' (screams). Actually, there *was* a sixty-piece 'symphony orchestra'. You couldn't actually hear them, however, such was the din that prevailed for most of the evening. But never mind. Also present were the RAF Apprentices Marching Band who roared in for a lusty climax (more screams). You couldn't hear them either, but there you go. And then, lo, from the back of the stalls, the Ambrosian Singers leapt into view and sang their heads off (even more screams). They were inaudible too; but that, I suppose, is show business. It was, said the handout, 'the ultimate in pop presentation.'

What you *could* hear were The Brothers Gibb, Barry, Robin and Maurice. They gave us 'Massachusetts' which claimed 4 million world-sales; 'World' with Barry Bee Gee gyrating himself into early arthritis; 'New York Mining Disaster', their finest lyric although straight Beatles, and a single (which flopped) called 'Jumbo'. It was, perhaps, a long way from their Christmas debut at Charlton-cum-Hardy in 1956 where they played with the aid of two toy banjos and were - at their own admission, 'awful'. Ironically, Charlton-cum-Hardy was the home of the first girl-friend of the great British composer, Sir William Walton.

Their words could truly be said to have brought the pop world into fresh realms of experience - such as boredom, pretentiousness and plain silliness. Sincerity was everywhere - really and sincerely. We were assured that the sun *would* shine, that the rain *would* fall, and that the world *was* round. For the preservation of these truths, fans had chained themselves to Buckingham Palace. The Queen made no comment.

But they were big, very big. And pure. 'I will personally object if any of them decides to get married,' their manager Robert Stigwood, who had also produced the Albert Hall show, told me. The group then signed a million-dollar contract for an American Tour and promised their manager: 'We will not get married.' Unfortunately, Barry Bee Gee was already married - but, he revealed, he and his Birmingham wife were parted.

They also signed for a United Artists colour feature film, 'Lord Kitchener's Little Drummer Boy'. The lads were to play a variety act who are press-ganged into the English army during the Boer conflict. 'So that's why we won the war,' wrote one commentator. Alas, the strain of it all proved to be so great that Robin Bee Gee collapsed and was put under 'sedation'.

Tony Blackburn, another thinker, and BBC Radio 1 DJ, announced that he wanted to meet God, and Simon Dee preached at St. Paul's. Jonathan King - now in prison for paedophilia - was so overcome by the power of pop words that he said of a new record by Ray Stevens: 'I am stunned by the entire organism.' Said Keith Reed, creative leader of the Procol Harum: 'I'd like to become such an accumulation of knowledge that finally I'd explode.' And explode he did, during the new summer 'season' of pop/folk festivals which grew up - at places such as Sidmouth, Broadstairs, and even Harrogate.

For those who believed in Art, this debauchery must have seemed - and indeed, did seem, like the end of the civilised world. Distinguished commentators spent vast fortunes of public moneymaking documentary films about Civilisation to prove that everything would be all right in the end. None other that Daniel Barenboim himself took over London's South Bank for his own summer festival in an attempt to restore confidence in classical music. Whilst Boulez announced that he wanted to blow up opera houses, BBC Promenaders were able to vote a new piece a hit or a miss. The distinguished conductor, Sir Colin Davis, looked as if he were being touted to take over from Mick Jagger.

Meanwhile, back in the pop factory, things were going from bad to worse. A group called, (appropriately so it seemed), The Crazy World of Arthur Brown appeared to some like the Day of Judgement - an absurd and malicious joke. With Vincent Crane on organ and Drachen Theaker on drums, vocalist magician ex-petrol-pump attendant Arthur Brown thundered his way across America with devastating results. In Detroit, three men ran from the ballroom where he was performing, convinced he was the Devil; in Miami, police stopped the show saying that it was 'harmful' to young people. His act, said *The International Times*, was 'the all time high in erectile music.'

In 1967, he had stunned the Windsor Pop Festival by arriving on stage lowered by a crane and sporting a horn-shaped metal helmet ablaze with a sinister cow-gum substance. With his face smeared with hideous Red-Indian daubings, his cloaked body writhing and squirming like an octopus in labour, his voice - at his own admission - a cross between Little Richard, Tom Jones and Maria Callas, it is little wonder that his act became the hottest property on the University dance-underground-prayer-meeting circuit.

Describing himself as the Prince of Eternal Dark, Defender of Omnipotent Forces, keeper of the Leaden Key and Herald of the New

Dawn, he was not likely to appeal to those who believed that pop music was intended as light entertainment, the breakfast wallpaper of those too preoccupied with Art to accept the possibility of musical experiment.

Arthur Brown wanted to shock people into listening; to attack the audiences. 'You all stink - raise your armpits,' he shouted during an appearance at London's Marquee Club where he broke all box-office records, outgrossing The Who, Jimi Hendrix and even The Rolling Stones. Born in 1944 in Whitby, Yorkshire, he had been to London University but was thrown out for making grand Zen gestures during lectures. After a spell as a sewer-farm worker, he tried Reading University where he got a degree in philosophy. He then taught at Leytonstone High School, but after three weeks was told by his Head to get his hair cut or leave. 'What sort of choice was that?' Brown told me. He tried Paris where he used to come on stage wearing a bucket on his head, carrying a mop and shouting, 'Statue de Liberté.' He tried London where he was seen and heard by Pete Townshend, leader of The Who. It was an ideal chance since Kit Lambert and his organisation, Track Records, (who also manage and produce The Who), were about the only record company farseeing enough to cope with such as Arthur Brown.

Crazy though he may have appeared, The World of Arthur Brown was nonetheless the renewal of an articulate attempt to provoke a reasoned response to pop. His fantasy songs - he wanted to call his first LP 'Tales from the Neurotic Nights of Hieronymous Anonymous', embodied the aphoristic wants of his generation; 'Man is the perfect computer. Believe in machines'; or 'Truth is a misleading advert for reality. And vice versa'; or 'Better hate than never'; or - best of all - 'Heaven - will the Russians reach it first?'

Arthur Brown was not the first to notice that pop music could tap something deeper than booby wooby booby. The Beatles and The Rolling Stones and the Soul-Presley tradition from which they sprang, had long-since realised the same thing. But suddenly, as if in reaction to the old-timers who continued to dominate popular taste, a growing number of those inside pop music began to make considerable claims for its role in contemporary society. Eric Burdon of The Animals, Pete Townshend of The Who, Paul McCartney, John Lennon, Manfred Mann, Donovan - all became aware that they were on to something bigger and stranger than anything previously attempted by 'popular music'.

Their views may be self-contradictory, self-parodying and even plain wrong, but if we are to understand pop and what pop has come to mean for a great number of people, then it is essential that we know what these views are. Most of the communications media at the time showed no inclination whatsoever to let us know the reality of what's going on. They preferred tittle tattle to truth. Not a lot has changed.

'My ambition,' Donovan told me, 'is to see *all* the arts come bursting out into a summer colour.' He went to live in an idyllic cottage deep in Hertfordshire, surrounded by books of old English fairy tales and relics of peasant Mexico where he had previously gone 'to think'. He planned to bring out a pocket book of children's poems with a record in the middle. He wrote two exquisite ballets, was asked to write the music for the National Theatre's 'As You Like It', composed the soundtrack for the film 'Poor Cow', and wanted to buy a Greek island for 'contemplation'. His favourite word - inevitably - was 'beautiful'.

Donovan Phillips Leitch, born Glasgow 1945, had made his first appearance at the St. Alban's Folk Club in 1964, after three years as a hobo on the road. He always described himself as a minstrel, and when performing doesn't sing, but whispers confidentially. Comparisons with Dylan made both angry - although songs like Donovan's 'Catch the Wind' and 'Universal Soldier' had that same restlessness which colours much of Dylan's music and words. They were also both slight of build, had unruly black curly hair and a sagging jaw. The snide comparisons, however, caused Donovan to disappear and reorganise his talent. When he re-emerged at the Albert Hall on 15 January 1967, it was immediately apparent that a major talent had arrived.

With a backing of strings, woodwind and harpsichord, he led the audience through a wonder world of Chinese gardens, King Arthur, gipsies and tinkers. He murmured sonnets beneath a screen showing delicate art nouveau slides; and a beautiful person whom he discovered on a farm near Naples 'amongst goats and ducks and dogs', with long auburn Rossetti hair, danced a sarabande in accompaniment. 'Don is an occult of the religion music, someone who is part of a deeper thing than a revival of something that was dying,' his publicist told me. With eyes the violet grey-green of a Scottish mist, he seemed like a magic elf, graceful, delicate and fragile. 'Pop songs are like books,' he told me. 'Today, no-one has enough time to read novels. So you get Lennon and McCartney writing a novel called *Eleanor Rigby* - which takes just three minutes to digest.' If you went to interview him you were likely to be asked to remove your shoes; he didn't like bright lights and hoped that photos of him 'would have a high art content'.

This mood, this style achieved its synthesis in one of his songs called 'Jennifer Juniper'. She lived on a hill, with lilacs in her hair, dreaming. A cor-anglais chanted a sad little descent over woodwind and strings backing. The melody had charm and simplicity; it was economical and relaxed. The lyrics were tender and without specific 'message' or 'significance'. But altogether the song had a Chekovian disappointment, an ethereal longing which sighed us to sleep during the lazy days of summer. It was all in a word - beautiful.

The simultaneous arrival on the scene of another strangely beautiful person, whose very life and career seemed to summarise all that had happened so far, marked the beginning of the end - or, if you prefer, the beginning. This strangely beautiful person was Jimi Hendrix.

Chapter Five

'When I was a little boy,' Jimi Hendrix told me, 'I believed that if you put a tooth under your pillow, a fairy would come in the middle of the night and leave a dime. Now, I believe in myself more than anything. And I suppose, in a way, that's also believing in God. If there is a God and He made you, then if you believe in yourself, you're also believing in Him. So I think, everybody should believe in himself. That doesn't mean you've got to believe in heaven and hell and all that stuff. But it does mean that what you are and what you do, is your religion. I can't express myself in easy conversation - the words just don't come out right. But when I get up on stage - well, that's my whole life. *That's* my religion. My music *is* electric church music; if by "church" you mean "religion", *I am* electric religion.'

Petula Clark called him 'a great big hoax'. 'For all I know,' he told me, '*everyone* could be laughing at us. But if they are, I'll cry all the way to the bank.' It is widely reported that the Daughters of the American Revolution tried to have him prosecuted for obscenity, but in fact the much publicised 'prosecution' was a promotional trick to persuade the American West Coast Underground Press that he was 'intellectually and socially OK'. One LP was packaged with such effrontery that many English provincial shops refused to stock it. 'We've never had anything like it,' said a dealer in Hull. Boots and W. H. Smiths came up with the perfect British compromise. They stocked it, but would not display it, and when sold it came in a brown paper bag.

When in London, Hendrix lived in a house once owned by Georg Friedrich Handel. 'I didn't even know this was his pad, man. I haven't heard much of that fella's stuff.' Handel wrote the Water Music where Hendrix once counted the banknotes. 'But I dig a bit of Bach - now and again,' he told me.

When his manager had first spotted him, he saw him as 'the governor rebel of all times. A monster. A wild beast. The original man you'd never let your daughter marry; a giant bogey-man.' 'He's so sincere about his music,' Eric Burdon of The Animals told me, 'that one of these days he will probably make a human torch of himself on stage.' Jimi Hendrix, said the *New York Times*, is 'the black Elvis.'

His full name was James Marshall Hendrix, who, together with John 'Mitch' Mitchell, an ex-child actor from Ealing, and Noel Redding, a rock 'n' roll bass player from Folkestone, became The Jimi Hendrix Experience.

Like the Soul brothers had discovered earlier, if you happened to be coloured and American and ambitious, you had three options. You could join the military, you got into sport or you became a musician. Hendrix was 15 when he started playing professionally. For his first gig at Seattle, Washington, he got 75 cents and 3 hamburgers. Soon he was earning 30,000 dollars a performance. In just three years, he climbed from being a down-and-out in Greenwich Village to being one of pop's highest paid artists. When he was 14, he was expelled from Garfield High School. 'I wonder if my old school teacher digs me now', he told me. 'She was a good looker but she got me thrown out. I was talking to some chick during the lessons and this teacher got mad. I said "What's the matter - are you jealous?" And that was the last time I saw *her*. Maybe she's now a Daughter of the Revolution.'

Later, he went back there to play - just him and the school band in the gymnasium. Although it was 8 in the morning, the entire school turned out, and first class was cancelled as a special tribute. The town he ran away from, Seattle, gave him the freedom of the city. 'Man, that's quite something,' he told me. 'The only keys I expected from *that* town, were the keys of the jailhouse. When I was a kid, I was always gone on wearing hip clothes, but the only way to get them was through the back window of a clothing store.'

So he got arrested. He was jailed again for taking a ride in a stolen car. 'I didn't know it was stolen, honest.' His father was a landscape gardener, he told me - 'he was very level-headed and religious. My mother had a good time - always dressing up and that, and didn't take much care of herself. She drank a lot and died when I was about 10. My dad was very strict. He taught me that I must respect my elders.' Hendrix remained almost unnervingly polite. 'When I was a kid I used to hate having my hair cut. I wanted it to grow long to hide my big ears, and I would have to avoid my dad whenever it got *too* long. I'd sneak in and out of the house and try not to be noticed, but eventually he'd always spot me and sit me down in the hall under the lamp and shave it all off until I looked like a skinned chicken. And all the other kids would just laugh.'

He left home at 15 and never went back. He had a half-sister, Genevieve (his father remarried) whom he'd never seen, and lots more for all he knows. 'I once sent Dad some money, but he sent it back.' He joined the Army Airborne and got to Spec.4 - or corporal, but he broke his ankle on his 25th jump and got hung up on the discipline. He began to play on just about every rock 'n' roll tour going - on the 'Solid Gold Soul' circuit, where you could be fined 5 dollars for getting a step behind. King Curtis, Ike and Tina Turner, Chuck Jackson, Jackie Wilson, Joey Gee, The Isley Brothers, Otis Redding, B. B. King and Little Richard - you name them, he played with them. ' "The King of Rock and Rhythm" - that's how Little Richard used to describe *himself*, he explained to me. He used to say that on stage he was the only one who was allowed to be pretty. One night I put on a frilly shirt but got dragged off immediately. "Take off that shirt", he told me. So I did.' But he began to miss out on tours, settling his hotel bills with the manuscripts of songs he'd just written, in lieu of payment. He began to revisit his Cherokee grandmother on the reservation in Colorado where he'd previously spent all his summer vacations. His part Mexican and part Negro blood made him restless. He wanted to be an actor. He wanted to be a painter. He didn't really know what he wanted to do. Like many of his contemporaries at the time, he was struggling to find an outlet for what he knew to be inside him and which he knew could not be satisfied within the established so-called cultural framework.

He went to New York. He was always broke - so broke, in fact, that a girl friend bought him his first new guitar. He was playing one night at the Club Wha in Greenwich Village when Linda Keith, at that time girl-friend of Rolling Stone Keith Richard, heard him and took Chas Chandler - 'the walking hill' of The Animals - along next night to hear. 'I remember thinking', Chandler told me later, 'that this cat's wild enough to upset more people than Jagger.'

Chandler went into partnership with his own manager, Mike Jeffries, and persuaded Hendrix to come over to England. 'He didn't think we had amplifiers over here', said Chandler. 'He thought we still used gas.' He arrived in London in September 1966 and was nearly put on the first plane back when the immigration officer discovered he didn't have a work permit. After a lot of fuss, he got a one week temporary visa. 'We'd had enough trouble getting him a passport let alone a birth certificate which, of course, he'd lost', the ever-patient Chandler told me. Chandler and Jeffries promoted him as a grotesque, voodoo witchdoctor, the epitome of evil. 'We spent £5,000 before Jimi did a single gig.' They lured drummer Mitch Mitchell from the Georgie Fame band. Fond parents had sent Mitchell to the Corona Stage School, and fond parents were later to give Mitchell a twenty-first birthday cake which was a full-scale replica of a snare-drum and sticks. Noel Redding they lured from Folkestone. He'd been on the road 6 years and was saving up to buy a nightclub in Spain.

The temporary visa got extended to three months, but it was not until they were playing together one night in Munich that the penny which was to turn into millions of dollars for them as well as for a host of others, dropped. Hendrix was pulled off stage by some over enthusiastic kids and as he jumped back on stage he threw his guitar before him. When he picked it up, he saw that it had cracked and several of the strings were broken. He just went crazy and started smashing everything in sight. The audience got on its feet and cheered, and The Jimi Hendrix Experience was launched.

He began to play his 240 volt guitar with his teeth, behind his back or under the leg. According to his mood, he'd smash it up or set it on fire as he did at the Monterey Pop Festival. 'I like to entertain myself on stage', he told me. 'I get tired of just standing up there. Our music isn't all that organised. We just get on stage and start calling off the tunes. We never have a set programme - we just play it by ear. My influences, I suppose, are like those of most other people - Chuck Berry, Buddy Holly and Muddy Waters. But I never think about how to describe my kind of music - until people start asking me and trying to categorise it. Let's just call it freak and funky music.'

But again - like most other people who have had a real influence on pop music - Hendrix did grow up in the Soul and blues tradition. In his smoky, grating voice, you can hear echoes of McKinley Morganfield (Muddy Waters). It's almost as if Hendrix *is* Muddy Waters' Hootchie-Cootchie Man come to life. Another of Muddy Waters' songs, Rolling Stone Blues, gave birth to The Rolling Stones who did muchto popularise - and vulgarise - that kind of sound. But the twitching Mick Jagger could evoke none of the power and soul that was Hendrix's birthright.

'My music is hungry', he told me with omnivorous confidence. He soaked every number with himself and then bombarded the audience with overt, sexual, aggression. Eric Burdon told me at the time that 'if you really want to see where the mind of an American Negro is at, go and see Jimi Hendrix. Technically, he's a wizard on the guitar. But his music is all so disturbed and explosive.' Hendrix himself steered clear of any kind of political involvement, although he sent a cheque for 5,000 dollars to the Martin Luther King Memorial Fund. Because of his 'pop-music image', he like others realised that direct participation would be more a hindrance than a help. But flower-power, of which he was the self-confessed high-priest, did - he believed - help somewhat towards the colour problem in the United States. 'Coloured artists', he told me, 'daren't go near some Southern audience in the past. But since flower-power, much of the violence has gone.' He resented the implication that Negro culture was being exploited more for the benefit of white people than coloured people. He told me: 'I always say, "let the best man win" . . . If you play the music - OK. Whether you are black, white or purple. If someone likes your music enough to be inspired by it, then that's fine. It's silly to say that this or that kind of music can only be played by coloured people. Really, some people seem to think from their kneecaps. Colour just doesn't make any difference. Look at Elvis. He used to sing better when he sang the blues than when he started to sing all the beach-party stuff. *He* could sing the blues - and *he's* white.'

Hendrix was coloured in every sense - a 'Cherry-Blossomed Mick Jagger' was how Ray Connolly once described him. Like a six-foot parakeet, he tip-toed about the stage adorned with multi-coloured clothes woven out of my old mother's herbaceous borders, his sweaty neck dangling with witch-craft charms, his hair like that of an electrocuted porcupine, standing up as if in fright of his face. He was a bird of paradise lording it over his territory. 'The earth's my home', he explained to me in a more modest moment.

Out of 12 giant cabinets housing 48 loudspeakers, came bursting the songs that have brought him fame - 'Hey Joe', 'Purple Haze', 'The Wind Cries Mary', 'All Along the Watchtower'. The sound was essentially no different in intensity from that of a great number of other new groups. It was vast, wrenching, and spluttering. Hendrix masturbated with his guitar, appeared to suck off the audience, grins, clowns, apes and just kept on playing. He was self-conscious and melodramatic, like a neolithic musical gypsy rampaging around the sensibilities of the young. It was orgiastic, and he knew it. 'Lots of things we do are dangerous,' he told me, 'but life itself is dangerous. Nothing is really worth bothering with that isn't *full* of danger.' The philosopher-mathemetician, A. N. Whitehead had once noted that it was 'the business of the future to be dangerous'; in the same pattern, Hendrix declared that he was writing music for the twenty-first century. But at the rate he was going, neither he nor the twenty-first century would be around to experience it.

Like Elvis, The Beatles, Bob Dylan, and The Rolling Stones before him, (and for the same reasons) Hendrix eventually appeared less and less frequently. 'I'm frightened of becoming an American version of Dave Dee,' he told me; 'part of pop slavery - part of the what-cornflakes-for-breakfast scene. I'm tired of the attitude of fans that they've bought you a house and a car and now expect you to work the way they want you to for the rest of your life.' His LP - 'Electric Ladyland', the one with 21 nudes on the front cover that caused all the fuss in Smiths and Boots, is - like much of pop music, very much a personal document. 'Apart from a little help from my friends such as Stevie Winwood of Traffic and Buddy Miles of Electric Flag, it's all done by us', he told me. 'We wrote most of the songs, recorded and produced it. It has a hard, rough feel on some of the tracks. But it's US.'

It begins with a ninety second sound-painting - a picture in sound of the heavens. 'And the Gods make Love', he sings. 'When I was a kid, I was always painting scenes on other planets. "Summer afternoon on Venus" and things like that. I never wanted to go to the moon too much. But I always wanted to go to Venus or Saturn. Some place that could show me some kind of scenery.' In one song, he sings:

> O strange beautiful grass of green
> With your majestic silken scenes
> Your mysterious mountains I wish to see closer,
> May I land my kinky machine?

But from what and from whom are he and his fellow musicians in pop really escaping? From the racist society which bred them and whom they have repaid with a violent, wounding music? From the limitations of the puerile musical language into which they have unwittingly slipped? From the relentless, hotel room to hotel room struggle that is called 'touring'?

Like a stampeded convict, Hendrix was being burnt up with the desire to get away. He was a firm advocate of pot. 'I think smoking pot must be legalised in 5 or 10 years,' he told me. It seems to me to be silly to be sent to jail for smoking a natural plant, when you've got winos and drunkards out in the streets begging for money and nobody seems to care about this. Some people will kill for a few cents to get a drink. Also, it's madness to classify all drugs under one heading. Pot is completely different from hard drugs. I really don't see how anyone can put a needle in themselves. I had pneumonia when I was young and I used to scream and cry every time they put *that* needle in me.'

Jimi Hendrix
Ralph Steadman

He liked dead flowers, Chinese and Japanese canvases, brocade, and lace and beads. He returned to England for a mini-tour to avoid his group splitting up. Redding had kept on insisting that they play in England again - where they started. Redding had already made an album with his own group called 'The Fat Mattress' which he recorded with the ex-Flowerpot Man Neil Landon, Engelbert Humperdinck's drummer Eric Dillon and bass player Jimmy Leverton. Mitch Mitchell had gone jamming with Lennon and Clapton. More and more, the best musicians in pop were no longer content just to play in 'groups'. They preferred to play with other musicians whom they admired rather than join a collection of mediocrities whose only advantage was a collective packaging which appealed to the teeny-boppers.

In a sense, the Experience was already over. The musical gimmickry, fire-crackered though it remained, no longer satisfied any of them. Gone were the days when Hendrix could shout with conviction during the song 'Stars That Play With Laughing Sam's Dice' which is all about a trip on a space rocket called 'Butterfly Rollerskate', 'I hope you're enjoying the ride - I am'. The ride, just like Beatlemania had done, turned sour. That Electric Ladyland cover - 'a very classy bit of work', Chris Stamp, co-manager of Track Records which released it, told me. Hendrix didn't like. When 'All Along the Watchtower' was brought out here as a single, Hendrix didn't even know what was on the flip side. When he visited Sweden, 30 leading hotels refused to book him. He was even arrested and fined £250 for supposedly smashing up a hotel room - he doesn't remember too much about it. His demise was the same as that of a hundred successful pop stars before him. On his last tour of the States, things got so out of hand that a counterfeit ticket ring was in full operation in New York, Texas, and Arizona. 'You've got to be progressive,' he told me at the time. 'Take Presley. He's still got plenty of fans, but the only *progress* he's made is on his bank statements.'

'I am what I feel,' he told me. 'I play as I feel and I act as I feel.' His one stroke of luck was to be signed up as a recording artist - like Arthur Brown had been - by Track Records. It is perhaps not surprising that many of the more progressive and stimulating sounds of pop came from these comparatively small and inexperienced record companies - such as Elektra, Apple and especially Track; after all, some of the best pop musicians had actually begun to seek refuge in these smaller companies - The Beatles in Apple and Hendrix in Track - away from the big commercialised Bernard Delfont-type combines.

Track Records eventually cornered 6 per cent of the British market (at a gross of nearly half a million pounds a year) with songs like The Who's 'Magic Bus' and 'Pinball Wizard', Hendrix's 'All Along the Watchtower', and Arthur Brown's single, 'Fire', which became a million seller and got to No. 2 in the American charts. Chris Stamp and his partner Kit Lambert, together began to revolutionise the recording industry by demonstrating that quality alone counted. With careful promotion and devoted musical production, quality could bring its just rewards. Plans for the future included an opera and a full-time orchestra. Technically, they were already in the future. While everybody talked about making stereo singles, Track actually did it. Jimi Hendrix's singles, although the label never admitted it, *were* in stereo.

But this lucky marriage could not prevent Hendrix's creeping awareness that he was worn out, an exhausted man - physically and musically. 'I used to write thousands of tunes, but I don't seem to get around to it now,' he told me. 'You can say my music is erotic and whatever you like. I don't care. What others say or think just doesn't worry me. People still mourn when other people die. That's self-pity. The person who is dead isn't crying. When I die I want people to just play my music, go wild, freak out, do anything they want to do. Enjoy themselves. The mechanical life - where cities and hotel rooms all merge into one - has killed that enjoyment for me. So I've just got to get out. Maybe to Venus or somewhere. Some place *you* won't be able to find me.'

His plea could have been the plea of John Lennon or of Mick Jagger. Like them, Hendrix wished only to be left alone to do his thing.

But those who would not let him do so, grew in number. As the claims for pop became more extravagant, so did the demands for its extinction. It was slowly branded as a useless, neurotic nuisance. So it withdrew, and strived for a proper understanding of itself. Whilst the clatter went on outside, it gradually built up a corpus of work which, even if it was not liked, could not be ignored. The annoyance of those who had already attacked it, thus took on a more savage tone.

Chapter Six

'When I read the Scriptures and I see what happened to Sodom and Gomorrah before they were destroyed, I can see that what was happening there is exactly what is happening in London today. After I was converted, after I became a Christian, I met different Christian people who told me that all the time I had been a pop star, they had been praying for me. They had been praying that God would literally smash everything that I did so that I would be saved out of that dreadful life.'

Terry Dene - in the late fifties, the wildest of the rockers. The original teddy-boy. Now, forgotten. A gospel singer. An evangelist. Has worked, for periods, as a packer at a Scripture Union Bible Centre. His pop career ended when he sold his life-story to a Sunday newspaper with the title, 'Shame made me want to be dead'.

'I just felt that I had to come out of my heathen surroundings and seek God. So I prayed to God and asked him to forgive me for the sins I'd committed. I asked Jesus to come into my heart and save me from a profession in which many of the people involved had attitudes which were evil. I don't think that playing a musical instrument is evil in itself, but it's such a *false* life. It's a heathen life. Barbaric. After all, I found that people were worshipping me and that's idolatry. I sometimes go back to old show business parties but I find the atmosphere so oppressive that I have to go upstairs and pray. The money I got made me terribly selfish and terribly self-centered and I began to think "Am I going to have to answer for what I'm doing?" I can't bear to think of my former life in show business. It was unspeakable. In a sense, I was afraid to live and afraid to die. It was a very conflicting situation. I thought about suicide but eventually I came to believe that I was predestined to serve God.

'Sometimes, you know, I was made big offers to go into films or this and that. But always the schemes fell through. Nothing ever came off and I began to wonder why this was. Now, of course, I know that it was the unseen hand of God at work. God intervened many times and prevented me from doing something drastic.

I owe my present position to a group of Christians called the Mobile Evangelistic Crusaders. They gave me the message in Trafalgar Square. Once I was in Dublin - we had an open air meeting there. And I said to the people, I said, I understand, I said, why you're going into public houses, I said, and bingo halls and all these places, I said, and listening to pop music, I said, because, I said, if I didn't know Jesus Christ, I said, that's where I would be, I said.

'If one walks in the way of wickedness, as it were, one sort of enjoins oneself to falseness and falsehood and one very soon becomes a part of it. I mean, my former life only brought me a certain amount of periodical sort of false security. The pop world *is* heathen - and it's getting worse. They're scraping the bottom of the barrel as far as *material* is concerned. And as a result, the spiritual condition of the young people is - pretty sad.'

*   *   *

'So these days, it's not "this is a good song with a good theme and a good chord change and a great construction with a great artist singing it". As I've said, it's art for art's sake and money for Christ's sake. If it sells, who cares?'

In 1969, when I interviewed him, Eddie Rogers was a 50-year-old, wise-cracking, Jewish, Ex-Tin Pan Alley publisher. He wrote what he described as the ultimate Tin Pan Alley expose called with amazing perspicacity 'Tin Pan Alley' - and the 'retired'. He had worked as - among other things, a driving instructor.

'I'll tell you an interesting thing, why Tin Pan Alley is called Tin Pan Alley. Tin Pan Alley was originally Denmark Street; it now covers a much greater area but it was originally just Denmark Street. Now when *I* started in the business, there were eleven music publishers and eleven music publishers only. But there were *hundreds* of artists 'cause in those days they had the music hall, so there were more *artists* that there were singers. Now the artist used to come down to *us*, to see what new songs *we* had. He'd just walk down Tin Pan Alley with us song pluggers standing in the doorways of our various offices, and we'd grab him. We'd yank him upstairs into our office and play the new tune to him on the piano which is another thing song pluggers don't have to do these days is play the piano; all they need to play is the gramophone. But in those days the pluggers used to *know* something about music; they had to play the piano. We used to grab this artist, take him upstairs and play our new song to him.

'Meanwhile all the other pluggers from the various publishing houses round Denmark Street would get dustbin lids, saucepans, tin trays, anything, and bang them like mad outside the window to try to kill the plug. That's why it was called Tin Pan Alley. Interesting? Now this created a wonderful atmosphere, a *wonderful* atmosphere. You *knew* that if you contracted an artist, this artist would sit down with you for an hour, a day, a week sometimes, working out how this song should be sung, where the emphasis should come, work out his routine, what cities he should play in the next six months, and so on. We'd plug the song 'cause we *knew* it was a great song, and we'd stick with it maybe a year, two years, as long as it took.

'But now it's rush, rush, rush; clap the artist or the group into the studio, make the record, get it out on to the air. Rush, rush, rush, and in six weeks the song is dead and buried. Out of the fifty records a week released in this country, *you* hear probably fifteen of them. This is a terrible thing.

'There's no Bon Hommy any more. I couldn't phone up a disc jockey and say: "Oh, uh, is that Mr. Murray? Oh, this is the ABC publishing company here." And he'd say: "Oh, yeah; well drop dead." You know. I used to say: "Hi, Pete, Eddie." "Hiya, Ed, what can I do for you?" The whole business was based on that, do you understand? It was all done on the Bon Hommy, the old pals act, because he *knew* I would phone him with something that was *good* for him. And we had a nice little arrangement with the B.B.C. which meant that the groups we like were certain to get played on the radio. So we had it all wrapped up.

'But these days, you'd get eleven or twelve calls a bleeding minute with young kids saying, "Great record man." There's a *great* musician around by the name of Jack Emlo, who *I* would put in the top half-dozen jazz accordion players in the world; he's that good. Now *I* used to go up to Jack and I'd say: "Jack, we've got a new song here." He'd look at it and say: "Yuh, that's *in* next week, Ed." Now I saw a kid going up to Jack Emlo, a young plugger who went up to Jack Emlo (who's a *great* musician), and says: "Uh, Mr. Emlo, I got a knock-out record." And Jack says: "Oh yes? How does it go?" He said: "I'll tell you, it goes like this: booby wooby booby wooby". Now Jack's too polite to say push off so he said, "Yes, but it's not quite the sort of stuff I play." Now this kid was so bloody ignorant he said: "Oh, well um, uh, well what we going to do then?" And Jack, being such a nice guy, says: "Well, have you got anything else?" And so help me, this kid said: "Oh, yeah, well, we got another one but I ain't learnt it yet".

'In the old days we were *fussy* about what type of song went out. We were worried about whether the lyric was married to the melody. If the lyric said something about "we all climbed up up up the mountain", the *music* went up up up up the mountain and we all came down down down down again; it was *important*. Fifteen or even ten years ago, the writers and the publishers were *artists*; they would sit together for hours changing one word that didn't seem right. Now it doesn't matter. "I *l·o·v·e* you"; you know, this is music? If it doesn't fit, so make it fit, even it it *is* bad musicianship and bad lyricism. Nobody cares nowadays whether the song makes sense, lyrically, musically or morally. Morally, especially. I mean look at 'Bend It'. Now *look* at 'Bend It'. Take it in its entirety - the way it sort of slowly starts and works up and works up; what's this, what's this? It's musical copulation. And that's what it's *supposed* to be.

'The whole thing has *nothing to do* with music - nothing to do with lyrics. It's a commercial property. Nobody buys a *song* any more; they buy a sound on a record. You want four things to make a hit record. The right artist, singing the right song with the right treatment at the right time. It doesn't seem to matter that in general the musicianship is bad.

'There's a famous singer in the business now - a standard singer earning a lot of money; I was on five of her record sessions and on all five of those sessions there was just one note she couldn't get because her voice wasn't good enough to get it. One of the session singers steps forward and puts that note in. With a little bit of tape splicing afterwords, (done by a guy who gets twenty pounds a week for tape splicing), this girl makes a hit record and earns a thousand pounds a week. And the tape splicer is now out of work, looking for a job.

'Half these bastards can't tell a crotchet from a quaver. Come to think of it, they don't know a crotchet from a bleeding crowbar let alone a quaver. Some poor ice-cream gets seven or eight guineas a session and makes a hit record for an artist who goes out on the road and earns a hundred pounds a night. But why should *he* make a fortune for somebody else? What's more, these so-called pop stars can do no wrong; they could go and fart the Anvil Chorus and they'd be number three next week. Now in the old days, it didn't matter how big the artist was.

Look at Vera Lynn. She was the sweetheart of the forces; an international name. But if she turned out a bad song it just didn't happen, because the *song* was important. But look at Tommy Steele; great fellow, don't misunderstand me. More talented than enough. He's got a load of talent, Tommy. But I can remember when he was voted number one guitarist. Number *one* guitarist. He's never played a guitar on a record in his life. It was either Roy Plummer or Bert Weedon playing the backing for him. And this was ten or fifteen years ago. I mean, this has been going on since time immemorial.

'And look at those charts. The charts are based on the returns of sales from certain record shops, which are supplied by various record shop managers. Now, a record shop manager is in business for one reason and one reason only; to sell as many records as he can. He bases his business on what he *hopes* is his knowledge of the business. A new record comes out. He's issued a printed circular from the record company saying: "Buy this record by Charley Flog and the Hipsters". Right. He thinks: "Well, that must be a hit", so he orders twenty-five copies. Six weeks later he's lumbered with them; he hasn't sold them.

'Now in the record business there's no sale or return; you buy 'em. If you don't flog 'em, it's just too bad. But *he's* lumbered with these records, so what's he going to do? He puts them on his returns, of course, and sends them to a paper which runs the charts, hoping that his returns will put Charley Flog *into* the charts, so that the kids will say: "Oh, blimey, it's in the charts, I haven't got it", and go out and buy all his old stock. I know one paper that takes its results every Monday from twelve dealers in the London area; now don't tell me it's difficult to find out which those twelve dealers are. I mean there's more ways of killing a cat than choking the bastard with cream; the pluggers find out which the twelve dealers are, and go round and say: "I love you forever" is in the charts this week and here's fifteen quid to prove it. Or if they want to be a bit more extravagant, they can go round and *buy up* enough records from these twelve dealers. It may cost a hundred quid, but if the record gets into the charts, his group will be able to earn a hundred quid *a night*. So it's obviously worth it.

'And then there's sex. Well, I hardly need say anything about *that*. Of course they're selling sex. Musical copulation, as I've said. You could see it with your own eyes; all the girls in the front row masturbating like mad. In the audience! And this fella used to go round with a ruler and smack 'em. Elvis Presley, and this is general knowledge, you can check this, was banned in several States in America because he had a piece of rubber hose in his tight jeans; a piece of rubber hose! And so when he used to cavort and perform, what else would this suggest?'

*   *   *

Derek Taylor, brilliant Press representative for The Beatles. Elliptical and allegorical, witty and honest. An impossible man in an impossible job - but always very nice.

'I remember I once took on a big lumpy group. It was a mistake and I knew it. And as those five faces came in week by week and said, "Are we in the magazines?" I would have to say: "No, not yet. And the reason you're not there is you're so bloody ugly". And they'd think that was funny. But it was true. They were so ugly and simple and decent. And nobody wanted to know about them.

'I suppose there's always something in everybody which is worth not only illuminating but enlarging and expanding; say: "Never mind, look at this bit of him." Tell the people. Tell the people the truth, because they want to hear it. They really don't want lies. I think the liar, the romantic liar, is nice to have around now and again because he spins such yarns. Mr. X was in Majorca, then he was in Australia. He was in every campaign during the war; if everything the good liar said was true, Mr. X would be 104.

'But the *big* lie, of course, is the age lie. It's a small thing but it's a big lie. And it's always told for financial gain. It's not told to help the group or to convey that in the group which is meaningful; and it's not told to keep the public informed. It's told to make extra money. The second big lie is, are they married or are they not? I once took on The Beach Boys, a very big American group, all of whom it was thought were single. They had one married member and he was a cute little chap. They said to him: "You can be married but we're all single". But, in fact, the whole damn lot were married. So one day I said: "let's get it out; put the pictures of their wives out right away." And funnily enough, it worked. Everybody thought - how lovely.

'I think that you should not put the artist in a position where he's going to be embarrassed to sustain what it is that you've given him. If your client is not literate then he shouldn't have a ghost column. I ghosted for George Harrison when I was on the *Daily Express*. He had a weekly thing; 'George said' or something. I wrote it almost without punctuation because I knew that if George was ever interviewed, he would speak exactly as his column spoke. The mistake that most publicists make is that they think *themselves* to be the stars. They're not. They're just the mediators; but they don't see themselves in that role. They become name-dropping whores.

'Bob Dylan has never had a press agent. And he vanished for fifteen months to make a new album. Without any publicity. When the new album came out (John Wesley Harding), without pre-publicity, it was a winner. Because the album was good and because Dylan is all there. So I think people like me are irrelevant. And yet, when I think about it, I'm not quite so sure. Let me tell you how I met The Beatles. I first saw them in New York and I absolutely couldn't stand the sight of the man who was speaking for them. Their Press agent, you know, at the airport. There were these four lads doing the very best they could, being themselves, and there was this bald man in a blue serge suit, shouting at the Press, and I thought: that man doesn't belong somehow. He should go. But I didn't know how to do that, without taking his job.

'*Everybody* has an image; but equally everybody wants to see things in you. They see a shadow, they see a halo, or they see a threat or a joy - and that comes through, image or not. Image building is one thing, but the *image* is in all of us. And if there's a magic in the group, then it shows. That's what happened with The Beatles. They don't consider themselves as Beatles. They don't *feel* Beatle when they go out. It's like going to a fancy dress ball dressed as Hitler which I did one Christmas. It was a good Hitler, but I didn't feel like it . . . I was getting Hitler responses from people, from waitresses and that, but I still felt like *me*. Well, The Beatles get Beatle responses and yet they also feel ordinary and themselves. *Other* people have demanded that they be leaders. *Other* people have demanded that while they're there, somewhere, whether it's India or London, as long as there's a Beatle *somewhere*, then all's well with the world. I think if they were to die say collectively and dramatically, and of course if a Beatle *did* die at this time it *would* be dramatic, it would be incredible, what would happen round the world. Because they give hope; because although the world is in such a shocking state, as always, there they are. Grinning and maharishi-ing and still being commercial.

'But *they* have never been conscious of creating this kind of worship. Everybody was hungry for something to worship, and along came The Beatles.'

*   *   *

Tony Hall, in 1969 sort of 40 and sort of very hip. A professional spokesman and publicist and promotion-man. As In-Touch and groovy as only the In-Touch and groovy *can* be.

'The things that are most important to us are the integrity of the artist, the complete and utter dedication to their music and their art, a belief in their sincerity as people, and a genuine desire on our part to be creative.

'I think that the appreciation of beautiful sounds must be latent in you. I personally have been listening to and involved with music in some way or other since I was five years old. And music is my entire life. You know, literally. I often work twenty-hour days, at promotion, because without promotion I don't think *any* record stands a hope in hell. Now can you imagine. Every single producer and disc jockey has on his desk a pile of seventy new singles a week. Well, maybe two of those singles will carry a little stamp saying, "Tony Hall Enterprises"; well we hope that the DJ will pick these two records out, and give them extra attention. Because he *knows* that we would not allow our names to be associated with any record that we did not consider to be extremely good of its kind.

'I think *creativity* is tremendously important; it's amazing how few producers can create spontaneously. And the old pals' act is, of course, also very important. Contacts are the most valuable things in the world; and friendships, really genuine friendships. We try to make as many real friends as we possibly can. Out of these friendships come goodwill and integrity. I've been in promotion for thirteen years, and I've never cried wolf in my life. If I'm in trouble with a record, I will come right out and say, "Please help me, I've got this manager breathing down my neck; I'm desperate for a play of this record." But you've got to sell with genuine honesty, and a very honest sincerity. So of *course* I would have to consider; is the group pretty? is its hair right? Are the little girls going to swoon? These are *important* questions.'

'But for the general public these often seem to be the *only* questions. What the *public* demands has usually got very little to do with honesty and sincerity. At the moment we're going through the dreariest period of pop music I can ever remember in thirteen years in the record business, and we - in our own humble way - are trying to make it less dreary. Not because the music is dreary, but because the whole business side of it is dreary.

'The public will only buy what they are allowed to hear and see in the greatest quantity. They will buy records that they hear most on the radio; they will buy records by artists that they see most often on television. But television producers are obviously governed by ratings; they know that to get the highest rating they will have to put on safe, middle-of-the-road shows featuring safe middle-of-the-road music and artists who are familiar to everybody in the family. I don't think we've had a single TV show in England since "Ready Steady Go" and later, "How it is" (before that was sterilised by Mr. Right-about-Art and then killed), that has had any real genuine concern for pop music and that has consequently tried to expose new talent. And I think this country desperately and obviously needs one. I would also like to see twenty-five different radio stations in this country, because I think that the more radio stations there are, the higher the standards would be on each station.

'If the public doesn't *know* about all that is happening in pop music - because it's never allowed the proper opportunity to hear it or see it, how can it possibly dismiss it all as rubbish? It's judging something that it's never heard or seen. So the really interesting question is - *why* has it never heard it or seen it?'

*   *   *

Kit Lambert, dapper son of Constant Lambert, godson of Sir William Walton. Co-manager of The Who and Arthur Brown; eminence grise of Track Records whose chief star - apart from The Who and Arthur Brown, is Jimi Hendrix. Articulate and funny about anything you cared to mention to him. Later died, derelict.

'I used to have great difficulty in persuading promoters to book The Who; this was *before* they had a hit record. It's difficult for everyone, but I found it particularly difficult. I'd say, "Well, their art is very violent". And they'd say, "*violence*? that's the *last* thing we want. We don't want any trouble in *our* clubs." So eventually we had to promote The Who ourselves; we just couldn't get them *any* bookings. The first thing we'd do was flood London with half-price tickets for a concert at the Marquee Club in Wardour Street; you know, great big ones with pictures of the group on. On thick cardboard; not like cheap giveaways. Then we literally dragooned in such fans as they had from those early days; I made sure that *they* were there. Even paid their bus fares for them to get up to the West End, so that we could get some warmth going.

'And finally we'd cover London with posters; we'd stick them up on banks, anywhere. We would go round *every* night with a van. As the banks tore them down, we'd put them up again. We put posters in the most outrageous places. We had a big van, with flat sides. It was about ten foot off the ground. We'd drive around in the best places, places like Trafalgar Square, or Piccadilly Circus. But everywhere we went was always guarded by the Police. So we'd drive the van in between a wall and the policeman, and park it. We found that if you covered the whole wall with posters, the police didn't notice. If you only put up one, they *would* notice it. But if you put up twenty posters in a square and have them absolutely symmetrical, then drive the van away, you'd be amazed how the police didn't notice. We'd leave the policeman standing there thinking, funny, you know. Something's wrong, something's different, funny, you know; but they weren't able to spot it. Maybe the posters would only be up there for an hour. But that would do the job.'

*   *   *

Anthony Burgess - distinguished novelist & critic. One time lover of pop - but not of its pretensions. Author of 'A Clockwork Orange'.

'I like pop as I like coca-cola or wrapped bread or fish fingers. They're instant and they give an illusion of nourishment. But I get very frightened when intellectuals start elevating pop to the level of important art. When *they* say such and such a record is great, *I* have to say, well Beethoven's Ninth Symphony is great. Tristan and Isolde is great, Mahler's Song of the Earth is great; do they mean great in the same way? I presume they must. They must be making out that pop contains the same elements of emotional satisfaction and intellectual complexity as Beethoven, Brahms, or Wagner. This doesn't seem to me to be possible.

'Even the best songs of The Beatles are only simple little lyrics written by young men of no great education and no great knowledge of our literary past; they do a very simple job very adequately. But nonetheless they deal with simple little emotions, suburban little emotions; they deal with adolescent love, with rather vague aspirations of adolescents which are not backed up by any knowledge of the world.

They're short-breathed, like the music, sentimental with a little fashionable toughness added to them. But they're incapable of dealing with the sort of thing that Dylan Thomas dealt with; the emotions one feels on seeing a child killed in an air raid. The emotion one feels when somebody dear to one has died. The emotion one feels on seeing the birth of a child. The emotion one feels when one hears that a civilisation has foundered. This is the sort of material which *great* lyrical poetry is made out of. All The Beatles do is deal with - well, a lonely old woman who's died and the priest doesn't care very much after all, and shall this girl leave home and go to London or not, or will I love you when I'm sixty-four or won't I? These are very vapid sentiments, and they're treated rather vapidly.

'I think it's significant that pop groups consist of young people. You can't imagine a very aged pop group consisting of people my age, unless we were doing it as a nasty gimmick. Satire, I think it would be called. Of course, the adulation of youth is not a new thing; it's an old convention, but economic circumstances have contrived to make youth a profitable social group to appeal to in the field of simple pleasures, simple entertainments. The significant thing about the worship of youth today is that it is manifested almost physically. Blatantly. Long hair from Biblical times has always been associated with great strength; when Samson had to be brought down, his hair had to be cut off. In the 18th century grown men used to wear wigs, to be like Samson. Now long hair is a prerogative of youth, it's a symbol of sexual virility. At the same time the lean hips, the lack of a belly, these two must be emphasised in a particular kind of dress.

'But I think it's probably illusory to suppose that youth contains *any* virtues, other than the mere fact of being young. It's good to be young because one is vigorous, one is handsome, one lacks superfluous flesh. One has hopes. It's an admirable period to live through but at the same time it lacks *content*. Just as music itself has - as content - music; so, *all* that youth has - as content - is youth. Youth produces *nothing* except youth.

'I remember an old proverb which says that youth thinks itself wise, just as drunk men think themselves sober. Youth is *not* wise; youth knows nothing about life. Youth knows nothing about anything except a mass of cliches which for the most part, through the media or pop songs, are just foisted on them by middle-aged entrepreneurs and exploiters who should know better. What's more, there seems to be a half-baked conviction that pop music has some kind of *religious* significance; that to like pop music, to admire it and listen to it, is not merely an act of enjoyment but also a religious act.

'I think the reasons for this are moderately clear. The first is that there's a tie-up between pop music and a kind of popular art of protest. The happening of protest in Trafalgar Square, the rather more deliberate and organised happening of protest which you find at these Albert Hall meetings when people with guitars sing songs about the war in Vietnam, about how good the Vietcong are, and how if you fought Hitler in the last war, as I did, you somehow became a fascist. Secondly, there's a tie-up with the practice of taking opiates of some kind; the practice of taking drugs, which may induce a sort of hallucination, a hallucinogenic vision, which is thought to be religious.

'But when we start thinking that pop music is close to God, then we'll think pop music is aesthetically better than it is, and it's only the aesthetic value of pop music we should be concerned with. The only way we can judge Wagner or Beethoven or any other composer is aesthetically. We don't regard Wagner or Beethoven or Shakespeare or Milton as great teachers. They're merely there to provide a very complex entertainment. And we judge them on their ability to do this.

'Now when we start claiming for Lennon or McCartney or the Maharishi, or any other of these pop prophets, the ability to transport us to a region where God becomes manifest, then I see red. We've become completely satisfied with our little long-playing records, ten pop numbers or thereabouts a side; this is great *Art*; we've been *told* this. We've been told this by the great pundits of our age. And in consequence, why should we bother to learn? There's nothing more delightful than to be told: you don't have to learn, my boy, there's nothing in it. Modern art? There's nothing in it. Learning German? There's no German literature, why bother to learn German. Go to Singapore? There's nothing in Singapore you can't find in Carnaby Street. When you're told these things, you sit down with a sigh of relief; thank God I don't have to learn, I don't have to travel, I don't have to exert myself in the slightest. I am what I am. Youth is youth. Pop is pop. There's no need to progress, there's no need to do anything. Let us sit down, smoke our marijuana, (an admirable thing in itself, but not the end of anything). Let us listen to our records because life has become a single moment, a single moment in eternity . . . We're with God; finis.'

*   *   *

Bernard Delfont
by
Ralph STEADman

Kit Lambert again, speaking in 1969.

'My father, who was a classical composer, brought me up to mistrust musical snobbery of any kind. The music he was writing when he was nineteen and twenty was full of jazz idioms, which was considered unthinkable by the musical elite. When his music was played at the Albert Hall, people were shocked. They couldn't understand how someone of his talents could hang around with such as Louis Armstrong rather than with classical musicians and the whole Establishment BBC crowd of Queen's Hall followers. Fortunately the musical frontiers are now beginning to disappear; classical influences are being absorbed by pop and pop by classical. And I really think there is more valid new creative music being made at the pop end. I don't see any good classical composers emerging at the moment. I certainly haven't heard a decent new symphony or a decent new opera in the last eighteen months and I think that the whole impetus has passed to the younger generation and to the excitement that is generated in pop.

'But what worries me - and this is why musical snobbery in England still persists, is that the Establishment, the Arts Council, would happily spend money on assisting some small opera group or some travelling theatre company to help them got off the ground, but wouldn't dream of financing some interesting pop project that might not in itself be commercial. But I think they may have to. I can see a Beatles opera on at Covent Garden. Ten years from now. I bet you. Because opera as we know it now, is absolutely defunct. One needs a completely fresh approach. And I think pop is going to provide it.

'People seem to think that everyone in pop has loads of money - but this just isn't true. Often to do anything worthwhile, you really have to struggle. When we started managing The Who we had a capital of £5,000 - which was the savings I'd made from working in movies. And it looked very rough at one time; I mean the £5,000 vanished in four or five months and we were down to practically nothing; shillings. It really was very close to the nail, and several times during the two years after that people came and took the furniture away. In fact, to be exact, they came in four times and took the furniture away. It's very depressing when you're managing a group and you're supposed to be making money, and you arrive and there's a big furniture van on the steps of your office and a big bloke's carrying out your desk. And there's a man standing there saying: "Seize Christopher Lambert and deliver

him unto the Governor of Brixton Jail." I couldn't believe it; this can't
be happening to me, you know? And as your group gets bigger, so you
have to get bigger and bigger treatment and exposure for them. Recently,
I had to spend a fortnight in Hollywood. My phone bill alone was more
per week than most people earn in a year. It was horrific.

'It's true that famous singles have been made for £20 or £30, and
have then earned millions and million of dollars. But these days, singles
production has become so refined that you can find yourself spending
several days in the studio to perfect a single which can therefore cost
thousands. And single sales have gone down during this same period. I
suppose a big record in America sells around half-a-million copies.
Always used to be a million. And in England any record that went to
No. 1 used to collect a silver disc for 1/2 million sales more or less
automatically. But now, a No. 1 record only needs 100,000 sales.

'So for us touring has become more and more important. Most pop
music was once entirely disseminated through vast promotional
expeditions. To keep the group before the public eye. When The Who
first started touring, they went around in a converted furniture van. It
just had shabby old armchairs in it. They often had to travel nearly
1,000 miles between two bookings. Now they have a whole special bus,
with beds and a lavatory in it so that you can sleep on the road if
necessary. But they still go around a vast amount. On a recent tour of
the USA, for example, The Who journeyed 15,000 miles in six weeks;
800 miles a day for an engagement was nothing. Increasingly the strain
of such tours has forced ambitious pop musicians away from live
performance and into the womblike recording studio. A song has thus
become an electronic creation. It exists in its true form *only* on record.

'Even so, The Who have always been very popular on stage. This is
because they have a direct sexual impact. They ask a question: do you
want to or don't you? And they don't really give the public a chance of
saying no. It *is* a sort of rape. I suppose that's what happened to me
when I first discovered them.

'I was looking for a new group to put into a movie that was, I hoped,
going to revolutionise pop film-making. And I used to drive around
looking for pubs or clubs with the largest number of motor scooters
outside. There was one very scruffy-looking pub in Harrow where there
was this huge cluster of scooters outside, and I went in and there were
The Who. They were playing there in this room with just one red bulb
glowing and an extraordinary audience that they had collected. They
were the loudest group I'd ever heard and they gave the whole thing a

satanic quality. It just seemed to me that this had to be the face of the late sixties.

'There was Keith Moon, the drummer, raised on a high stool dominating the group, battering away for all his life was worth. The rest of the group was playing on a stage made out of beer crates. And the ceiling came right down on top of them so that when Pete Townshend - the lead guitarist - was playing, he'd keep banging his guitar against the ceiling, and one night he physically poked a hole through the ceiling because it was getting in his way. It was only made of paper and cardboard, and he went straight through. This went down tremendously with the audience. And that's how the whole thing started.

'They also used to have trouble with equipment, like all new groups have. And so Pete, who's not the best tempered of people, would occasionally give the speaker cabinet a bang, and smash that up. It all escalated and of course Keith wanted to be in on the act. He had no guitar to break up and so he started the whole destructive drumming thing. And finally at one concert at Wembley, he more or less stole the show by building up into a drum climax which finally resulted in the whole drum kit disintegrating and falling into the audience with Keith left drumming on a single drum. The original symbolical drummer - at an execution. Now, the audience feels cheated unless they see X hundred dollars worth of equipment broken up under their eyes.

'And when The Who play live now, people *still* dance as if they are possessed. The rest just listen in a kind of frozen terror. There is a distinct feeling of the presence of evil. And of something which I can only describe as revolutionary; revolutionary in the sense of blood, revolutionary in the sense of a complete upheaval of everyone's ideas. And a feeling of violence and aggression and fury that is almost too sinister to handle.'

Chapter Seven

Paul McCartney - Composer:

'I was always frightened of classical music. And I never wanted to listen to it because it was Beethoven or Tchaikowsky and big words like that; and Schoenberg! A taxi driver the other day had some sheet music of a Mozart thing on his front seat. And I said: "What's that?" And he said: "Oh, that's the high-class stuff, you won't like that." He Said: "No, no, you won't like that." I said: "Well, what is it?" He said: "Oh, no, you won't like it. You know, it's high-class stuff. Very high-class. Highbrow." And that kind of way *I* always used to think of it; I used to think, well you know, that is - that's exactly what's going on in pop at the moment. Pop music *is* the classical music of now.

'*We* started off by imitating Chuck Berry, Buddy Holly, Elvis, Carl Perkins, The Coasters and all the old Soul-come-rock 'n' roll stars; we just copied what they did. John and I used to sag off school and go to my house or to his house, and just start trying to write songs like theirs. We'd put a Buddy Holly record on - and then after we'd listen to it several times, we'd sit around with our guitars and then try and something like him. We couldn't think of any other way of doing it; you can't just write a song out of the blue. *And* think of your own style and everything. The people we copied were all American, of course, because there was no one good British. There still isn't. I don't think there's anyone really on the British scene that's got that thing that the old rock records used to have. I'd much rather have an American coloured group singing one of our songs than us. 'Cause they do it better.

'Anyway, we were just searching for years to get our own style. You've got your Buddy Holly style and you've got your Chuck Berry style and your Bill Haley style, and we thought, well now we'll have to get a Beatles style. And so we tried all combinations of things, you know; take a bit of calypso and a bit of cha-cha; we were trying to do it like a formula. But eventually we just gave up and said we'll just copy Buddy Holly and that's that. So we used to go and play in places like

The Cavern and we'd start off trying to play a song exactly like Bo Diddley or exactly like Chuck Berry; exactly like the *records* we had listened to. Unfortunately, we couldn't ever get it *exactly* like the record. It always used to be a bit bumpier than the records, never as smooth. It was a bit louder, I suppose, and we shouted it a bit more. But eventually someone said, "Ah, that's a great style you've got there." What they didn't realise and what they still don't realise, is that it was only us trying to play exactly like the people we were copying. It was just that we weren't very good. So we could never get it exactly right. We still don't, you know.

'Obviously the most important influence on us was blues and soul music. We liked all of that. But we couldn't and *still* can't do it. It's like most white people; there's only a couple around that can - that can sound coloured. Most white singers are trying to sound coloured in some kind of way, you know that. But if it doesn't show in us, it's only because we can't quite make it. Our music tends to be a bit white, because we are. Mind you, that doesn't mean that, like some white singers, we wear gold lamé suits, and pink handkerchiefs with matching ties. That's all false and hypocritical. We wouldn't be able to write songs that were that slushy. Although, the first songs we wrote *were* pretty rough. *We* used to write songs about blue moons:

> there's no blue moon that I can see;
> there's never been in hist-or-eeee.

I suppose gradually we just got a bit better at writing songs; we began to write more like we thought - and we have never thought very sloppily.

'But in spite of our crude beginnings, people still take our music and read absolutely everything into it. Take, for example, a line like "she was just seventeen". That becomes in the ears of some critics: "she was a seventeen-year-old nymphomaniac working on the streets of Broadway." What *we* meant was that she was just seventeen.

'Or take 'Yellow Submarine', for example. People got very worked up about that being a song full of deep and hidden meaning. But for us, it's just a kid's song. I was just lying in bed and I thought, wouldn't it be great to have a song like the songs you used to listen to on the radio when you were a kid, like 'The Runaway Train'. That was my favourite. Came over the hill and she blew. And I thought that was great that, 'cause it was just for kids. But nobody seemed to make them any more. So I said, it'd be great, we'll do one just for kids, and we'll have it about

JUST SOUNDS LIKE A LOT OF CACOPHONOUS HELLISH NOISE TO ME—
I COULDN'T AGREE MORE, ELSIE— DO YOU COME HERE OFTEN?

a submarine. And it's yellow, and I just imagined it underneath the sea so that we all lived in a yellow submarine. It was never supposed to be anything other than that.

'But it might mean all the other as well; I don't know. I've no idea if there's any Aeolian cadences or miasmic climaxes in it. As far as I'm concerned, it's just a song; just about people and things.

'But I can quite see why people *wanted* to see other things in our songs. 'Yellow Submarine', for example, did come out at a particular time when it seemed to mirror all the worries that were about at the time. So everyone said: "Oh, ho, ho, dig man, get your meaning, get the message." But it was only intended as a straight children's song.

'Occasionally, however, the critics do make complete fools of themselves. For example, someone said that the initials of 'Lucy in the Sky With Diamonds' were short for LSD. Well, no-one was more surprised about that than us. All that really happened was that John's son had come home one day from school with a piece of paper on which he had a drawing. John had said, "What's that? That's nice." He said: "It's Lucy in the sky with diamonds". It's like a Hollywood story. So John wrote a song about it and we recorded it - and that was it.

'In any case, I'm not an authority on our songs. I sometimes love listening to old album tracks, 'cause I've just forgotten them, you know. I was looking through an album the other day, and there was a song called 'Yes it is'. I couldn't remember how it went or anything. But I don't really play our music that much, so *I* don't know. I suppose it's better to leave the sophisticated write-ups to the sophisticated writers. We just keep trying to write songs the way we write them and not try to analyse them. You get into trouble once you analyse a thing, if you're doing it yourself. You get to a word and you've become so self-conscious of what you're trying to do, that it starts to worry you. After all, we're the last people to know about our songs, because The Beatles have never heard The Beatles as such. We can't - if you look at a snapshot of yourself, you don't really see it objectively. You're looking at what tie you were wearing or whether you were looking nice in the snapshot. But anyone else would just look at the snapshot and say: "Oh, that's good, that's a snapshot of so-and-so."

'Nonetheless, I think that all the intellectualising has got out of hand. We started off as a rock group, just a rock combo, just playing what we wanted to play, and we're *still* doing that. Of course, in the meantime we absorbed a lot of influences. We've had a lot of things happen to us. We've got famous in the meantime. We've got money in the meantime. Everything's had its influence. We went to India and George got interested in Indian music, so he wrote Indian music into us. Nothing's ever that permanent with us. There's no master-plan driving us all along. We're very fidgety people. We gave up being on stage, for example, because we were tired of it. We'd done a lot of tours of America and we were really just finished; physically knocked out. And one day we said, OK, let's pack this in, all this touring. Now, we actually miss some aspects of it. For instance, just singing. I always used to sing all the time. But now I only sing when I'm writing a song or recording it. And that's not most days. So I miss singing out loud - the pleasure of doing that. We might easily perform live again. There'll come a time when we'll want to do that again.

'Likewise when Brian Epstein died we found ourselves committed to record deals, music publishing contracts, films, and so on. So we tried to look and see whether we could do any better and get better deals. And in doing that, we just got together a few experts. But we didn't really *plan* it. The idea of running our own affairs just snowballed from that simple beginning. All we wanted to do was to provide the kind of business situation that we always hoped there would be when *we* were trying to get a record contract or get into films or do anything.

'*We* had always had to go to the big man on our knees and say: "Please can we have a record or please can we make a film?" And most of those companies are so big and so out of touch with ordinary people that we *always* had trouble. But now, instead of us just taking all the profits out, and being fat and rich, what we can do is re-invest it in things that we believe in. The bosses for the first time don't want all the money back. So we put it back and let other people who haven't got a chance, have a go. But not in the way that the Arts Council do, in a charitable way as if they were the big patrons. We just say: "Here's a bit of money, now go and do it." And you know - earn it. The whole scheme started off in chaos because we said we won't have any yes sir, no sir, you're the boss. But we've had to have a little organisation. People are now all working together, for this great aim. If it comes off, you'll know about it.

'Of course, it has brought its problems. For example, I once bought a couple of paintings. The very next day I read in the newspapers that I was now *sponsoring* this artist. I wasn't. I was just buying a couple of paintings. Nonetheless, there *is* a desire in us to get power in order to use it for good. I know it sounds a bit like a vicar getting up and preaching: "We can really make this place a good place to live in." I never liked preachers, and I don't like anyone preaching at me. Most people don't. That's why vicars aren't very successful in what they do most of the time. But if you've got power - and we obviously have - you've got to use it, and use it for good. Even if you are a group of just happy little rockers.'

*   *   *

Pete Townshend - dazzling lead guitarist of The Who. Skinny and thoughtful - still with a curious menace hanging about his large piercing eyes.

'I'm today's powerful young man; I'm today's successful young man. I'm not saying that in any egotistic way at all, but you have to face it. It is *us* and people like us who dictate the music formula; we dictate changing hair styles, the way people dress. This is what art is; this is what our music is all about. It *involves* people, completely. It does something to their whole way of existence; the way they dance, the way they express themselves sexually, the way they think - everything. But most importantly, our music tells you about *now*. Ultimately there's nothing left but the present. And by and large, the past two generations have made such a colossal mess of everything that they have to step down and let us take over.

'The world of pop and what it is achieving is unbelievable. I can't see someone like Benjamin Britten, sitting in his little studio doing his things (which I very much admire), getting through to the same kind of audience and having the same kind of effect. After all, pop audiences are the cream of today's music-listening audiences. They're not the classical snobs who sit by their poxy Hi-fi and listen to Mr. X (name censored) conducting. Not knowing that Mr. X (name censored) is completely stoned out of his crust and grooving to high heaven, thinking "what a *fine*, excellent recording this is, what a *fine* conductor Mr. X (name censored) is, really *fine*," and him not knowing what the fucking hell *is* going on. Almost for this reason alone, pop music and its incalculable effect is crucial to an understanding of today's art. It's crucial that pop should be considered as art. It's crucial that it should *progress* as art, and not return - as parts of it seem desperately trying to do, to the kind of factory-made, big-agency-controlled rubbish that it was before The Beatles came along.

'If you look at *any* form of art, you can find something in the best of pop which completely eliminates the old form. Completely eliminates it.

'If you think that Mahler's Ninth Symphony is overwhelming, I can play you a tape which I made in my studio at home which is *more* overwhelming. If you tell me that Italian opera is unsurpassable, then you're talking rubbish. If people dig Italian opera then let them dig it. I think we can do better - in today's terms. Italian opera doesn't say *anything* for today. Benjamin Britten, for example, is hung up on Purcell. So am I, but I think *I* was getting nearer to what Purcell was getting at musically in my song, 'I'm a Boy', than Benjamin Britten was in the whole of his work.

'I'm sure it will surprise a lot of people when I tell you that I can read music and I know how to arrange it; I also know all about counterpoint. But as soon as I had learned all the theory, I realised that it was utterly useless to me. All it allowed me to do was to understand what other composers were trying to do. And once you've understood, you've got to go on and use today's terms to produce new music, not yesterday's.'

'I think the most important musical development *we've* made in pop is in free form music. Complete abandon in music, completely uncontrolled music which does exactly what it wants. We don't allow our instruments to stop us doing what we want; we don't even allow our physical health to stop us doing what we want. Ours is a group with built-in hate. We smash our instruments, tear our clothes and wreck everything. The expense doesn't worry us because that would be something which would get between us and our music. If I stood on stage worrying about the price of the guitar than I'm not really playing music. I'm getting involved in material values. So I don't have a love affair with a guitar; I don't polish it after every performance; I *play* the fucking thing.

'Our actual *intention* is to play out all the adrenalin and all the aggression and all the things that are in us. We communicate aggression and frustration to an audience, musically and visually. We want to show the audience that we *are* frustrated characters, that we *do* wanna do it in front of them. I've written a thesis for Gustav Metzger - the auto destructive artist. I said that our audience is numbed by seeing violence in the same way that they're numbed by seeing a car crash. It's a traumatic experience. But it *does* release basic tensions - just like other people do when they fly off the handle. Lack of control and basic abandon are qualities that people don't particularly admire or respect in others; but at the same time, they don't seem to realise that they *themselves* have also got these things stuffed inside them. So our performances and our music have got much more to do with art and life than people imagine. Much, much more to do with pop music than anything else. Outside of football, there's been very little *real* expression of how we feel since the days when people ran around with no clothes on banging drums. It's all been sophistication and gloss.

'We're not out to blow people's minds, however. We're out to get through to them. It's too easy to blow someone's mind. All we have to do is to go on either stark naked or explode - blow our toes off or something; you can always blow people's minds. You know these guys that come up and say: "Wouldn't it be a mind-blower if we get 6,000 million kids all dressed in red uniforms and had a big freak-out in the middle of Ealing Common?" Sure it'll be mind-blowing, but what would it prove? At the moment, I'm very interested in getting complete control over my music. In other words, I would write a piece of music, arrange it, play every instrument myself, record it all myself, in my own studio, sing any part that needed singing, produce it myself and also distribute it myself. Complete control. The more control you've got over what you're involved in, the nearer the finished product is to what you intended. It will be good when every individual can make music in the same way that every individual can now paint a picture. Think how huge it could be; instead of the drab music classes that you have in school now, you could have something similar to an art class where everyone actually makes music themselves. This could be huge.

'I have to admit that I find it very difficult to talk about pop music, since to start with there isn't such a thing as "pop" music. There are many different kinds of music all called "pop". You can't say that the sounds I produce are the same as those of Donald Peers. They're totally different - but they're both called "pop". For me, my kind of pop is being the leader of youth, it's being in the present. But the more you talk about that, the more confused you become; the best thing is not to be talking but to pick up a guitar and be playing it. Because that's what pop music is really about. Pop music isn't me sitting reasoning out its role; it's me picking up a guitar and playing you a song. After all, even to go bang, bang on a guitar does get a lot of things said - although *you* may not like what is being expressed. Pop music is ultimately a show, a circus. You've got to *hit* the audience with it. Punch them in the stomach, and kick them on the floor. Pop music will cease to be any interest if it gets too interested in musical or lyrical obscurity, because when it comes down to it, its purpose and its value is in the creation of an immediate and overwhelming excitement.'

*   *   *

Eric Burdon - founder member and lead singer with The Animals. A Geordie, from Newcastle, England, who moved in the seventies to California where, he said, the opportunities for self-expression were greater.

'Now take the period from 1960 to 1968; you'll see that in 1960 there was a lot of hard rock stuff being sung. The Beatles were singing things like 'I want to be your Man'; 'Let me hold your hand'. The Rolling Stones were doing all rock stuff, Chuck Berry stuff. Everything was hard and solid. And then LSD came along and the music suddenly went all trippy and dreamy. 'Flowers that grow so incredibly high' and 'Lucy in the Sky with Diamonds'. Everything became much softer, much more hallucinogenic. And now that the drugs are gone, we're coming back again to the solidness; everybody's getting themselves together again.

'The people who've lived through the LSD experience went through a complete facet of learning, which must have been done some other way when my father and *his* generation were kids. Maybe they did it by going to war. I was talking to an air hostess who told me that she once worked for TWA, which was flying soldiers to the front in Vietnam. And she would watch a platoon of soldiers get on the plane on their way to Vietnam, and they'd be getting as much booze down their throats as possible, all bragging about wanting to get into battle and fight it out, all trying to grab a hold of the hostess. Now she'd watched the same platoon on the way back to America *after* they'd experienced combat, and they'd become *men*. They were dignified and quiet; they shut up and behaved themselves. So for them, that's kind of like an LSD trip. That's what it does to you. You go in like a mad bull, and you come out with your ego destroyed. You're a much more together person. The drug experience may not have proved much in the long run, but it has taught us that to be *deranged* is not necessarily to be useless.

'Most people think that pop musicians are idiots and we're only in it for sex and screaming girls. Well it isn't like that. Most of us have given our life to it and most of us spend twenty-four hours a day eating it, thinking it, walking it, talking it. I talk about nothing else. It's my religion. And it's a better religion than many of the others around.

'I don't give a damn whether I earn any money or not. If they took me to prison and locked me up in a prison cell, and all I had was a washtub and a bunk to sit on and four bare walls, I'd still be singing me mind out. It's me life. So the biggest thing that brings me down is when people come up to me and say, "Oh, you're in show business". Which is terrible, because show business has got nothing to do with pop.

'As we build up the whole materialistic thing which is getting bigger and bigger all the time, our spiritual thing isn't keeping up with it. Somehow, somebody, somewhere has got to find a way of making the spiritual thing catch up. And make it so that the everyday working man isn't brought down by religion or disappointed by it or made to think that religion is dull. The dated old Christian concept of religion makes me sick to my stomach. I wrote a song called 'Sky Pilot' in which I sang about this. We *still* send army chaplains into wars as if they were men of war; we did it in World War II, and we did it in Vietnam. Religion today is a failure because it doesn't get through to people any more. And what's more, it's no longer honest with itself because it still blesses the bombs that are dropped on people.

'But *music* can get through to *everybody* - and especially pop music. So for me, of course pop music *is* a religion - because I believe in it. In this sense, pop music is a crusade. It's also a crusade against all kinds of social injustice. I don't think that pop music was *caused* by any particular set of social circumstances. A violent world did not, of itself, produce violent music. But often - and only afterwards - you can see a connection between the two.

'For example, there was a race riot brewing up in New York several years ago. But for five days, everything remained quiet. Now it just happened that during those five days there was a music festival up on 125th Street. Most of the Negroes went there to hear their music and so it kept them cool and calmed them down when they heard their music, they felt better. When the music festival ended after five days, everything just blew up. *Obviously* music affects the mind. The people of India realised this centuries ago. They have ragas to wake you up in the morning, ragas to make you feel good in the afternoon, ragas to pray by. They know that certain music, certain tone levels, will affect the body. But in the West, on the other hand, scientists spend their time messing around with sounds to wipe out the human race. With vibrations. It makes you sick.

'What's fuzzing up people's minds today is that there is so *much* communication, but there's also a great lack of communication. That's because although the tools are there for communication, we're not using them right. Television is being misused, radio is being misused, the movies are being misused. The movies in Hollywood, for example, have told the biggest lie that mankind has ever told. When I first got to America, I'd seen so many Hollywood movies that made it look so colourful and comfortable that when I got off the plane at New York I actually expected that I wouldn't even catch a cold. Or if somebody stuck a knife into me, I wouldn't even feel the blade. I thought it would be plastic, like in the Hollywood dream. In fact, when I got there I found that there was just as much pain and just as much misery as there is anywhere else. But why had nobody told me *that*?

'The same kind of lack of communication has happened between the pop world and the general public. Most of the general public don't even *hear* the best of pop music, because TV and the radio conspire against it ever getting broadcast. All you ever hear on TV and radio is the music that is commercially successful. There's nothing wrong with that but it's only a tiny part of the story. So the public get confused as to what *is* pop music; and because they hear only the stuff that is not really very worthwhile, they come to think that *none* of it is worth while.

'I remember the first Beatle concert I went to. At the time, The Beatles were trying to make the switch from their loud "yeah, yeah" music where everybody went aah and screamed, to the more subtle and sophisticated music that they made later. Paul McCartney got up and sang 'There were birds in the trees and I never heard them singing'. But the audience were still screaming and screaming and screaming, whilst The Beatles were trying to make a soft gentle statement. And nobody was listening.

'Today, the kids are more hip. If you go to a pop concert today, the kids *don't* scream any more. It's just the adults, the older people, who still think that everybody's screaming. When we do a concert in America, a town will lay out something like 10,000 dollars for police protection. The local authorities still think "Oh we're having a rock and roll show downtown this weekend. Gotta get the cops in!" So the cops come along and they're all muscle and guns and everybody gets frightened. But there's no need for it.

'I suppose the main problem is that pop music is still very young. It's like a teenager. Like a teenager, it's disturbed. A teenager gets spots

The
Who
Ralph STEADMAN

on his face, he falls in love every day. But we're only at the beginning right now. The more we know about music and about sound, and in particular the effect that sound can have on people, the faster we will *all* grow up. And the faster we will realise that there's no need to split things up. There's no need to call it classical or pop or jazz; it's just music. Modern-day music. There's no such thing as rhythm and blues, rock and roll, or soul. If you listen to Ravi Shankar and then listen to some Scottish bagpipes, there's no essential difference.

'*Of course* pop music is the voice of the 20th century. During Mozart's day what we now call classical music was called pop music then - except of course that the word pop didn't exist. Today's classical music is being created right now. There are some people who realise that pop has got its finger on the pulse. In America, for example, they tried to ban Negro music several years ago on the radio. They tried to ban it from being listened to by white people, because they thought that the nasty, nasty oversexed Negro was leading them on a downhill run. Perhaps he is - I wish I knew.'

*   *   *

Donovan - once lived in the perfect country cottage, surrounded by heavy woods. Later he established a commune for himself and 6 others in Scotland. Each was paid £10 a week and each had to contribute to the complete welfare of the others. A spartan existence - Donovan himself had very few material possessions and lived peacefully - and in seclusion. This is what he believed in 1969.

'Pop music is a great camouflage. I think we're all glad of it really. Although it's not much fun being treated like an idiot, it's good in a way because it hides the reality of being very serious about your life. Consequently, we are left in peace.

'Also, the camouflage helps us to get through to people whilst no-one is watching. Before, a writer would come out with a couple of books. That's all either he or his publishers could afford. If they didn't sell, he was finished. Now we have plastic records which are just like books - except that *many* more people can get to them. The writer can put his words and his poems onto these records - and again because they are thought to be all part of pop music, they sell enormously well and the message gets through. In the same way, our music - which is serious music, doesn't die the death that much serious music and serious poetry has done in the past. No longer is it only the rich and the intellectuals for whom it is available. For whom it is even accessible. Now, a young fourteen-year-old mod-girl can hear this poetry - she may not like it, but at least it's there for her to hear. So pop music could become the great vehicle for sensitizing *all* the arts. Since it's usually thought of just as a "popular music", we can do all our different things inside it and for the first time be sure that we will be heard - and widely heard - simply because we are thought of as pop. And the reaction to it by the kids is in a sense much more pure than it is to the other "arts", because the kids don't feel the need to intellectualise it. It's just there for them to take or not.

'As long as we go on thinking of the arts as The Arts with a capital A, we will be in danger of killing off them all - or condemning them all to the museum and the library and the TV documentary. In the old days, a painter and a stonemason and a carpenter and a plumber were *all* thought of as craftsmen. They were not "artists" as if that were something separate. If you chopped a tree down, you were as much an "artist" as a man who painted the Madonna. I would like to see people realise again that painting isn't just something on the canvas; it's building your house or cleaning the windows or living or loving or falling in love, or walking down the road; Art is 3-D just as life is 3-D.

'Also I don't feel cut off from my generation in the way that many so-called "contemporary artists" do. I just feel that I am being called upon by my own generation to fulfil my little bit in the whole spectrum of today's Art. The Beatles have another job, the Stones another. But together we have been able to demonstrate that pop music is the best and clearest expression of our generation. When Paul McCartney sings about Eleanor Rigby, the whole of our generation *knows* that; the whole generation *feels* that and *sees* that.

'The star system which puts one man above another in the entertainment world, the big, glossy glittering world, has absolutely nothing to do with what we are trying to achieve. The older generation - our fathers and mothers - have got hold of this extraordinary fallacy that the world is in a very shaky state and that the younger generation don't really know how to take care of themselves. They grow their hair long and they're very wild and they're very frustrated. But the last generation has got nothing at all to do with the new generation. The new generation is growing, flying; the old generation is dying.

'I used to think in messages when I was younger, but I was slowly trying to learn *who* I was. So now, the message - if it *is* a message - is only a description of a beautiful feeling or a description of a beautiful object.

After all, this is not a message in itself, because it's sharing the beauty of the world with someone else. Maybe two wars, and seventy years of wars, have prevented the children from seeing the beauty of their surroundings. They weren't able to look out past the cities, and see the beauty of the sea and the winds and the sky.

'I don't think there's anything that ever happens to me now, that doesn't influence me. I read Tennyson and Wordsworth and the Medieval Minstrel poems. Also the sea influences me a great deal. The sea is big - bigger than anything I've ever seen on the earth or ever will. It's bigger than the sky because you can fly across the sky. The sea is the beginning of one world and the end of another, and the creatures that live on the sea, live half in the water and half out of the water. So they live in two worlds. The sea is deep and heavy. It's beautiful just to be by the sea because you feel so tiny. If the sea just wanted to come up that minute and wash you away, there would be nothing you could do about it. It must have been a beautiful experience to sail on the sea and find that you could sail for days and days and never see anything.

'Everything that you see is beautiful. It has been made not so that it can be looked upon and admired; it's just been made. Flowers are beautiful but they weren't made to *be* beautiful. They *are* beautiful. We can *only* feel an affinity with a beautiful thing, because the creation of the flower and the creation of the man are both beautiful. And when you give someone a beautiful thing, you're saying: look, how beautiful. You're humbling yourself in front of all nature and creation because you're saying: look, how beautiful. The whole world is so fantastically beautiful.

'I suppose I get a kind of religious feeling from nature. But I don't want my religion to have any particular name, because it hasn't got any name. The most pure God is no God because He is here all the time, whether you want to talk about Him or whether you don't want to talk aboutHim, whether you want to give Him a name or whether you don't want to give Him a name. He's still there; God for me is everything and anything that lives. Nothing can live without God and nothing ever exists without it being God. That's everything you see, touch, hear, feel, sing about, taste, smell. So I met the Maharishi and I learnt this same feeling from him. What He can do is to bring - for nothing - peace to people. And He gives you a sense of aloneness from which you can feel at harmony and at peace with the world. Not many people ever feel alone; the only time they're alone is when they go to the toilet. This is what meditation is.

'The Maharishi knows a way which is a very ancient way, of giving you a word so that you can go inside yourself; and inside yourself you discover a bigger space than is outside. This is God inside, huge, vast, boundless, vaster than twenty million seas, so vast you can't even measure it; skyless. And so you are humbled. Jesus was a yogi, a supersaint, and he told the people how to do it and they said "Yeah yeah that's great". Three hundred years passed and they'd forgotten about it and it all got twisted and corrupted. Look at the Church now and see how far it has removed itself from the truth.

'We all come from the earth, from God, from nature; and we all want to go back there before we die to be reassured and to feel the power of all things. That's why I love the sky and the sea; and that's why I sing about them. We all seek a form of devotion that fits our sense of wonder. Perhaps *my* form of devotion is expressed in the songs I write - which are called pop songs.

'But as a "pop star", I don't feel that my sense of wonder has *any* obvious outlet. For example, it doesn't make me feel successful. I felt successful when I went out this morning and found the sun rising. And I feel successful when I've written a good line of poetry. But success in the record business is different. I feel good from it, but I don't feel successful. The only thing it has done for me is to make me rich, and this has given me big dreams. I see great things in the future. I see all the writers together again and I see all the painters together again and I see all the film makers together, altogether under one roof, influencing each other and making beautiful things, controlling the whole market, all the markets, with all the art. Just how you'd imagine if you sat down, how you'd really like it; that's how we're going to make it.

'I'd like to get one of those old rambling houses in the country and just fill it up with orphans, hundreds of them; teach them to dance and paint and sing, like a school. You could raise the education level and submit plans for education for the whole country because you'd have all the best teachers under your roof and all the best scientists; you'd have *all* the best people - just like it happened in Greece, in the Parthenon. All the great minds of the world sitting up on top of the world, working it out. All the architects and all the cooks. And then you could change the whole country because as artistic awareness increases, people might not want their houses to be square any more, for example; they might not want clothes to look like they do now. They might not want a transistor radio to be square; they might want it to be translucent and be made of plastic, so you can look at the works. We don't want cars any more; we want electric buses.

'I get letters from all different types of people, from painters to train drivers, and they're all feeling the same thing; *our* dream. All the people I've spoken to, The Beatles and everybody, all have the same idea; to pull everybody together, and put all our ideas together and see what happens. Because for us, for the "pop stars", we can only spend so much money on food and clothes and cars. So you get to a position where you say: "Well, let's *do* something with all our money". For the first time in our lives it doesn't cost us anything to dream. The established forms of art like the cinema or the theatre, are going to fall if they don't realise that the new generation wants to change the set-up so that we can get greater artistic and social freedom. What nobody seems to have realised is that *we* can create that freedom on a grand scale.

'Pop music is just the beginning of the whole trunk. It will all just spread out. Because pop music is changing the scene anyway. Fashion will change, architecture, eating, everything; because we want it a certain way - and we're *going to have it.*'

*   *   *

On 1st April 1967, a letter appeared in the correspondence columns of the London *Times* which advocated firstly that marijuana be removed from the Dangerous Drugs List, and secondly that offences for 'pushing' the harder drugs such as heroin, be regarded more seriously. The letter spoke simply but eloquently in favour of the modest plea that objections to marijuana were primarily moral and not medical. Such a reasonable letter might well have expected a reasonable reply. But the reward of reasonableness was to be accused of inciting the young to enter upon a feverish world of mass drug addiction with the further charitable slur - as one Professor Camps told a Moral Re-armament Meeting - that probably the writer didn't understand what he was saying. After all, the writer *couldn't* know what he was saying because he was one of those 'pop stars'. And a South African to boot. The pop star was Manfred Mann.

Quintin Hogg, later to become Lord Chancellor, thundered into action saying that he hoped the Minister of Health would not be lured by 'pop' singers who wrote to *The Times* about 'letting-up on cannabis'. 'I fervently hope,' he said, 'that they find themselves in the Old Bailey and, however distinguished their position in the Top Ten, that they will be treated as criminals deserve to be treated. They have a responsibility to the young and when they are naughty, they must not only be punished but seen to be punished.' The irony of it all was that Manfred Mann had never smoked marijuana. He replied, somewhat precipitantly, by retreating into an imaginary artistic ivory tower saying that it was ridiculous to believe that 'Young people copied the example of pop singers' private lives'. People in the pop world hardly ever mix with outsiders anyway.

'Very little is really known about most pop singers' private lives anyway,' he told me. 'If you were to ask people what they knew about *me*, what would they say? Some probably think that I'm Michael D'Abo (Mann's lead singer), others that I've got a little mousy black beard and circular silver-rimmed glasses, sit behind an organ and look miserable. But if you asked a thousand people what I cared about, one or two might mutter "Oh, he takes drugs", but that's about it. Most people, however, believe or seem to want to believe what they read in the Sunday newspapers. It happens *every* week. An incredible collection of flimsy facts and massive headlines are combined with a tatty sort of moral stand; "is this what our youth is coming to?" It's so degrading. I just can't believe what they're writing.'

Manfred Mann came from Johannesburg. His real name is Manfred Lubowitz. He saved fifty bob a week for 3 years to escape from South Africa and arrived in England in 1961. A fanatical jazz pianist, he got a job at Clacton's Butlins. There he played in the Ken Godard Quartet for the benefit of the old ladies of Clacton - he tickled their fancies by playing rather bad send-ups of the popular tunes of the day. He met drummer Mike Hugg and together they formed the Mann-Hugg Quartet to keep them in business after the summer season finished. A meeting with a failed Oxford undergraduate, Paul Pond (later Paul Jones) who was nuts about pop music, persuaded them to try their hand where the money was. They were known as The Blues Bros., The Hipsippy 5, The Fats Fenby All-Stars and even Freddy Slack and The Cow-Cow Boogie Band. But the money didn't come. With bass-guitarist Tom McGuiness and three others, they all lived in a one-room flat in Forest Hill whose sole furnishings were a heater, 2 beds and 3 mattresses. 'You look back on the past in a romantic way', Manfred told me. 'You forget how terrible it was struggling.'

'The most misleading thing about me is the way I look - mournful, nasty and unpleasant. Most of the time the public sees me, I'm just sitting there like a mechanical puppet, pretending to play an instrument. So if the public doesn't really know what I *care* about, I don't see that I have *any* responsibilities to them at all - except to make a record that they like. If you want to follow pop people, you can follow Cliff Richard and go to Church every Sunday. Cliff Richard is a very popular bloke, but all the kids don't go to Church every Sunday. The Beatles went to meditate on the Ganges but I don't think everybody's doing *that* now. In the beginning, of course, one is conscious of one's image. I remember for about 2 years I denied I was married because I was advised to. My manager gave out that famous-last-words statement "I can categorically deny that Manfred is married", 15 times. But I was. One magazine will write a headline "Dylan digs us most, says Manfred"; or "Hermit Manfred moody, secluded from the world, listening to Bach with headphones on." All that had happened probably was that the dog had pissed on the carpet which the interviewer had thought was not the way pop stars behave.

'But we don't "behave" like pop stars, because we don't know what that means. My consciousness of other people is that they stare at me. They demand that when I go on stage, I've got to put on a sort of Mexican blanket so that they'll think: "Jesus, look at that, he's wearing a Mexican blanket!" I know I look ridiculous - and uncomfortable. The whole thing is hugely embarrassing. I'm not an animal to be paraded - opening charity fêtes and the like is intolerable.

'Actually, I've become a much more reserved person since I've got involved in the pop scene. I used to be a raver, but now, if I go to a party and get up to dance, everyone turns to see how I dance. So I can't dance any more - the whole thing has killed me. I have to stand around looking vaguely hip and intelligent which is what people vaguely expect. And since I can't make small talk, I tend not to talk at all for fear that somebody quotes me and uses it against me. I very often wish that one really *did* have an influence, that the pop world *did* symbolise something worthwhile and worth emulating. But it hasn't and it doesn't. Each hit record just postpones the need to look for other employment for a little while longer.

'But this kind of attitude is conspired against by the mass-media which tend to encourage mob-think and mob-response. And I believe that the mob is always wrong when it behaves like a mob. The police are just as wrong because *they* behave like an organised mob. What is happening as a result, is that you get one group of people thinking that they're young and hip and are going to liberate the world from all the old things and sneering at the older people who are sneering at the younger people and everybody is just terrified of everybody else. It seems to me, therefore, that young people - like the hippies - are even more intolerant than the older people they're sneering at. When all the young people of today have grown up and their daughters want to stay out at night with someone they don't like, how tolerant are *they* going to be?

'I don't think pop music is the pinnacle of any artistic achievement. There are those who think it's fashionable to intellectualise pop and there are those who think it's all rubbish. Neither are true. It's like making television commercials. Of course it's artistic, but it's also involved with the commercial world. Serious musicians who sneer at pop should try themselves to turn out a successful record. It's incredibly difficult. Pop music is probably the only art form that is totally dependent for its success on the general public. The more people buy a record, the more successful it is - not only commercially but artistically. So there is a continual compromise that musicians in pop groups whose musical skill is considerable - like Mike Hugg, who is a very fine vibraphone player - have to make, in order to create a sound or a tune that they know instinctively will sell. But compromise can be a discipline. Even so, I'm very pessimistic about my pop work and have a total disbelief that anyone will like any of the records I make. Every hit is our last, I tell myself. Musically, I much prefer to sit and listen to Bach.

'The main reason the pop world is so full of extraordinary people, however, is that no-one's our boss. I'm not answerable to you or to anyone for my living. I do a job and I work as hard as the next man. Harder. But no-one tells me what to do or lays down the law about the rights and wrongs of what I do. If I make a good record, the record companies fall over themselves to release it. Publicity appears from nowhere. PR men start talking about their "campaign". I'm quoted on drugs, abortion and cuckoo clocks as if I were the voice of God. And I too hate *talking* about music, because the people who talk most rubbish about music are musicians. But none of that really matters. Of my own free will, and out of the public eye, I've made something which you like and will buy. Of course, this means that we have to keep being successful and that's a drag and a grind, but in a funny sort of way it's as honest as most jobs. Tell me one that is more so.'

*   *   *

Frank Zappa; leader of the now defunct Mothers of Invention. Cunning and brilliant. American. A natural leader, of considerable eloquence. He had long, ringlet hair, a classic hooked nose and very white complexion. He'd pass as an Old Testament Prophet, or Jesus Christ - Hollywood style, or Frank Zappa. His film, '200 Motels' (of which I directed the visuals), is now reckoned one of the definitive statements of pop culture in the early 70s. Later, Zappa appeared with great success before the United States Congress as an advocate for youth.

'We're involved in a low-key war against apathy. I don't know how you're doing on apathy over there in the U.K. but in America we got a lot of it, boys and girls.

'A lot of what we do is designed to annoy people to the point where they might, just for a second, question enough of their environment to do something about it. As long as they don't feel their environment and they don't worry about it, they're not going to do anything to change it; and something has *got* to be done before America scarfs up the world and shits on it.

'Pop music today is the only living music in America. Most of jazz is really in bad shape, and concert music is basically just shit. They play the same stuff over and over again. There *is* a *slight* increase in the performance of contemporary works, but you would hardly call it a flowering of the arts. And all over the world there is what is called a culture boom - which means that more people are buying carefully packaged classical music at budget prices. "Get a little Mozart in your house" and make people think you know what's happening. Pop music, bad as it is, is better than most of the rest of what's happening.

'After all, pop music is primarily a very advanced folk art. It's electric folk art; and yet you have to admit that a lot of the people producing pop music, are bordering on musical illiteracy. I suppose it's great that people who do it on the glandular level can get in, do their thing, make their money and get out. It's *wonderful* that they have the chance to express themselves, because when you get right down to it, that's what the population here in the United States want to buy. Something on the glandular level. They want something that communicates to them on the same level at which they exist. That's culture in the United States, folks!

'When rock and roll first came out some years ago, it was renounced and persecuted just as it is now; it was called "underground" music, just as it is today. The simple rhythm and blues music of the very late forties and early fifties also seemed to frighten a lot of people; they kept talking about its lewd and suggestive rhythms. The lyrics were a bit too frank for the people of that era. I remember a song that was banned from the radio in those days called 'Annie had a baby'. "Babies!" everybody said - "you can't talk about things like that!" Mind you, don't think that nowadays those twelve - and thirteen-year-old girls don't look for that stuff. They call it 'The Bump". I found out this weekend. I heard these girls talking about it; "I saw Mick Jagger; he has a nice bump." Soul is bumping and humping music.

'But in the last few years, a few more people have begun to realise that pop music *does* express the social and sexual environment which has produced it. For example, one time we were playing in Greenwich Village, New York, and three Marines came in. This was just after a Marine had been stabbed to death in the Village, so there was this big rumour going round that the Marines were coming to the Village to do in the hippies, as if it were some kind of crusade. When these three Marines in full-dress uniform came walking into our rehearsal in the afternoon, it seemed like they were the advanced guard of an invading army. Instead, they were nineteen-year-olds who just wanted our autographs. So I said: "Well what are you guys doing tonight? Got some spare time?" And they said: "yeah, we were just gonna go out and get drunk". So I said: "Come and sing with our band. All you have to do is co-operate with us a little bit. When I give you a signal, you lunge at the microphone and start screaming 'Kill, Kill, Kill', just like they teach you in bayonet training." So they thought that would be swell.

'That night, at the performance, we come up on stage looking like we usually look; and then *they* come walking up on stage looking like they usually look, and the audience couldn't believe that they were on stage with us. United States Marines in full dress uniforms with the Mothers! There they were; and people were quiet and waiting for something to happen. So I gave them the signal, and they lunged for the microphone and started screaming, "Kill, Kill, Kill". The audience laughed. Then I had them sing their army songs. After it was all over, I walked to the microphone and I said, "thank you". And then I motioned to Ray, our lead singer, and *he* walked to the microphone and said, "thank you". And then I went back to the microphone and I said,

Frank Zappa by Ralph Steadman

"thank you", and he said "thank you", and we kept doing it until it got very redundant and we hoped to involve the Marines in this whole redundant unit, and expected *them* to go up to the microphone and say "thank you". I pointed to the first Marine; he walked to the microphone and said, "Eat the apple, fuck the core. Some of us love our mothers more". And there was dead silence in the room.

'Then we went into some electronic music, and the Marines sat down on the stage. I sent out during intermission for a large doll; a girl doll, about 5 foot tall. They brought it back, and during one of our hot numbers, I gave the Marines instructions to mutilate the doll just like they're trained to do back at the camp. And they did it. They just ripped the piss out of this doll; they stomped on it, they mangled it, they messed the eyes up. They really did a good job on it. When I showed the mangled doll to the audience, the Marines cried. They had become so involved with the music which was clearly expressing for them what they felt deep down inside, that they had shown us what they really are. The music had allowed them to demonstrate their true selves. They train those suckers, boy.

'What I think is interesting is that this involvement derives essentially from the music itself - the sound - and *not* from the lyrics. It was the *kind* of sound - its loudness, its aggressiveness, its simplicity, which affected them.

'For me, the words are just a carefully manufactured part of the packaging medium of the music. The words are more relevant to the album cover than they are to the songs. You have to stick the words on the music to sell it. People *still* demand to have some sort of verbal communication; people don't seem to be ready yet for straight musical communication. Everyone says that the words of pop songs are deeply meaningful and have a great satirical importance. For example: the hero in our song 'Brown shoes don't make it' is City Hall Fred. Fred is a mild-mannered pervert, who's responsible for making a lot of the laws governing social conduct among young people. Meanwhile, Fred dreams of having a bizarre relationship with a thirteen-year-old girl smothered in chocolate syrup. That's deeply satirical, I hope you noticed.

'Another one of the songs that ranks high in the list of meaningful tunes is 'Colony Vegetable'. A lot of people think it's a song about vegetables. Well, they're right. It *is* a song about vegetables. Americans are vegetables because they don't do anything; they sit back and let their government eat them up. Or take the words of my song 'Mr. Green Jeans'. I think they're very cosmic; you have to meditate on them a lot.

I'll recite to you the words from 'Mr. Green Jeans'. Spelled G-e-n-e-s.

> Eat your greens
> Don't forget your beans
> And Celery.
> Eat . . .

I forget what they are because they're *so* cosmic. Ah yes, I remember now.

> Eat a bunch of these
> Magnificent with sauerkraut mm mm mm Sauerkraut.
> Eat a grape, a fig, a crumpet too.
> You'll pump 'em right through. Do you?
> Eat your shoes, don't forget the strings, and socks;
> even eat the box you've bought 'em in.
> You can eat the truck that brought 'em in.
> Garbage truck.
> mm mm mm mouldy garbage truck,
> Eat the truck and driver and his gloves.
> Deliciousness, nutritiousness, worthlessness.

'And of course all the words are clean. So there you have it. Thank you, ladies and gentlemen.

   'You have to send everybody up, otherwise they'll get to taking you too seriously and then you're back in the culture camp. Of course we *care* about what we're doing. We're getting through to a great number of people and we've got to care. And *I* care that *you* should care. If *no-one* treats us with any respect at all, we may as well give up. And the only way we get respect is to keep on trying, and keeping on making good sounds and good songs. If the songs are good enough and strong enough, only the fools will put us down. Unfortunately, there are a lot of fools about.'

Chapter Eight

'Caring' took on many disguises. Some pop singers chose to appear as if they were deliberately affronting the sensibilities of 'shocked of Wimbledon'; others seemed to imitate the classical masters whom they apparently admired after all, but dare not to admit to doing so for fear of being cast out by their fellows. Others just went on creating a body of songs regardless of trends or fashions whose musical and lyrical stature was such that their capacity for caring could not be doubted. Pre-eminent amongst these was and is Bob Dylan.

Although Dylan is a key figure in the world of pop and has had a greater influence in recent years than any other single song-writer, he is not essentially in the mainstream of pop's development. He is a loner in every sense - a person difficult to imitate because of the very distinctiveness of his style. He can *only* be emulated and admired, and thus has had a great loosening effect on pop. Like his teacher Woody Guthrie, Dylan believes that he is 'trying to be a singer without a dictionary and a poet not bound with shelves of books'.

In August 1966 he had a motor-cycle accident which forced his withdrawal from the pop scene. As the months dragged by, rumours spread that the accident had damaged his brain or disfigured his face. Donovan, of whom Dylan once said 'Donovan who?', declared that 'Dylan has gone to the hills. He came to the end of his era, and he knew it'. But a year later, this untidy (then) 28-year-old from Hibbing, Minnesota, whose voice is like that of a dog with his leg caught in barbed wire, whose looks are those of Harpo Marx crossed with the younger Beethoven, and whose poems are to some the authentic pitiful outcry of a disappointed generation, returned, like Moses, triumphant. He produced a record called 'John Wesley Harding' which gave strength to his fellows, just as his earlier protest songs had given strength to a youth which had felt the need to protest and in Bob Dylan had found a spokesman.

The flinty music, full of savage melancholy, the drawling incoherent lyrics, the apologetic harmonica stabs, the steady, relentless country-

Dylan
by
Ralph Steadman

and-western backing of bass, drums and steel guitar, these are the characteristics of Dylan's sound and music. It's lean and pinched - like his voice. His subjects are intolerance and the loss of liberty; he writes in traditional ballad metres, using shifting patterns of 8 to 12 syllable iambic rhythms which adjust themselves as naturally to speech as to song. His images rumble forever in the imagination - 'with strings of guilt they tried hard to guide us'; or 'in the wild cathedral evening'; or 'money doesn't talk, it swears'. The commercial show-biz atmosphere was never for him; 'fat guys chewing cigars and carrying around gold records and *selling* songs, *selling* talent, *selling* an image. I never hung out there.' (Brian Epstein's office was covered in gold records.) He denied that his 'protest songs' ever existed. 'What I do,' he told me, 'is write songs and sing them and perform them. Anything else trying to get on top of it making something out of it which it isn't, just brings me down.' Nonetheless, his song 'A Hard Rain's a Gonna Fall' was clearly about the 1962 Cuban Missile Crisis, just as 'Oxford Town' was about the ordeal of James Meredith, just as the 'Ballad of Hollis Brown' commemorates a particularly bloody killing of a Dakota dirt-farmer; just as every song on John Wesley Harding was clearly inspired by a particular incident or incidents which jammed in the gullet of Dylan's imagination.

He often sang with a US flag as a backdrop and gave Press Conferences holding dolls. Could we assume he was married? We could assume anything we liked. He was born married. What was he doing at the moment? Nothing (he was just about to give 14 sold-out concerts). How did he feel? His toe nails didn't fit. Mockingly, he sings of writers and critics who prophesy about pop music. If they only kept their eyes open, and their mouths shut, they'd do a lot better. From a man so prejudice conscious, it's hard to realise that he was born Zimmerman, of German origin, the son of a cigar-smoking appliance dealer. He sings with a South-West American accent which is acquired - he speaks without it. He has sold countless millions of records but lives in comparative squalor. His career is one of increasing withdrawal into a never-never land of unseen dangers and nightmare, a twilight world of monsters and terror. However dark the previous songs, there was a desperate optimism which clung fiercely to the mind. Now even that has gone. His LP, 'Nashville Skyline', shows him struggling to get back to his roots in country and western music. One song, 'Girl From the North Country', is almost a re-recording of one of his earliest releases except that this time he sings it as a duet with Johnny Cash, one of the best country and western singers.

His previous record, 'John Wesley Harding', showed a picture of Dylan on the front cover, disguised in a half-grown beard and surrounded by three nameless Indians. It was like a Mental Institution passing-out photo; Dylan squinted mysteriously over his shoulder at the intruding camera. Songs began with lines like 'There must be some way out of here', or 'Oh help me in my weakness, I heard the drifter say', or 'I still don't know what is it that I've done wrong'. There were watchtowers everywhere; horsemen ride out of nowhere; he dreamt he was among those who had put St. Augustine out to die. The hint and suspicion of menace was everywhere. He sees the woman of his dreams and then notices that she walks in chains. He takes her by the hand and she responds by giving him her arm: 'I knew that very instant, she meant to do me harm.' The lyrics, half-spoken, half-sung, had that dying falling forever Dylan. They had dignity in an age which had none; they had eloquence in an age which had none; they had a terrible honesty in an age which had none. Dylan is the prophet of reasoned defiance. If one wanted a simple catch phrase by which to capture the moral force of pop music one should remember not only that you should never be where you don't belong, but also not to 'go mistaking Paradise for that home across the road'. As Johnny Cash told me: 'This man can rhyme the tick of time.' Someone else who had not mistaken paradise for that home across the road is again the irrepressible Frank Zappa. The 'disgusted of Croydon' would really warm to him.

'My aim was to *kill* Top 20 radio,' he told me. (Come back, Jimmy Young. All is forgiven.) 'Certain concessions must be made before a record is playable on the air. But I'm not in the business to compete with the makers of 'Hanky Panky'. That record will be played anyway because it won't hurt anybody. But it won't *move* them either. Top 20 radio is unethical, unmusical and its stinks. What's worse, classical music stations aren't much better either.' (Zappa scored Rock versions of Mozart's 40th Symphony and Holst's 'Planets'.) Zappa claimed he was trying to use the weapons of an unhappy society against itself to demonstrate the lameness of modern life; to demonstrate that America would *never* grow up because it cannot. To achieve this end, he invented the 'Freak Out' which he defined as a process whereby an individual cast off outmoded and restrictive standards of thinking, dress and social etiquette in order to express his relationship to his immediate environment and the social structure as a whole. It was a release of community energy, musically induced. 'We have so much pent-up anger and frustration,' Zappa told me, 'that we must find ways to expend it creatively - if only to avoid riot and destruction.' 'Necessity,' agreed Plato, 'is the Mother of Invention.'

Such a philosophical mood invaded the consciousness and thus often destroyed the logic of many of those who inhabited the bigot-infested castles of suburbia. Occasionally, an intellect as formidable as that of Zappa, did silence prejudice. Occasionally, a group as musically distinguished and as classically literate as The Fugs - another American 'underground' group, did silence abuse. The Fugs stood in the main tradition of Athenian comedy and Elizabethan Theater, savage and uncompromising satirists, comedians, philosophers and tragedians. They were not - as was popularly believed - slobbering, psychopathic, unkempt sex-fiends who were now coining millions out of a disturbed and confused youth. Their music had an heroic pessimism which was gentle but insistent. Their lyrics - often by poets such as Allen Ginsberg and Ezra Pound - bore constant witness to the barbarity of the society which made them. Their spokesman, Ed Sanders - a Greek scholar from New York University - had published four books of poetry, written an opera, 'The Peace Eye', and started the Peace Eye Pornographic Gallery of Art in New York. Their obsessions with disorder and poverty, racial injustice and sexual mores, made them an easy target for suspicion and ridicule. The adulatory fervour with which the cognoscenti greeted their every dropping, however, did make a proper understanding and acceptance of them almost impossible.

Still, they did a pretty good job at disguising what they were really up to; indeed, occasionally the disguise was so good that one began to wonder which *was* the reality.

For example, in Zappa's group - The Mothers of Invention - there seemed to be eight Mothers (approx.) in all, including a mythical girly called Suzy Creamcheese. (The Mothers dreamt up the name for a giggle, but their idiot public demanded the reality; so they just seized an unsuspecting hanger-on, changed her name and hey presto. That's show business.) In fact, rumour had it that in fact there were several Suzy Creamcheeses. Their first record, described as 'improvised insanity', sold over a quarter million copies and was called - appropriately - 'Freak Out'. As if to demonstrate its good lineage, it was dedicated to Muddy Waters and Phil Spector - with genuflections towards Stravinsky, Charlie

Mingus, Varèse, Boulez and Webern. It included such compositions as, 'I Ain't Got No Heart' (or 'a summary of my feelings in socio-sexual relationships') and 'The Return of the Son of Monster Magnet, an Unfinished Ballet in Two Tableaux'. Of The Two Tableaux, the first is a Ritual Dance of the Child-Killer, and the second - stylised as Nullius Pretii (no commercial potential) - 'is what freaks sound like when you turn them loose in a recording studio at one o'clock in the morning on 500 dollars worth of rented percussion equipment' (sic). This super-abundant cross-referencing was, perhaps, the Mothers' great weakness because almost no-one could follow all the implications of what they were playing. The ultimate in mockery of the listener came when they released another LP called 'Absolutely Free'; which, of course, it wasn't.

Zappa told me: 'Flowerpower? It sucks! It's a lie - all those flower children would be better off staying at home. They go to a love-in and then go home and talk about who was at the love-in and who wasn't. I think a lot of the people who buy our records must be mental. But there's no reason, is there, why I should speak subtly to people who aren't subtle? The *American* idea of Youth always assumed that all rebels finally joined the herd. But the fact that we haven't, doesn't mean that you can ignore us. Even if you don't like the idea behind our music, you have to listen to it because it is everywhere.'

The Mothers' music was most frequently listened to on LSD trips, like that of Country Joe and the Fish, Big Brother and the Holding Company and The Beatles' Sergeant Pepper'. 'Good for sales,' Zappa told me. Yet paradoxically no-one was more derisive of the wastefulness of the contemporary 'scene'.

So this derision erupted into a violent send-up of the whole self-indulgent shambles that we liked to pretend was our popular culture; a deliberate sneer at the herds of flower-gazing junkies that passed themselves off as the new enlightenment. What with the Marareesh and all stations East, and his gospel of supreme meditation - in silence, of nothing at all - with meaning, the Day of Judgement was already at hand and the best we seemed able to offer by way of atonement was processed turge like Engelbert Humperdinck, Frankenschmelt Rosensick (sing us one of the old songs, Frankie) and, of course, Tiny Tim. Tiny Tim epitomised the honey-schmaltz of the good old days and all the mealy-mouthed show biz 'caring' that the new generation of pop stars sought to replace with a more lasting honesty. In his performances he was the walking, talking parody of all that the thinking end of pop music was fighting against.

painful. His voice wavered and cracked. He stumbled over words and fumbled around like some blasted, demogonised cat. The jazz-flavoured blues that he intoned, lacked the bitterness of Dylan, lacked the insistence of Jagger, lacked the irony of Lennon, lacked the simplicity of Donovan - in fact, they lacked just about everything, except what Hardin calls 'their legendary quality'.

Legends come and go very easily in the pop world and again have little to do with 'caring'. Some have the most bizarre beginnings. A group called The Love Affair scored a great success with a song called 'Everlasting Love' - a success, that is, until they admitted a little smugly that they hadn't themselves actually played on the record. They had hired session musicians. As a result, one affronted TV producer said 'We're not having those thugs on our show'. 'The statements (the group) made about "Everlasting Love" ', said another, 'were thoroughly harmful to the pop music industry.'

After the fiasco with 'Everlasting Love', their 24-year-old manager John Cokell said that the next time 'the studio will be crowded with unbiased witnesses and a commissioner for oaths.' It wasn't. And anyway, the practice of using session men who can earn a fortune per week whilst making pop singles, was common knowledge. A group called The Plastic Penny was actually invented to fit a record already made. What is disheartening is the strange reaction of both the Musicians' Union and the groups themselves to this musical sleight of hand - or ear, if you prefer.

On the one hand, Hardie Ratcliffe, general secretary of the MU, was busy going into print to assert 'the moral claims' of session men. 'The whole business is spurious . . . for too long the pop groups have climbed to prominence on the backs of talented musicians. Pop is as much related to music as Bingo is to Mathematics.' Actually, there was statistical calculus relating the last two and much avant-garde music that is not pop has about as much relation to today as jam pudding to starving Chinese. It was unfortunate that the Musicians' Union usually hold their branch meetings on Friday nights - the one night on which many pop musicians cannot attend because they are working. The MU accordingly attacked pop musicians for not being interested in Union affairs, despite the fact that pop provided much of its revenue. A foreign pop group always encountered difficulties getting a work permit here. Not so the 'straight' musician such as Andy Williams or the second triangle player for the Boston Pops Orchestra. Curious.

Session musicians are sometimes thought of (mistakenly in my view) as hacks who are paid a fee to do a job. This is not to belittle what they do, nor prevent them from doing it well. But it is to admit that what they do is essentially different from what the pop record producer or performer does, which is to create a commercial sound that is food in itself and will sell widely and thus communicate. Paul McCartney can't read music but he composes great songs.

On the other hand, the groups themselves behave with maximum childishness when 'found out'. When The Love Affair admitted on TV (to boost sales?) that they had been bad boys, the compère Jonathan King (now in prison) quipped: 'they should be complimented for owning up in front of 5 million people. Pop is, after all,' he said, 'a deeply lovely word.'

What matters is the sound on the record. Provided those who made it are properly rewarded, the means by which it is made are of little consequence. Inventive pop music is increasingly the preserve of the recording studio and all that therein is - session men, electronic gadgetry and other sinister goings-on. Phil Spector, a young New Yorker, was probably the first to realise the potential of recorded sound. His famous releases which included those of The Righteous Brothers and Ike and Tina Turner and international hits such as 'Spanish Harlem' and 'River Deep and Mountain High', were characterised by a colossal wall of echoing vibrations. Like the most advanced of The Beatles' songs, live performance of those songs which would reproduce the sound as on disc, was inconceivable. But if the final sound on disc is good, then that's all that matters. If it's not, forget it. It just won't be noticed.

But in an attempt to *get* noticed and convince you that its subject matter is dealing with higher things, some pop music did reach farcical proportions.

'Joseph and the Amazing Technicolor Dreamcoat', for example, was an attempt to describe in simple-minded pop words and music the story of would you believe Joseph according to the book of Genesis. It was scored for orchestra, called with perspicacious accuracy, the Joseph Consortium, a schoolboys' choir called with accurate modesty, the Wonderschool, a strangely inaudible and inarticulate beat-group called with modest perspicacity The Mixed Bag, and a loose fitting ensemble of strings, percussion and woodwind just called - presumably for want of a better name - The Ramases III Orchestra. Undoubtedly it succeeded totally, being as it is totally simple-minded.

Addressing the 'poor old Pharaoh', Joseph says

> All these things you saw in your pyjamas
> Are a long-range forecast for your farmers.
> Find a man to lead you thru' famine
> With a flair for economic plannin'.*

That's about the level of the lyrics, or poetry as it was called. And now imagine Mantovani *without* the strings, the Boys' Brigade Reserve Band, the wondrous rising organ of Hackney Wick Empire, the levelling hand of a Tin Pan Alley arranger, and that's the kind of sound, or music as it was called. If Joseph was the beginning of a major breakthrough - the 'pop oratorio' that its promoters claimed - then it could only be the beginning of the end, I wrote in 1969. How wrong I was.

The point is that the best pop music was primarily concerned with energy, frenzy, pity, power - all short and sweet. The moment it tampered or aped the large-scale forms of classical music, it banged its own death knell. It had neither the musical discipline or virtuosity, nor the lyrical subtlety with which to compete. It had great instrumentalists like Clapton or Baker, but no great composers. It had mastered the miniaturist art of song. But that *is* a miniaturist art, incapable of symphonic or operatic scope. This is not to dismiss it or necessarily to denigrate it, but merely to acknowledge its proper place in our scale of aesthetic values. Instinctively, there was something palpably absurd about the dedication of those bent on creating pop operas - Pete Townshend of The Who wrote his opera called 'Tommy' and Andrew Lloyd Webber, the composer of 'Joseph', later had a string of international hits - because the language to sustain such an endeavour just did not exist. Even the best musicals rely heavily on a good plot, flashy staging, star acting and above all, style.

By comparison with the worst of this genre, Joseph is a random hotch-potch of trivial words set to trivial music, aimless, thoughtless and amateur. The occasional catchy tune is drowned in a swamp of indifferent orchestration played by an uneasy marriage between groovy guitarists strumming witlessly to themselves, and bespectacled MU

---

* This excerpt reproduced with permission of the joint copyright owners Norrie Paramor Music Ltd., of 5 Denmark St, London, W.C.2, and Novello & Co. Ltd. of 27 Soho Square, London, W.1

members blasting away and really feeling part of the scene. Man, this is where it's at, you could hear them cry. But imagine what *would* have happened if a great composer really had come along - a Stravinsky of the pop world. The raw material was there, but not - as yet - the articulated, controlled and purposeful creativity.

As the song says: 'Well stone the crows, this Joseph is a clever kid.' Well so he was, but he still needed to do something with that cleverness. Never mind, as a friend said during one of those longeurs beloved of all opera, referring to this particular pop creation; 'there's a lot of it about, you know.'

There was one musical, however, which did at the time seem to be stretching out towards the possibility of a full-scale pop work, the musical 'Hair'.

'Hair' was variously described as a musical be-in, an American tribal love-rock musical, a McLuhan era freak out or the apotheosis of a sex-crazed generation. It was written by two actors in their 20's, Gerome Ragni and James Rado, and could make some claim to being the most dazzling American musical since 'West Side Story'. Whatever else it might have been, it was the first pop-music musical.

Performed on an open stage by 20 harum-scarum multi-racial kids and a pounding, thumping 5 man band, it shouted and implored and loved and wooed and laughed and electrified in a manner that had the audience on its feet clapping and stamping and cheering over and over again.

There was no plot as such. Berger is kicked out of school. Sheila in between making protest posters, loves Berger; Jeannie love Claude. Claude, who gets drafted, loves Sheila. Claude and Sheila make it together. Dialogue was spasmodic and ad-lib. It tended to be about understanding adults who miss the point; it was anti-war, anti-dishonesty; pro-life, pro-love, pro-sex, pro-joy, pro-music, pro-colour, pro-fantasy. The up-tight 'rational' world of the older generation is mostly hypocritical, stupidly restrictive and ultimately cruel and violent. The 'Hair' of the title is hippie hair, 'long, beautiful, shining, gleaming, steaming, flaxen, waxen, long, straight, curly, fuzzy, snaggy, shaggy, ratty, matty, oily, greasy, fleecy, down-to-there hair'. Hair is a personal protest flag against a world in which manliness is exemplified in short hair and crew-cut aggressiveness. When Claude's hair is cut by the Army, it is for him social castration. Like Samson, he becomes helpless against a hostile social mechanism.

On this level, it sounds like any other protest piece, inarticulate and opinionated. What gave it the touch of genius was the breathless music of Galt MacDermot. It had an unflinching and unfailing generosity. Unlike the songs of Tim Hardin, Hair *did* smack of The Rolling Stones in all their cynical, up-beat mockery; it *did* smack of Dylan in all his nightmarish sweetness; it *did* smack of Lennon, in all his warm coldness; it had passion and power and it cared.

With the American musical, sometimes thought to be the American way of life, clutched by a money-spinning thrombosis; with opera, sometimes thought to be the only way of life, flailing about like a wingless bird; with the avant-garde seized upon their annual pantheistic ritual (at the time it was a string band mistakenly described as incredible), the pop world and its opera 'Hair' emerged triumphant if only because it embodied Life in a way that other modes of expression did not. If ever the young had a worthy anthem, that was it.

What 'Hair' also did was to serve as a reminder that nothing is so sad as the walls that are erected between different forms of artistic self-expression. Even within a given style, we seem determined to discriminate between high-art and low-art as if we really knew what such definitions meant. So, whilst all pop music - even if it is labelled 'Opera' - is written off by some as worthless and trivial, even within pop music it is often a matter of acute snobbery that one should distinguish between 'folk', 'rock' and the 'blues'. One group that is determined to knock down these absurd and pernicious barriers, both within and without pop music, was The Pentangle.

For those who insisted that pop music was exclusively gaudy and vulgar, the music of The Pentangle came as a bit of a surprise. It was relaxed, gentle and poised. For those who insisted that pop was just a noisy aberration of the mid-twentieth century, the baroque, ornamental delicacy for The Pentangle was neither heard nor believed. Like the best of pop, the group stood in the main stream of English music - folk in origin, classical in tone, and popular in emotion. Although commercially their records were increasingly successful, they were distrustful of such success; nor did they enjoy large-scale concerts, in spite of their stunning debut at the Albert Hall in 1968 - 'you lose contact with your audience', Bert Jansch, their lead guitarist, told me. They were happier going back to London's Horseshoe Club where they started three years ago. They had no leader - preferring to work as a 'cooperative', had no snazzy stage act and were not remotely interested in the perks of show-biz. Their repertoire includes Italian medieval lyrics, Tallis 'Laments', and John Dowland's 'Melancholy Galliard'. They preferred songs with a beat of 7 in a bar - 'it added an element of the unexpected', Jansch told me. They were cool, before that word became a cliché, elegant, cunning and witty.

The two guitarists - Jansch, a 26-year-old Glaswegian ex-nursery-man, and John Renbourn, a 25-year-old folk idol, were both well established names in the folk world, before they teamed up with bass-player Danny Thompson and drummer Terry Cox who were rated among the best jazz session men in the business. The fivesome was completed by 25-year-old Jacqui McShee, a bird-like lady with a voice as dark and hard as icy water. Not a gimmick in sight; not a multi-track, feed-back, howl-round sound to be heard; not a whisper of crass publicity or of dubious musicological significance in vision. It was not so much a fusion of styles or even of peoples, but a direct, uncomplicated need to express themselves which found a harmonious fulfilment in their articulate music making - impeccable, quiet and honest.

Needless to say, they had to struggle in England where the demands on pop in newspapers, radio and television, centred round those charts. Like Hendrix, Cream, Ten Years After and 50 others before them, The Pentangle went to America for a more sympathetic hearing. You might have justifiably concluded at the time that in England there was no room for quality - at least not in pop.

Certainly, the capacity to care as demonstrated by English musicians seemed to be diminishing in spite of the eloquent protests of singers such as Donovan. 'Caring' is still thought to be 'an underground activity' and therefore dangerous and drug-ridden. So, not surprisingly, much of the best music did seem to come from the 'underground', was thus mostly ignored by Radio and TV and consequently, initially, had a hard time financially.

But if you cared about contemporary music and its power to express now, then groups like Pink Floyd provided a terrifying glimpse of what might be and of what is. Suddenly the description 'pop music' became with them an irrelevant label for what many thought was neither popular nor in many ways, music. A harsh, relentless juxtaposition of animal sounds, of heaving monotonous, pulsating tones, of fragmented whisperings and half-heard, half-familiar snatches of melody, their music and music like it triggered off psychological fears too deep for words, too complex for easy assimilation and too full of wonder to be thought cheap. Their music was primarily a sustained attempt to harness in sound our crazed, demented, agonised ambitions. A sense of horror and melancholy pervaded every song, and the dominating mood of their music was one of evil.

Pink Floyd first startled the London scene with a concert at the Commonwealth Institute. Previously, they had been horded by the underground as the ultimate psychedelic freak-out. Loudness became a totally new concept when sheltering from the barrage of strident chord-clusters and flashing light patterns that they inflicted upon an unsuspecting audience. A song could last for 20 minutes - such was their skill at polyphonic improvisation. Encapsulating the violence, both aural and visual, onto a single 45 disc, proved impossible. Their first release - 'Arnold Layne' - got to number 20 in those charts; their second, 'See Emily Play', got to number 5 and their subsequent two, 'Oranges and Apples' and 'It Would Be So Nice', nowhere. In spite of the lack of any real commercial success, Pink Floyd remained uncompromising in style, in tone and in purpose - a pilgrimage which eventually struck real gold. And if what they the others were doing was just a beginning, then pop music was about to be wrenched from adolescence into an aggressive maturity.

With music that depended upon relentless ostinato melodic and rhythmic motifs and upon endless pedal notes whose grinding insistence gave the songs their menace and power, the temptation to devise sounds whose effect was just repetitious and boring must have been enormous. Those who disliked Pink Floyd found this harmonic sameness the least palatable aspect of the music; but somehow they charged their bare musical fabric with such nervous electricity that - as with Beethoven - the very simplicity of the material became its strongest potential.

Their songs were symphonic in construction, and through a combination of sound effects, backwards-tapes, feed-back and echo, produced the first wholly science fiction music to have emerged. Unlike Cornelius Cardew or even Stockhausen, whose futuristic dabblings seem by comparison erratic and uncoordinated, Pink Floyd managed to blend sounds - *all* sounds - so that they conveyed deeply felt convictions with a clarity and directness whose authority was unmistakable. One song in particular, 'Set the Controls for the Heart of the Sun', with its energy, its anger, its science fantasy, its longing and its musical brilliance, said it all.

Like many classical composers, Pink Floyd often wrote to commission. For Peter Whitehead's dreary film, 'Let's Make Love in London Tonite', they contributed a notable score which said far more about the nightmare scene depicted than all the pictures put together. For Paul Jones' film, 'The Committee', they screwed up the paranoia contained therein to an almost unbearable pitch. They turned up with devoted regularity at be-ins, sit-downs, freak-outs and throw-ups; they believed - like Benjamin Britten - that their music should be useful and to the living. For to live amongst the living is to care.

There was one English group in particular who cared; Cream.

They played together for only two years - but during that time almost singlehandedly gave pop a musical distinction which only the deaf could not acknowledge. Admired by Leonard Bernstein, their records sold more copies in the 24 months of the group's existence than the Bible had sold in the previous 24 years.

What Eric Clapton, Jack Bruce and Ginger Baker did was to show, as The Beatles had begun to do, that the *form* of pop music - eight-bar phrases, primitive harmonic progressions and nursery rhyme lyrics - was pathetically unable to cope with all that pop music was beginning to want to express. The Who overcame this restrictiveness by bursting into free-form improvisation which often finished up in the physical destruction of everything in sight. Cream just played and played until they were exhausted. Clapton on lead guitar - straining and soaring against The Dark Ages of music which still, in spite of Stravinsky, seemed to want to believe in 4/4 and the common chord. 'Improvisation and performances which constantly renew themselves - that's our goal', he told me. Jack Bruce - making his harmonica talk, whilst his voice dragged every last syllable out of some profound disquiet. And Ginger Baker - 'You get to a position or a feeling that you're not playing the drums; you're not playing your instrument', he told me. 'It's playing you'. It was he who had persuaded the other two to combine their differing talents in a trio whose virtuosity was to stagger the musical world. It was also him who enabled the other two to develop their free-form playing. His playing was and is fragmentary but insistent, devious but relentless, meandering but precise. To Jack Bruce's counterpoint, he gave rhythm, and to Eric Clapton's technical virtuosity, he gave shape. On their first tour together, he practised so intensively that he left behind him a trail of hotel bills for broken furniture.

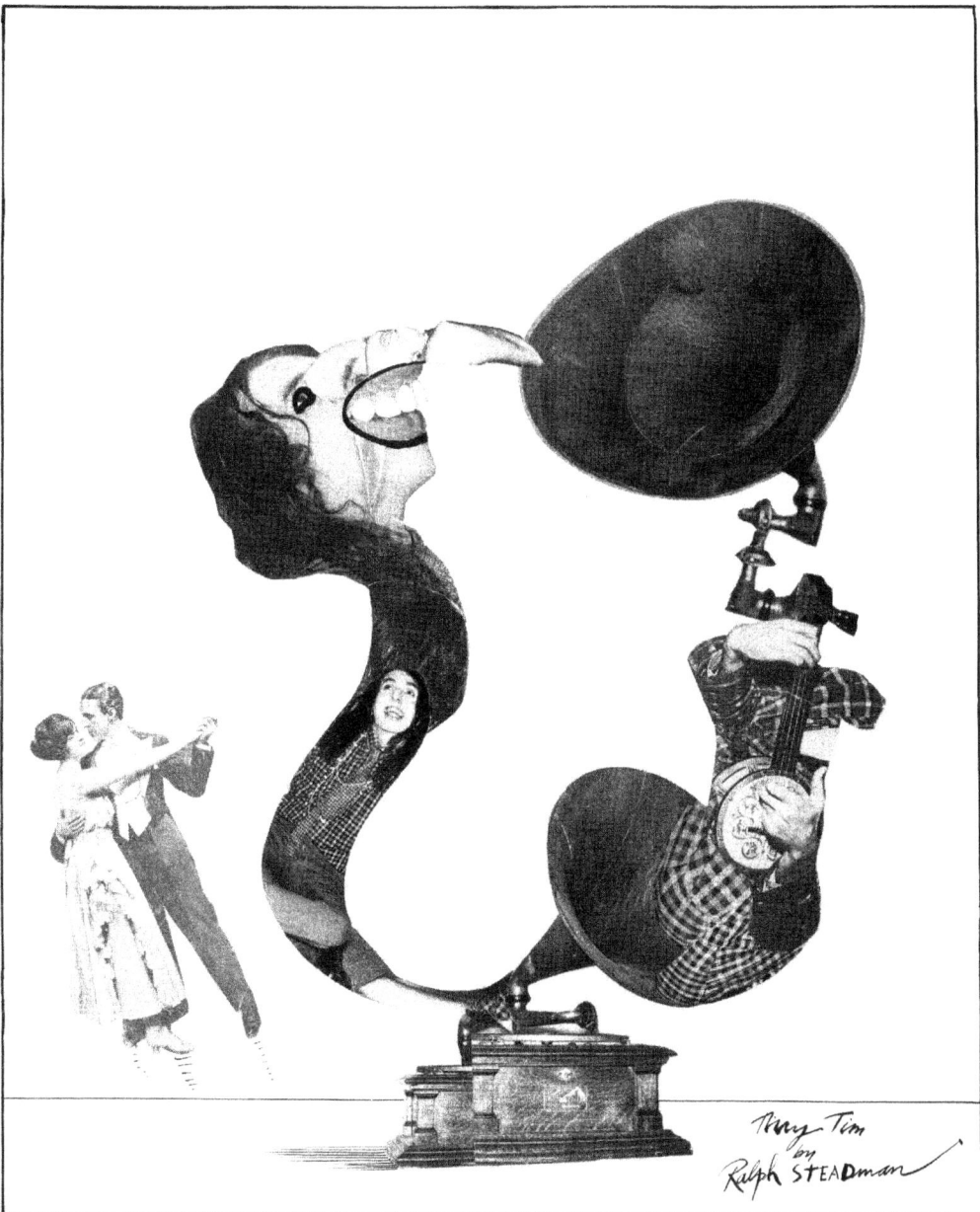

Tiny Tim
by
Ralph STEADman

In concert after concert, in San Francisco, Los Angeles, Sacramento and San Diego, it was they - and not The Beatles or Benjamin Britten or even The Rolling Stones - who consolidated, probably for the next 10 years, the total pre-eminence of English music-making in America. The days of Elvis Presley's domination seemed a long way away.

When Cream started, each member was the other's favourite performer - so it was inevitable that they should join forces. They may not have been the greatest musicians or the greatest poets of the age - but together with The Beatles, they were getting through to the greatest number. Their motto was simple; 'forget the message, forget the lyrics and just play'.

The best pop has thus had to resort to technical mastery and musical virtuosity as a refuge against unthinking prejudice and criticism. Cream exemplified this virtuosity; and if by technical mastery we mean mastery of the simple resources at the disposal of pop music, then musicians such as Simon and Garfunkel also fulfilled that need.

Paul Simon was a shy, diffident New Yorker who got the equivalent of a First Class Degree in English Literature at Queen's College. Art Garfunkel was a student at Columbia University working on his Ph.D. in Mathematics. Both were in their mid-twenties when, as a singing duo - Simon and Garfunkel - they displayed in their records a mastery of orchestration, from the simple chordal acoustic-guitar antiphony to the full-blooded lusty bombast of organ and brass. They also displayed a mastery of vocal-lyricism - restrained, apologetic, fragmentary - 20th century madrigalists whose understated counterpoint gained them the misleading reputation of the ultimate urban folk singers. Above all, they displayed mastery of poesy. To the clichés of hippiedom, they gave clarity. To the desolate fears of their elders and self-appointed betters, they gave compassion. To the indifference of the society in which they existed, they gave a fresh awareness. Pop music, after all, because of its limitless appeal - which has no class, no age group, no prejudice inherent in it - has, almost in spite of Frank Zappa, become the first truly mass satire. What it says, however trivial, reaches a vast audience with an immediacy whose effect is incalculable. If - as with Simon and Garfunkel - it can say more than just love is blue, then in its intention at least, it is deserving of proper consideration.

Thus, one of their albums called 'Bookends' deals with the grotesque casualness with which we underestimate loneliness, cruelty and all manner of personal tragedy. A mother screams to save the life of her child now perched upon a ledge, threatening to kill himself. 'He must be high on something', an onlooker laughs. A policeman says:

> The force can't do a decent job
> 'cause the kid's got no respect
> for the law today.

The whole scene is described as 'a freaky holiday' which never even makes the *New York Times*. At one point, actuality recordings snatched in old people's homes, are woven in. 'I am an old man', a voice croaks. 'Because I couldn't get any younger, I had to be an old man. That's all.' Old friends sit around on their bench, like Bookends. Old Roger - the draft dodger, is observed 'leavin' by the basement door. Everybody knows what he's tip-toeing down there for.' The San Franciscan hippies are just 'Fakin' it'. All the insincerity, false ideals, false editorial authority, false concern for balance and apparent reasonableness, the mindless cocktail tittle-tattle that sustains our every conversation - this is the subject matter of Simon and Garfunkel. 'I like what I see to be heard and understood', Simon told me.

Mike Nichols, who chose them to write the music for his fashionably successful film, 'The Graduate', described their songs to me as 'dilemma singing', which quality Garfunkel admits to being the only honest way to express what they experience. Amazingly, there is not one jot of didacticism in the translation of that experience into song. Their only intolerance is of 'people who are always sure they're right'. 'Why is it I feel compelled to write about this pain I see?' Simon asked me. 'Because I'm here, that's why'.

As the Hippies sing in 'Hair': 'This is the dawning of the Age of Aquarius . . . '

Tiny Tim was, in fact as well as in essence, unbelievable. He spent two hours every morning in the shower, made himself up regularly with a compound of Aida Grey Peach milk cleansing cream and pore cleanser, Root of Life night cream, Polly Bergen's Oil of the Turtle Soap, Johnson's Baby Lotion and Whisper Mouth Spray. He sang with a tuneless screeching falsetto, reproducing note for note the singing style of 1910 and performed with a miniature ukulele (which for protection he kept wrapped in an old cardigan). In 1968 alone, he collected around £500,000 from public performances and the profit from his LP 'God Bless Tiny Tim' which sold 35,000 copies a week. He was forever clutching a shopping bag, in which he kept his diet of pumpkin and sunflower seeds, wheat germ and honey. He looked like a hairy spider, *and* is American.

He'd previously turned up as Emmett Swink, Darry Dover and Larry Love the Singing Canary; but his real name was Herbert Kauhry. The son of a Manhattan Lebanese textile worker, he claimed that all his talent is owed to the Lord Jesus. Until his recent and televised marriage, he was worried about using any lavatory other than the one in his parents' flat. He didn't believe in kissing or holding hands before marriage and thought that for modesty's sake skirts should be round the ankles. He bought his 'thirties clothes second-hand and kept them semi-permanently in mothballs; all of his tweed jackets and baggy grey slacks were chosen by his mother,' he told me. Sex was a word he could not bring himself to mention - he had to spell it out, and children he referred to as 'blessed events'. Not surprisingly, he failed to pass the I.Q. test for the army and had been booed off more variety talent shows than he had greasy hairs on his hook-nosed, rabbit-teethed head.

Still, no self-respecting modish flat or semi-detached could afford to be without its Tiny Tim Album prominently displayed, unless that is you cared about music.

Tiny Tim was the apotheosis of the Cult. He was more talked about in show-biz circles than any pop star since W. S. Gilbert. He was described as a lost lithograph by Toulouse-Lautrec with the voice of Eleanor Roosevelt; he performed like a clockwork squirrel in a downtown Lesbian joint with a repertoire that droned from a diseased version of 'Tiptoe Through the Tulips' to a grotesque squawking of 'On the Old Front Porch'. Tuneless, witless, mindless and pointless, he skipped around the stage like a pregnant gazelle blowing kisses to the audience whom he addressed as 'beautiful people' and 'dear, wonderful friends'. He expected our 'dear, lovely Queen' to be at his Albert Hall Concert because he *knew* he can 'bring a little happiness to her heart'.

If he was anything more than the brainless nut he would have us believe, it could only be that he had a quality of freakish inviolability. He was so stupid, he could only be pitied. A sophisticated defence might have been that he was exploiting the nostalgic glamour of vaudeville and that his talent lay not in parody or mere imitation, but in genuine recreation. Certainly his songs and manner of presentation had a sincerity and naïvety that was difficult to dismiss. Maybe we were just suckers for the good old days, because he was 'trying to bring back the happiness that was part of the beautiful tunes in days gone by'. He sang, he told me, because he was 'full of sunshine'; maybe he had gotten sunstroke when young.

Tim Hardin was another singer whose songs were mistaken by some as the epitome of 'caring'. Asked why he thought his hit song 'If I Were a Carpenter' had been so successful, he replied with a meaningful pause. After a meaningful shrug, he mumbled: 'Like - it's corny. (Another meaningful pause.) But it's got co-ordinated corn. Like, when you hear Ray Charles sing 'Lord, Lord'. That's corny, but it's so together it becomes poetic.' Amongst purveyors of his corn have been Cilla Black, Marianne the Faithful, The Four Tops, Bobby Darin, Peggy Lee, Scott Walker and the ever lovely Cliff Richard. These were the beautiful people chosen to record the songs and spread the word of Tim Hardin, self-styled American genius, composer, poet, guitarist, pianist, singer, ex-Marine, one of the real legends of his own lifetime, who said to me of his songs: 'They are true, I don't have the imagination to make them up.'

Heralded by some as 'the musical event of the century', *this* month's Messiah said: 'Pop music isn't good, and no good songs have success. It all depends on how much money companies have to spend on them.' His grandfather was another immortal, John Wesley Hardin - the same as was beatified by Bob Dylan, and like all the true immortals, he suffered. 'On record, you can hear me crying with fatigue. I'm usually sick at the time. The sound that most people know me by is the sound of me, wasted.'

Born in Oregon, of classically minded parents, Hardin drifted around Greenwich Village, mumbling. He worked in the Night Owl Cafe, along with The Lovin' Spoonful and The Mamas and Papas, and took up the electric guitar at a time when most village musicians were hung up on the acoustic sound. His concerts, he told me, could be

Chapter Nine

A book was published in England in the late sixties called 'Innovations'. Its editor was a Mr. Bernard Bergonzi, Senior Lecturer in English at the University of Warwick, and it was concerned with analysing contemporary culture - its value and its importance.

It was primarily concerned with the new cultural modes of the 1960's, Pop and Op Art, discotheques, concrete poetry, LSD and all the paraphernalia of psychedelia. Did they represent the disintegration of what he calls the 'Modern Movement' and the beginnings of a self-destructive 'Post-Modern Period'? Or did they denote nothing at all since they are only the confused and debauched off-shoots of the traditional Arts which admittedly were then in a bad way?

So we read: 'Few of us have really understood how the Beatle hair-do is part of a syndrome, of which high heels, jeans tight over the buttocks etc., are other aspects, symptomatic of a larger retreat from masculine aggressiveness to female allure - in literature and the arts, to the style called camp.' He went on to explain how that style had been permeated through 'the invention of homosexuals'. We also learned that drug-taking was 'womanly', because it permitted 'the penetration of the body by a foreign object which not only stirs delights but even (possibly) creates life!' Like ice-cream? And so on, and so on.

It was not so much that the questions raised by the book are formulated in terms that - right or wrong -would have been unintelligible to the artist and particularly to the pop-artist actually in there doing it, actually wrestling with his sensibilities; nor is it necessarily that such questions could only parasitically describe the intellectual climate from which they germinated. They could rarely throw any light onto the perpetual twilight in which what we insist on designating as art is somehow born. What really made the book and others like it totally fatuous, was that speculations about Art or even books about pop music are useful only as long as they remain speculative rather than assertive. For since the artist deals in a world of possibilities and not of facts, it is a complete waste of time to assert that which cannot be asserted, and to factualise that which can only be fiction. As Stravinsky pointed out in his 'Dialogues and a Diary' (*not* quoted by Mr. Bergonzi): 'I do not understand the composer who says we must analyse and determine the evolutionary tendency of the whole musical situation and *I* can only follow where my musical appetites lead me.' Which is precisely what the pop world has done. The clothes that people wear have nothing to do with a 'retreat from masculine aggressiveness to female allure'. 'I only wear what I wear and behave publicly in the way that I behave', Manfred Mann told me, 'because society which demanded and created me - *expects* that I should dress and behave in that way. If I don't, then I'm being naughty and have to be punished.'

In direct contrast to W. H. Auden, who wrote:

> Art is *not* life, and cannot be
> A midwife to society.

Janis Joplin told me: 'What we really want to do is to create a real emotional experience for the audience; to send them away with the feeling that something has happened.' 'My intention', agreed John Cage, 'is to affirm this life; not to bring order out of a chaos nor to suggest improvements in creation, but simply to wake up to the very life we're living, which is so excellent once one has got one's mind and one's desires out of the way and lets it act of its own accord.' The painter Rauschenberg said exactly the same thing. 'I consider myself successful only when I do something that resembles the lack of order I sense.'

Like Beckett's heroes, we believed that we can't but we must go on, even if that going on is bound to look absurd, a very old-fashioned thing to be doing in a situation which we could show to be absolutely new. Since we have little or no idea why we are going on or where we are going, Art can only be an attempt to speculate upon the nature of the journey. Thus it becomes - Camus' phrase - the cry of the mind exhausted by its own rebellion. The artist, says Henry Miller, who becomes thoroughly aware, consequently ceases to be one. And in the 1960s the trend among the accepted Arts - such as painting, theatre and poetry - was towards awareness, towards that blinding self-consciousness in which no present forms of life could possibly flourish, let alone Art.

'We have no Art - we do everything as well as possible.' Marshal McLuhan once quoted this Balinese saying approvingly. While it is probably true that McLuhan escalates extraordinary insights into iron-clad generalisations, and that his dogmatic style and messianic tone obscure the fact that he is essentially an aphorist who uses his formulations not to establish 'truths' but to establish what he calls 'probes', all he too is saying is 'I want observations, not agreement.' McLuhan believed that you can only think about Art in exploratory and speculative terms; there can be nothing substantive and definite about it. He shows how Art and Education were previously presented to the public as consumer packages for their instruction and edification. But now - through the communications media, primarily TV - the new mass audience is involved immediately in Art and Education as participants and co-creators rather than as consumers. Art and Education have become new forms of experience and have thereby created new environments.

Once upon a time there existed a tribal encyclopedia of oral and memorized wisdom which was the property of tribal man. The art of writing enabled man to organise knowledge by categories and classifications; what Plato called the *Ideas*. With the origin of classified data and the subsequent visual organisation of knowledge, there came also representation in the arts. Representation is itself a form of matching or classifying unknown to pre-literate native artists. Today we are again returning to non-objective, non-representational art, because in the electric age we are leaving behind the once essential world of visual organisation of experience. With the advent of electric circuitry and the instant movement of information, Euclidean space recedes and the non-Euclidean geometrics emerge. Lewis Carroll - a mathematician by training - was perfectly aware of this change when he took Alice through the looking glass into a world where each object created its own space and conditions. To the visual or Euclidean man, however, objects do not create time and space. They are merely fitted in to space and time. Bertrand Russell observed that if the bath water got only half a degree warmer every hour, we would never know when to scream. New environments have reset our sensory thresholds. And these, in their turn, have radically altered our outlook and expectations.

Sartre therefore believed that what we have previously thought of as Art is subversive of civilisation. The true function of Art should be to help us to find our way back to the sources of pleasure that have been rendered inaccessible by our capitulation to cultural dogma. In other words, to recapture the lost laughter of infancy. The pop world, therefore, understands Art as the extension of life, since what we now have is one world, endlessly rocking and rolling in the electronic cradle. Art is not a criticism of life - as Matthew Arnold wanted us to believe. It is a celebration of it.   And the most obvious and immediate celebration of life, inhabits the pop world.

Admittedly, youth is no guarantee of understanding. But with the syntax of 'serious' music no longer rooted in the contemporary vernacular, and with 'popular' music at last escaping from just being a simplification of grander techniques and devices - as it was arguably for instance with such as Crosby, Sinatra or Benny Goodman - the best of pop music today is able to delight the listener out into the open, amaze him off his guard and so educate him through entertainment. Thus, pop culture has shown us that somehow we have got to escape from the formal Education and Maturity that we seem to value so highly. Burn your books is for once not just an idle and incoherent threat. It is the only course of reasonable action left to us.

If you want to know about the cut-out novels of William S. Burroughs, or how Jackson Pollock drips paint onto his canvas from a safe distance, or about Christian Wolfe - a composer who believes that his music goes in no particular direction (it isn't going anywhere, or making progress, and hasn't come from anywhere in particular - it's just static), or about poems which depend for their effect upon graphic space as an organising agent whereby the poem becomes an ideogram, a sign, then Mr. Bergonzi's collection of essays and books like it will acquaint you with the gossip. But if you want to experience and so understand these things, you've got to first open your mind to the powerful stimuli that are about you - of which the most immediate and accessible are television, which often misunderstands what it is and thus diminishes much of what it touches, and pop music.

This is a proposition which many will find intolerable - and with some justification. For example, there was once a pop club within a stone's throw of London's Royal Opera House, called The Electric Garden. It was eventually closed after a large number of police visits, but if you had visited it in its hey-day and had ventured past the Jesus figure guarding the golden gate, you would find inside what was described as the Ultimate Revelation. Slouching Jesus - him with the blonding wig - grumbled at you in some obscurantist jargon, took your money, and without explanation showed you a door marked Ladies. A few torn-out pages of *The People* newspaper promisingly headlined 'Would you let your daughter go here' and showing naked - yes, *real* naked girls (well, partly) 'disporting themselves', were stuck up on a hastily painted wall. The excitement mounted; the music pounded; painted girls with smiles flickering dangerously on their lips wafted by on the dreams of their obsessive imaginations; coloured lights and staccato patterns raced across the walls, pulsating in a closed frenzy. Around the floors were scattered the Freemasons of Youth, a mystic gang of shoddy, uncombed, sparkler-waving, Hindu chanting children, aged 10-30. The smell appropriately was of dead flowers, heavy in the basement air. Hieronymous Bosch would have recognised the scene. So did the journalists - lots and lots and lots of them - who gathered vulture-like for the pickings, hot from their formica desks at the *Daily Stench* gossip columns, anxious to feed the civil servants of Wapping and Raynes Park with the suburban satisfaction of this twentieth century peep-show.

Another example is, of course, sex. Enter the *Daily Stench* again. What's usually forgotten by the puritanical critics, however, is that sexual maturity is occurring one year earlier every decade. So it is inevitable that this increased awareness should show itself in pop music and all that surrounds it. The American pop magazine *Rolling Stone* printed an extraordinary interview with a 'groupie' called Anna. A groupie is a girl who follows the groups around for musical and sexual satisfaction.

'It's kinda fun,' she said; 'some of the limelight falls on you. You're in the room. You're involved. If a chick is *that* beautiful, she'd be, I mean, offended if the (pop star) didn't come on to her sexually. There are all sorts of scenes . . . with two people, three people, seven people. A guy in a band can easily handle two or three chicks in a night. It's very, very groovy, if two people can just forget that sex really means nothing when it's just sex. Love and sex don't go together. And like if you can look at it for that, then you can groove watching the person you love making love to someone else.'

Eric Clapton told me that having all these chicks eager to ball him gave him a sense of power. The realisation that it wasn't even your body or your face they wanted to make love to, but your name, changed his mind. And Mike Bloomfield of the Electric Flag summed up the whole tragicomedy when he told me that 'they just want to talk to the cat, see where he's at and watch him do his thing. And the only way they can do that, is to *give* him something - and the only thing most of them have to offer is their cunts.'

To make matters worse, there was very often a total failure of communication between the pop world and everybody else. Its most eloquent spokesman such as Ginsberg and the ageing Ungaretti had often by their idiosyncrasies partially hidden the debt of the new to the old. So adolescent were we in our Oxford B.A. (2nd class) adulation of the pop world, and so uneducated in our understanding of its out-pourings, that the vulgarity and cheapness and pitiful silliness of many of its spokesmen often blinded us to the worth and tradition that was embedded rock-centre in its music and words. When pop-star Cat Stevens, a singer, told me 'messages are very important to me. I have written two songs which have very deep messages. I don't know whether I shall release them, though. They may not be understood', he must expect only laughter. He was assuming an importance not manifest in his work, and an influence not guaranteed by his selective popularity. In its propaganda sheets, the pop world frequently mistakes abuse for proper criticism and personal graffiti for illuminating biographical comment. *The Record Mirror*, for example, had a column called My Scene by Tony Hall (see Chapter 6). 'Dig this sad, little tailpiece' he wrote . . . 'the other afternoon, a Very, Very Important Popstar in Indian garb, his glowingly beautiful wife and two phenomenally talented painters . . . went to a public garden. In the sunshine, the flowers and the lake were too beautiful for words. Then the park-keeper yelled "Everybody out . . . you long-haired layabouts are all the same. Vandals and hooligans." So, though the word *is* spreading, reaction and ignorance - through upbringing and not-questioning between right and wrong - is still there strongly . . . By the way the V.V.I Popstar forgave him.' There *must* be a truth there somewhere.

But the real evidence, apparently, for the worthlessness of pop, he told me, often came from the music itself. The entire output of The Monkees, for instance, seemed to some to have been derived from a Massachusetts computer programmed with Beatles fall-outs and the Oxford Book of Nursery Rhymes. Trash such as this only confirmed the dogmatists in their belief that the scene was one of unmitigated sentimentalism and trivia. Admittedly much of it was. Much of pop *did* rely on jargon and poor relations; some of its spokesmen became masters of the form of intellectual cheating known as 'the generalisation'. George Harrison, for example, could go to India for a few months and return to tell the world how to find inner peace. It was as if the Reader's Digest had come to life. Of course, much of pop had no sense of discipline or of sensible purpose. Its style was confused and its pose imperfect. It often surrounded itself with the trappings of some semi-Oriental cult and retreated into non-think land; since McLuhan, we have become vulnerable to the media and so pop became adept at manipulating the media. Jim Morrison of The Doors, for example, had a coolly calculated sexuality - he was known to spontaneously fall off the stage into the arms of the teenies at exactly the same point in consecutive concerts. But this is not the point, nor is it the whole story. After all, there are some who believe that modern 'serious' music consists - more or less exclusively - of Havergal Brian, Cornelius Cardew, or Gian Carlo Menotti. If so, whatever happened to Shostakovitch and Britten and Stravinsky?

And for those who doubted the value of *pop* music, it is worth remembering the musical wilderness which they would presumably have us prefer. A wilderness of which concert-going had often little more than a coughing, spluttering, who's who sensation, where gramophone record and the perfection supposedly mixed and trapped thereon, is the optimum of musical appreciation, and where 'new' music is so bankrupt of harmonic or melodic or rhythmic invention, that it has to resort to assorted gurgles as an excuse for its paucity of imagination. Nonetheless, gurgles may be better value than Brahms - and it is possible that gurgles do represent the latest flowering of the imagination. Like the concertos for tooth-brush and quintets for piano legs. Jack Westrup, the Professor of Music at Oxford, recalled a critic who wrote of 'modern' music that the 'slapped trombone is a glorious sound'. 'A glorious triumph of complete absurdity,' added Westrup, 'before an audience of 25 people may, for the time being, satisfy a composer who walks blinkered through the world. But this is not the reward that serious artists seek.' Peter Yates, however, in *Twentieth Century Music*, describes in awed tones an exercise carried out at San Francisco's Tape Music Center. 'The four glass sides of a tropical fish tank are painted with musical staves and with little squares indicating arco, pizzicato, etc. Four instrumentalists sit one at each side. Six fish, white or black, are placed in the water and swim behind the staves and boxes to furnish notes and instructions. Several weeks of practice were needed to enable the players to keep up with the fish.'

Can you wonder that the musician who took his artistic inheritance and tradition with anything like a proper sense of wonder, increasingly cast a nervous eye towards the much ridiculed upsurge pounding away in the other camp.

But even this nervousness was nothing new. Classical music has frequently been enriched before by the folk and popular idioms. In

1240, the most popular song of the day 'Sumer is icumen in', existed also in the handwriting of a monk of Reading Abbey, with religious words written beneath the secular ones which were in the Wessex dialect. Presumably the monk was intrigued by this 'popular' tune and noted it down in the expectation that it might be adapted for ecclesiastical use. This tendency was, however, firmly put down by Pope John XXII who issued in 1322 a decree condemning 'certain disciples of the new school who truncate the melodies with hocquets, deprave them with descants, and sometimes even stuff them with upper parts made out of secular songs. In consequence, wantonness increases.' Bach's 'Inventions' and 'Suites' are often little more than scarcely disguised popular dances. Mozart and Beethoven loved folk songs and popular ditties of all kinds, particularly those of Scottish and Turkish origins - 'Rondo a la Turk', 'Sonata in A', 'Il Seraglio', 'Eroica' and the 'Bagatelles'. Schubert wrote endless ländler - Austrian peasant waltzes, and even Mahler in one of his bleakest songs, 'Wo die shönen Trompeten blasen' adapted a harmless 'popular' tune.

In the last century, Stravinsky had a known addiction for Shorty Rogers, the jazz trumpeter, which showed itself in the trumpet part of Threni. His piano piece 'Rag-Time' is more than an acknowledgment of another tradition. Darius Milhaud in 'La Création du Monde' represents the primeval incantations of the gods Nfame, Nébère and Nkwa by a three-part jazz fugato over a percussion accompaniment derived from jazz arabesques. Milhaud also used night-club tunes in 'Le Boeuf sur le Toit' and Vaughan Williams in his Sixth Symphony uses an accompaniment immediately recalling 'The Teddy Bears Picnic' over which he weaves a medium-tempo blues tune played in close harmony by the trumpets. Musical analysis is always such fun! But not without its instruction. It seems to be OK for classical composers to absorb pop influences - even if the end result is indifferent - although somehow blasphemous (even if irrelevant) that Pete Townshend should actually know about counterpoint.

In Gershwin and Kurt Weill (pupil of Busoni, the great Bach transcriber), moreover, the world of music found at last two composers of stature for whom the terms 'classical' and 'popular' music were redundant. Gershwin, in particular, realised that popular music had something individual to contribute. He saw that some popular music could teach classical music a thing or two about the communication both of excitement and of intensity of emotion; and that it was popular music and *not* classical music which often more accurately captured the mood of today. Some have dismissed Gershwin as a composer of light music who just dabbled in classical forms. Others, however, believe that in Gershwin the world of music had found a composer whose classical training *preferred* to express itself in the popular idiom. Just as in T. S. Eliot, the world of letters found a poet whose romantic pessimism also preferred to express itself frequently in the techniques of the music-hall.

> This is the way the world ends
> This is the way the world ends
> This is the way the world ends
> Not with a bang, but a whimper.

echoes not only the jingle of a jazz song, but its sentiment.

The credit list of this cross-influencing is endless and really proves nothing except that a musician is a musician and will respond to any aural influence that attracts his attention. Folk-song in pop (Bob Dylan and others) is an exhumation of the past comparable with the revival of Art Nouveau. And the current vogue of pre-classical music such as that of Cavalli and Monteverdi is mirrored in pop by the revival of 1920's vaudeville songs, such as 'Winchester Cathedral', 'Finchley Road' and 'Peek-a-boo'. Eleanor Rigby has an Alberti bass: and the Procol Harum's 'Whiter Shade of Pale' is a straight lift from poor old Bach. Sergeant Pepper was described by one critic as a 'Tin Pan Alley *Dichterliebe*', and Judy Collins told me 'in the future we will have pop song-cycles just like classical lieder; but we will create our *own* words, music and orchestrations because we are a generation of whole people.' Van Dyke Parks, a young American pop composer, wrote what he called 'Song-Cycle'. The Nice planned a concert with the New York Symphony Orchestra and Pink Floyd wrote a piece for themselves and the London Philharmonic Orchestra. Psychedelic music - like that of Pink Floyd - might very well be the realisation of Oscar Wilde's dream of 'Curiously coloured, scarlet music'.

A tune like 'Stop the Blues' from the musical 'The Girl Friend', however, demonstrates indirectly the musical snobbery that has always crippled free-thinking about pop-music. Parts of 'The Girl Friend' bear a striking resemblance to certain tunes by the sixteenth-century composer, Edmund Turges. These same tunes had been roundly condemned by Dr. Burney in his *Survey of Music* - because 'they smacked of a groover's ditty'; in other words, they had been condemned because they smacked of pop music.

But one thing pop music has certainly contributed is a new fascination with the techniques of the recording studio. Even Benjamin Britten was converted.

Britten had once spoken unkindly of the gramophone record in his speech accepting the Aspen Award for 'services to music' in Colorado, 1964. It was, he thought, a sterile and ultimately self-destructive way of making music. He changed - according to some - because he too had come to realise that making a gramophone record, at least in stereo, was a completely different kind of activity from making music in a concert-hall or a private room. It has its own special disciplines and its own special rewards which are different in kind though not in spirit from what we have previously thought of as music making. The Canadian pianist, Glenn Gould, foretold the day when the concert-hall would be abolished and all music appreciation would derive from the gramophone and the hi-fi set.

In a sense, pop music only exists on the gramophone record, or CD as it became known. In 1969, apart from some weekly Sunday evening concerts at the Saville Theatre (which soon ceased altogether), and the occasional big event where the amplification equipment is usually so badly tuned that a battle develops between the outraged pop-group and the beleaguered, defenceless electronic equipment, 'live' pop-music is almost non-existent, at least for the general public.

Moreover, the language of music is such that it can encompass all sounds, including those not usually given the status of music and including those which derive solely from the recording studio. The onus is on the composer to develop a language whose effectiveness and power can communicate with his audience, even if that effectiveness can only be accurately achieved on a recording. If he can communicate the fragment of an idea with the smallest tap on the side drum, or if he needs the whole electronic paraphernalia of a recording studio or of a happening in clubs like The Electric Garden, then the bungling stupidity that surrounds him will eventually be forgotten.

But ultimately it is not the style or the environment or the technique or the cross-fertilisations which are important. It is what has to be said; and for many people what has to be said now, is being done not in the Wigmore Hall or the Third Programme or any of those critic-infested village festivals at Edinburgh, Bath, and the like, but in the world of pop music - in spite of the police.

Unfortunately, what has to be said has become confused and obscured by a plethora of 'words about pop music', explaining it, analysing it and classifying it. So anxious are we all to secretly identify ourselves with every half-trend, every quarter-development that in learned magazines we throw ourselves upon the altar of significance with pathetic desperateness. Defunct magazines such as *The Listener*, or Mouth of God as the heathen called it; *The Daily Worker*, or Mouth of the Devil, as the unconverted called it; *Nova* or Antiqua, as the sexually normal are heard to whisper; *Queen* or 'seen sharing a joke with' as the left-out are heard to grumble - all these devote acres of newsprint to 'Pop - we give you the inside facts behind the inside facts which, since we can't print them because we're not really involved, or interested, or concerned, here is a rewrite of the record sleeve which was written by some illiterate copy-writing gnome aged 104 who thought Dame Nellie was the greatest thing to come out of the black continent', which is, consequently, completely useless. But you pays your money and you gets your candy.

All you have to do is scan them quickly, remember a few boring phrases you've probably heard a thousand times before anyway, and you will be thought well-spoken amongst the nodding-acquaintance fraternity of Notting Hill and the BBC Club. Many is the friend seen clutching his *Melody Maker* and *New Musical Express* of a Thursday or Friday; many is the friend who leaves same on his office desk - like the Bible at a hotel bedside. I am the Way, the Truth, and the Life says the columnist; and we believe him.

Such is the super-abundance of 'pop-criticism' that our actual understanding of the music, like that of art or of politics, is now indistinguishable from the language in which we are accustomed to express that understanding, and from the media in which that language is formulated. Now since this language - assaulted as it is by cheap journalistic banter, jingoistic television, instant mini-think weekend-reviews, advertising mumbo-jumbo, jargon of all sorts - is thoroughly debased, the cliché has become the only real thought pattern. To capture our responses to pop music or symphony concerts, we rely on an endless stream of pathetic little catch-phrases as if these were the only way to reassure ourselves that all is well in the world of Art. What's more, we pretend that knowledge is no more than the reconciliation of any new data with this already debased language, forgetting that a stupefied kid listening mouth-a-gape to Ravi Shankar might possibly be nearer to a proper understanding of Shankar than a Cambridge-educated trendy with a slide rule sticking up his ass.

So, on television we confuse understanding with the greater and greater assimilation of this trivia. Inductive thought is forbidden - a dangerous, heretical and confusing process. In music criticism we have come to confuse understanding with knowledge of a greater and greater repertoire, or of comparative performances, or of hagiological tid-bits, or of Third Programme Kultur. In our adulation of pop, we have come to confuse understanding with the insideness of the news and the secret fear of seeming old. To be old, after all, is unforgiveable, for with age comes understanding.

The end of the sixties in the U.K. were, alas, not notable for the increase of such understanding. The Commercial Radio stations known derisively as the 'pirates' were smashed out of existence thus destroying the possibility that pop music might get a proper hearing; trial by jury untouched for nearly 700 years was suddenly, without so much as the whisper of a public outcry, effectively diminished and the reasonable doubt enshrined therein rendered an impossibility. The police managed to make life impossible for the only two experimental pop clubs in London - UFO and The Electric Garden. There was also the celebrated case of Michael Hagger, a popular singer, jumped on twice by the law partly because society had decided that the great social menace of the year was drugs (and not greed, selfishness, petty theft, promiscuity or ignorance) and partly because someone had decided that Youth must be punished for forcing the pace. Protest is no longer fashionable. At the end of the sixties, the liberal newspapers paraded a tired journalism which relied on innuendo and hearsay. There has been no great moral debate - the House of Lords rejected the Abortion Reform Bill. No Putney Debates, no trial of Sir Thomas More, just a few late-night television banter programmes called appropriately 'Your Witness'. Nervous half-statements made during the programme were taken as Divine revelations. Truth was the result of a vote and columnists in *The Times* thought the Day of Redemption had come.

Apparently locked in terrible struggle against the slow crushing of understanding was London's 'Underground', in many ways the spokesman for all that the best of pop represented. It had its own vocabulary, dress, stimulants, entertainments, publishing houses, communication network and shops. It even had its own legal aid - 'Release'. 'If you are arrested,' read the handout, 'you are advised to insist

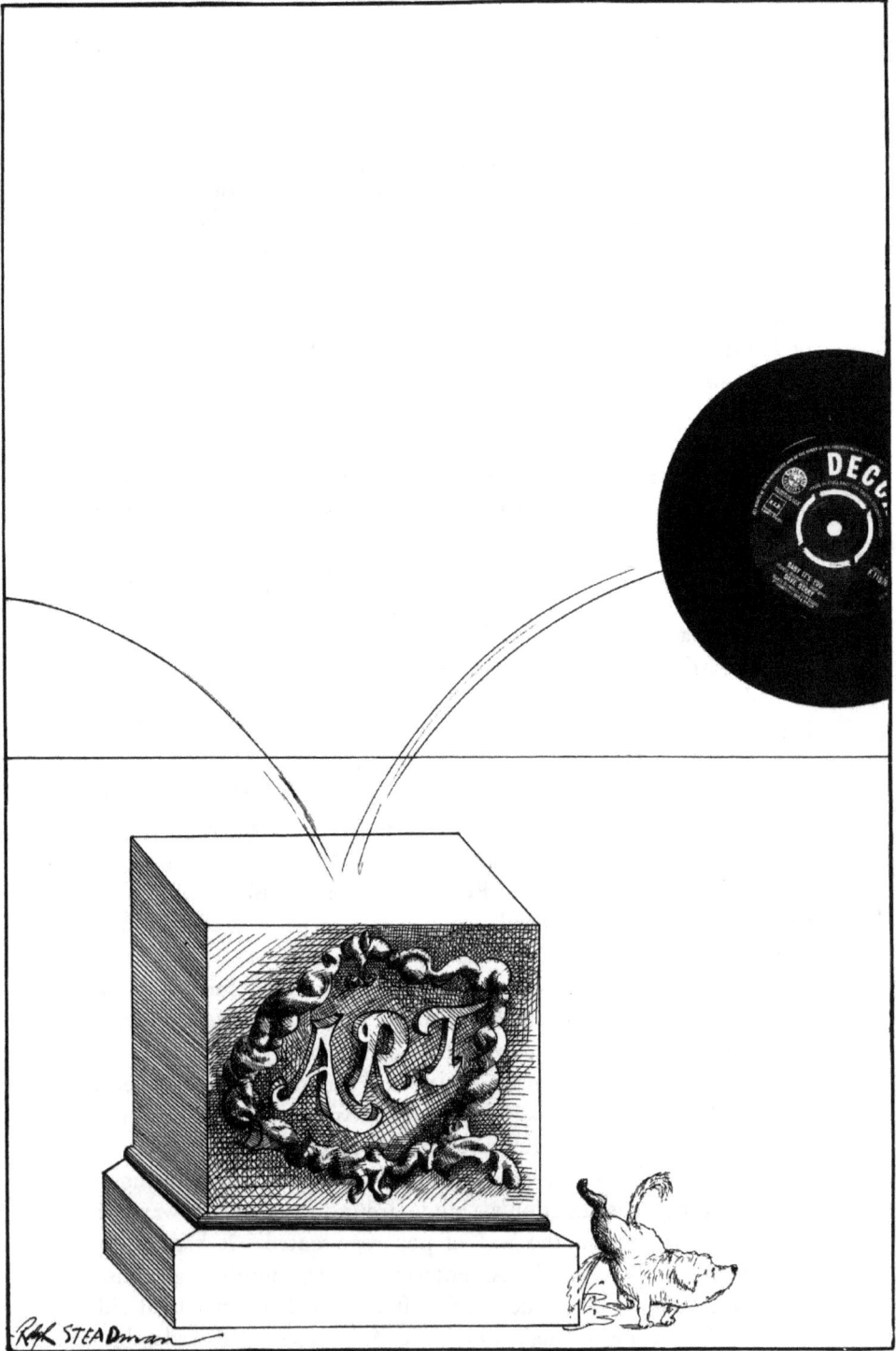

on telephoning the number on the handout, to make no statements, not to discuss the matter with which you are charged, and to be polite to police officers.' The Underground housed all manner of being; hippies, flower-power, black-power, popstars, perverts, adolescent trendies, drug-addicts, professional layabouts, middle-aged boppers, transcendentalists - all moving in a twilight world and groping for a new truth. They sought an alternative and better life than was their father's. So they grasped at every mystical shaft of light as if it were the whole truth, and searched for a dignity and purpose which all their decorative art and gaudy embellishment did not seem to provide.

There were some who viewed this onslaught as prophetic evidence of the final and total debauchery of the 20th century. Like the evidence for dismissing ninety per cent of pop music as rubbish, there would seem to have been much to support them. The Arts Laboratory in Drury Lane, for example, pioneered by American Jim Haynes, offered you a choice between Erik Satie's 'Vexations' which consists of eight hundred repetitions of four tiny themes for solo piano (performance time four hours), experimental films using two frame cutting, negative phasing and random construction, a 'light thoroughfare' through which you walked, or participation in 'The People Show No. 15', in which the audience was shut inside four cages and was deafened alternately by others smashing iron bars against the cage. Alternatively you could listen to the music of The Mel Davis Group and be persuaded to join in improvisations (on a basic script by Jeff Nuttall) about paranoia and the difficulties of communication.

Or again, there was the Fashion Group known as 'The Fool' whom some accused of being just a clumsy imitation of the worst excesses of Art Nouveau, without the latter's elegance. Sometime of Holland, Simon Postuma, Marijke Koger, Joske Leeger and English manager Barrie Finch, seemed to provide the Underground with its style. Lennon's piano, Harrison's fireplace, Cream's drum-kit, posters galore and clothes by the mile - all had that post-Beardsley Middle-European peasant look. Rich, highly-patterned, multi-coloured fabrics - mostly from Liberty's - were piled segment upon segment to provide a patch-work quilt which passed as a 'modern garment'. It was the ugly person's answer to the problem of how to become a beautiful person - just cover yourself in coloured rags.

The posters were mostly the product of a brilliant Australian, Martin Sharp, and an organisation called 'Haphash and the Coloured Coat' - the trade-name of Nigel Waymouth and Michael English. They began by advertising the activities of the first psychedelic night-club, UFO (Unlimited Freak Out). Again, to the unkind critic, these meandering colouring books were little more than a collage of other men's hard-won visions - Bosch, Magritte, Blake, Disney and alchemists' illustrations. They were pastiche, of itself, of itself, of itself. Like much else in the Underground, it passed for art because none other was known about. Yet it also provided the Underground with the excuse to believe that it was destroying the myth that the visual imagination exists only in museums and art galleries and the BBC Art programmes.

But for those who really wanted to be convinced of this total debauchery, the most reassuring evidence must have come from the columns of *The International Times*, the Underground's main newspaper. It had a circulation of 45,000, and if anything could be taken as the voice of the Underground and of the Pop milieu in the late sixties in the U.K., it could stake an important claim. The Underground and the Pop World were quick to deny that they had any commonly agreed code of behaviour or morality; yet it is clear that certain beliefs were held in common, and these found expression in the columns of *The International Times*. If one wants a coherent and cohesive explanation of what it is that the pop milieu and its prophets and apologists were about, one could do worse than look back to *The International Times*. It was not the voice of the pop world, but in England at least it was the pop world's most eloquent spokesman.

Intellectually, it was fashionable to dismiss the paper as childish and nauseating, opinionated and vulgar, selfish and crassly ignorant. Undoubtedly, its use of language was often semi-literate and pseudo-intellectual, as much a prey to jargon as the governmentsand publications which it attacked. Often, it was unreadable and plain stupid. 'Help a hash-man in Turkey by blowing up a dustbin in Savile Row', it chortled. Not surprisingly, when it first appeared in 1966, it aroused intense fury.

The New Statesman dismissed it as 'American anti-socialist beat-nikery'. *The Times* thought it was the 'kiss of death' for all rational debate. 'A flower children's comic' was how the *Sunday Telegraph* described it, whilst for *The People* it was simply 'anti-white'. The *Morning Star* predictably sneered at it as being 'completely destructive' whilst *Encounter* wrote it off as 'slovenly and amateurish'. When you consider that its contributors include such amateurs as Norman Mailer, Dick Gregory, Ezra Pound and Bertrand Russell, and such flower-children as Allen Ginsberg, William Burroughs and Morton Feldman, and such anti-whites as Claes Oldenberg, Buckminster Fuller and Alexander Trocchi, it becomes hard to understand the harsh attacks made upon the newspaper.

The International Times included passionate and sustained attacks upon unnecessary literary and theatrical censorship, arguing its case with immense resource and courage. If the argument continued and develops in the same vein, it was thought, then the laws of libel would have to be changed to accommodate it. It campaigned for the legalisation of marijuana with a greater intelligence than the rest of the Press put together. It attacked remorselessly a recent British Home Secretary for his apparent lack of concern about Prison Reform and about police domination - one headline ran 'Arrest the Home Secretary - wanted for Evasion'. The subsequent article listed case after case of police brutality - written by 'a qualified criminal'. One quoted a man arrested at 2 a.m. whilst walking home, for reasons totally unknown to him. 'Suddenly the door (of the police interrogation room) opens and a police sergeant strides in, and slams down two things on the table. Leering offensively he spits out "take your pick". On the table is a gun and a carrier bag containing a few pounds of hashish. Next day "the man" appears in a magistrates' court charged with unlawful possession of a firearm and of using threatening behavior. The magistrate remands the man in Brixton prison for a few weeks, taking care to congratulate the sergeant on his initiative.' Even allowing for the obvious prejudice of the writer, for his ignorance of the various civil liberties organisations, for the overt propagandist nature of the piece, at least someone cared sufficiently about freedom and its application or lack of it in our society, to write and keep writing with passion in defence of it. And that - curiously - has become an increasingly rare phenomenon.

Another of its favourite topics was censorship - it had a regular column called 'Censorshi*' which claimed to keep you up-to-date with the latest in obscenity trials. Jean Straker, William Burroughs, Jim Dine, Robert Fraser and John Calder appeared frequently. The now defunct Lord Chamberlain was pillaged relentlessly. One issue quoted at length the distinguished actress Gladys Cooper: 'Once it was glamourous to go to the theatre. Now it's all so dirty. Elegance is an old-fashioned word and if a play is described as well constructed it is an insult . . . . All this political stuff pours through the television set into all these people's little homes and they don't understand it. Once, only the right things got through - why can't it be like that again?'

Press censorship also did not escape. About communist China and the lack of news information coming from there in the sixties pre-Nixon's famous visit, the magazine was most revealing. During an eight-day survey of the world's Press, the magazine reported that of the twenty-eight incidents which received a mention in either the London *Times*, the *Telegraph* or the *Guardian* only three had not appeared earlier in the foreign press. But no fewer than eighty other different episodes had been reported in the foreign papers without so much as an apology in the all-seeing, all-knowing English newspapers. During the Red Guards' calamitous riots in the early sixties, the British newspapers somehow 'forgot' to mention, for example, the destruction of whole villages - both property and persons - in the name of Chairman Mao. In Wuhan, the Red Guards beat victims with sticks until they lay lifeless on the ground. Men and women were paraded with sandbags around their necks to bow their heads. Their faces were blackened and they carried placards listing their alleged crimes. 'Most of the victims . . . were elderly people, attacked apparently because they did not have to work and were living a more comfortable life than their neighbors.' As the magazine pointed out with understandable anger, all one quality newspaper (*The Telegraph*) had done was to contribute a series of articles purporting to demonstrate conclusively that the existence of the Red Guards was of only minor significance. It seemed 'more concerned with providing pleasant reading' (not to mention a digest of the week's cultural tittle- tattle) 'than with reporting the news'.

One of the most startling contributions *The International Times* made was a front page 'Christmas Message' to the Queen. In a sense, it included the Ten Commandments of contemporary Pop - explaining nothing about the music itself, but capturing perfectly the mood which purveyed much of the best of it. Moreover, the 'Christmas Message' could very well have been distributed with advantage to every Bishop and Jurist in the land, to every Politician and Moralist and to every fifth-rate, fat, bespectacled theatre, television and pop critic.

The magazine insisted that the following problems were not being sufficiently or satisfactorily dealt with in the tacitly accepted present structure of politics, diplomacy, finance and culture. It listed twenty of which these are some:

1) the nature of legality and crime;

2) the monopolization of temporal authority by businessmen through government, and of spiritual authority by priests through the churches;

3) the newspaper . . . monopoly over the masses and the consequent denigration of man's highest symbolic achievement to date, the written word; this has also led to the delegation of the responsibility of ferreting out the relevant truths of existence to anonymous advertisers who thus support uncreative writers called journalists;

4) the legal perpetration of official interference in the communications media;

5) the blind spread and acceptance of atheistic and dialectic materialism. God (if he exists) does not need verbal solicitors;

6) the need to remove sex, death and drugs from the taboo status they presently enjoy;

7) that the reign of usury still standing between a man and his desire and need to do a good job, must finally come to an end;

8) that the debate of truth must be continuous and consequential in the world of acts, and that survival at all costs is too expensive for the present day depleted state of man's spiritual fund;

9) the depletion of the earth's natural resources to satisfy artificially created cravings;

10) that love need not remain a banal cliché, but is and must be a constantly original and divine verb.

If even a few of these propositions were achieved, it said, California Dreamin' would become a reality.

These suggestions hardly seem worthy of the *Sunday Telegraph's* sneer of 'a flower-children's comic', or the 'anti-socialist beat-nikery' of the *New Statesman*, or the 'anti-white' of *The People*, or the 'kiss of death' of *The Times*. For the pop world in the late sixties, they represented a coherent and comprehensive attempt at a moral code which was both relevant and practical to our human condition. One searches in vain amongst the fashionable intellectual magazines of the time, or in the endless philosophic diatribes from the professional moralists (whether secular or cleric), in the hope of finding an alternative code. Only the psychologist and psychiatrist seemed willing to admit that being men of science they could offer no more than particular solutions to particular problems. The others, however, claimed a greater weltanschauung. In fact, they offered little more than the psychologist could suggest - and often much less.

How ironical, therefore, that this ambitious moral fervour should have come from the pop milieu and its newspaper *The International Times* - derided and stigmatised though it was as being nothing more than an example of the sickness of 'London's Underground', the scribblings of a randy collection of hairy, toothless, drugged layabouts. The pretensions of these 'drugged layabouts' which embodied many of the pretensions of pop, were colossal, as were their prejudices and their malevolent and spiteful attacks. Collectively and individually they were ego-mania personified. Their literary style was frequently so flip that it was meaningless. But at least they and the pop world believed in something, and that surely was preferable to wishy-washy, slightly left-wing, probably middle-class-oriented, well-meaning and ultimately selfish nouveau liberalism.

In 1969, I wrote that if we go on siding with those who think that pop music and its ambitions are the garbage of a civilisation, then it is surely incumbent on so-called serious music to provide an alternative language and an alternative text adequately expressing the age in which we live. This is not to suggest that instant popularity is the only yardstick of success for serious music. Much great music has taken a long time to be appreciated fully. Monteverdi took 350 years. Perhaps that Californian fish-tank - for better or worse - *does* entail the beginnings of a truly universal musical language that will ultimately be of more interest and have more 'content' than the entire output of pop.

But to many people, this seemed unlikely. And to these same people, the fact that serious music seemed to have failed so far to produce an alternative, was a measure of the extent to which it is probably unable to do so. It was also a measure of the extent to which, perhaps, we ought to have begun considering pop music as the embodiment of a new and purposeful language. After all, pop helped remove the self-consciousness from Art and gave it a sense of exhilaration.

It was surely time, therefore, that we forgot that pop music was probably born under a bad sign. For within its embrace, as John Lennon wrote in his song 'Dig a Pony'.

> You can celebrate anything you want.
> You can penetrate any place you go.
> I told you so.
> You can radiate everything you want.
> You can imitate everyone you know.
> I told you so.
> You can indicate anything you see.
> You can syndicate any boat you row.
> I told you so.

If anything described the mood of young people at the end of the sixties, that is probably it.

The Pop Singer
by
Ralph STEADman

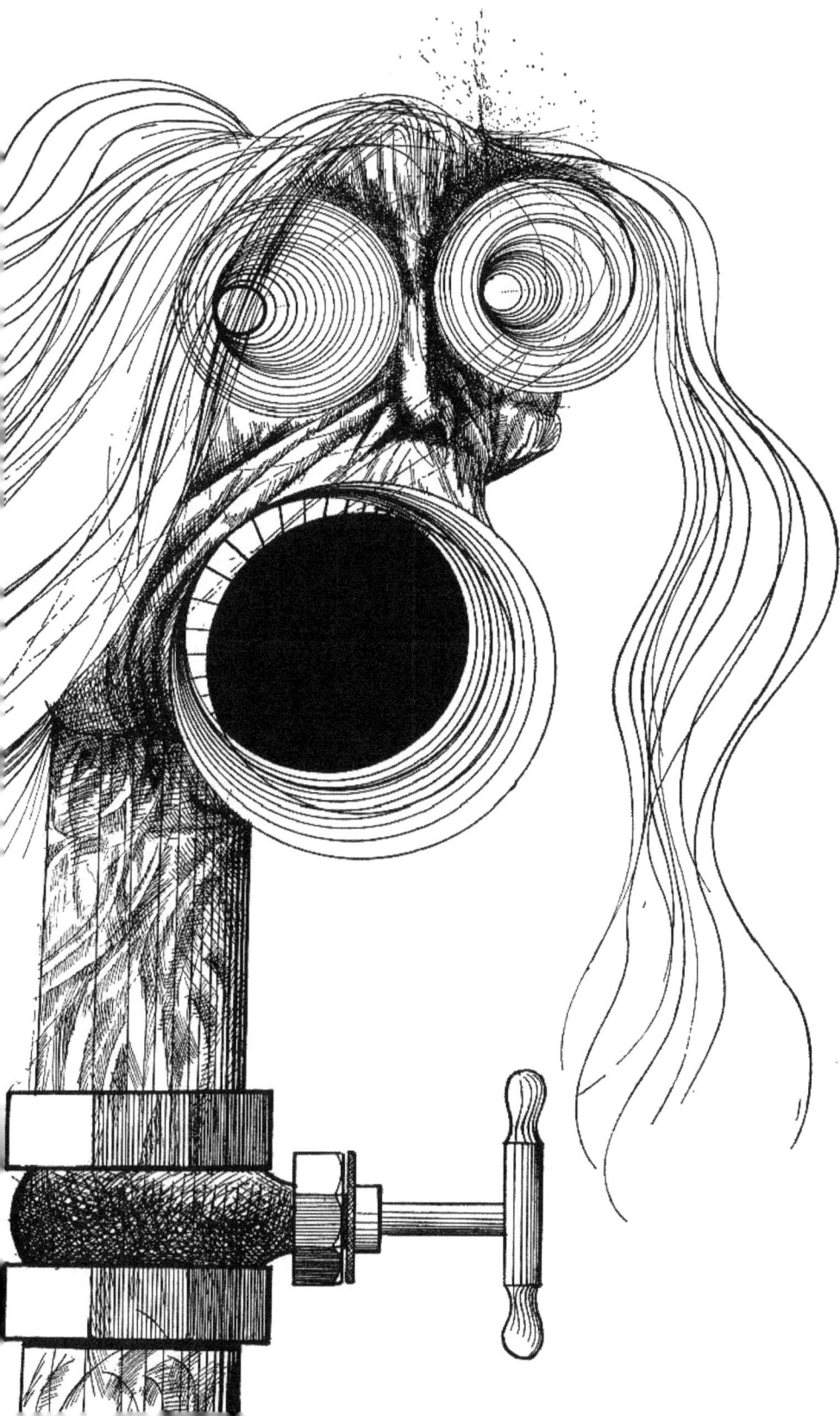

GONZO
Books

There is still such a
thing as alternative
Publishing

robert calvert
centigrade 232

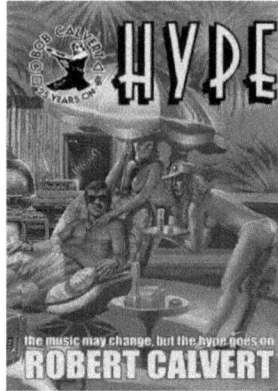

the music may change, but the hype goes on
ROBERT CALVERT

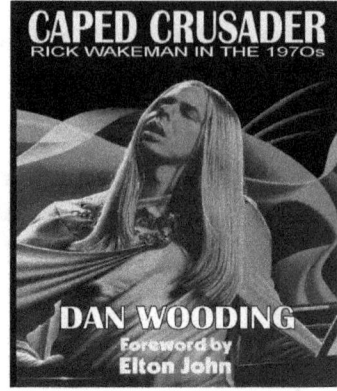

CAPED CRUSADER
RICK WAKEMAN IN THE 1970s

DAN WOODING
Foreword by
Elton John

Robert Newton Calvert: Born 9 March 1945, Died 14 August 1988 after suffering a heart attack. Contributed poetry, lyrics and vocals to legendary space rock band Hawkwind intermittently on five of their most critically acclaimed albums, including Space Ritual (1973), Quark, Strangeness & Charm (1977) and Hawklords (1978). He also recorded a number of solo albums in the mid 1970s. CENTIGRADE 232 was Robert Calvert's first collection of poems.

Hype   'And now, for all you speeding street smarties out there, the one you've all been waiting for, the one that'll pierce your laid back ears, decoke your sinuses, cut clean thru the schlock rock, MOR/crossover, techno flash mind mush. It's the new Number One with a bullet … with a bullet … It's Tom, Supernova, Mahler with a pan galactic biggie …' And the Hype goes on. And on. Hype, an amphetamine hit of a story by Hawkwind collaborator Robert Calvert. Who's been there and made it back again. The debriefing session starts here.

Rick Wakeman is the world's most unusual rock star, a genius who has pushed back the barriers of electronic rock. He has had some of the world's top orchestras perform his music, has owned eight Rolls Royces at one time, and has broken all the rules of composing and horrified his tutors at the Royal College of Music. Yet he has delighted his millions of fans. This frank book, authorised by Wakeman himself, tells the moving tale of his larger than life career.

"So many books, so little time."
Frank Zappa

THE NINE HENRYS
By Peter McAdam

TERRY DENE: BRITAIN'S FIRST ROCK & ROLL REBEL

DAN WOODING

King Squealer

MAURICE O'MAHONEY WITH DAN WOODING

There are nine Henrys, pur
ported to be the world's
first cloned cartoon charac
ter. They live in a strange
lo fi domestic surrealist
world peopled by talking
rock buns and elephants on
wobbly stilts.

They mooch around in their
minimalist universe suffer
ing from an existential
crisis with some genetically
modified humour thrown in.

Marty Wilde on Terry Dene: "Whatever
happened to Terry becomes a great deal
more comprehensible as you read of the
callous way in which he was treated by
people who should have known better
many of whom, frankly, will never know
better   of the sad little shadows of
the past who eased themselves into
Terry's life, took everything they
could get and, when it seemed that all
was lost, quietly left him … Dan Wood
ing's book tells it all."

Rick Wakeman: "There have
always been certain 'careers'
that have fascinated the
public, newspapers, and the
media in general. Such
include musicians, actors,
sportsmen, police, and not
surprisingly, the people who
give the police their employ
ment: The criminal. For the
man in the street, all these
careers have one thing in
common: they are seemingly
beyond both his reach and,
in many cases, understanding
and as such, his only associ
ation can be through the
media of newspapers or tele
vision. The police, however,
will always require the ser
vices of the grass, the
squealer, the snitch, (call
him what you will), in order
to assist in their investiga
tions and arrests; and amaz
ingly, this is the area that
seldom gets written about."

"Outside of a dog, a book is
man's best friend. Inside of a
dog it's too dark to read."
Groucho Marx

LUNAR NOTES
ZOOT HORN ROLLO'S CAPTAIN BEEFHEART EXPERIENCE
BILL HARKLEROAD
with BILLY JAMES

THE EMPIRE OF THINGS
SELECTED WRITINGS 2003 - 2013
CJ STONE

The Time of Feasting
mick farren

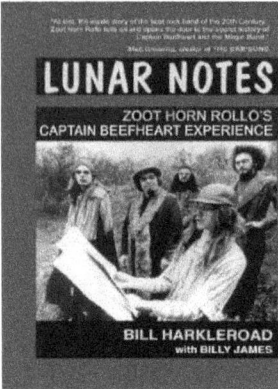

Bill Harkleroad joined Captain Beef heart's Magic Band at a time when they were changing from a straight ahead blues band into something completely dif ferent. Through the vision of Don Van Vliet (Captain Beefheart) they created a new form of music which many at the time considered atonal and difficult, but which over the years has continued to exert a powerful influence. Beefheart re christened Harkleroad as Zoot Horn Rollo, and they embarked on recording one of the classic rock albums of all time Trout Mask Replica - a work of unequalled daring and inventiveness.

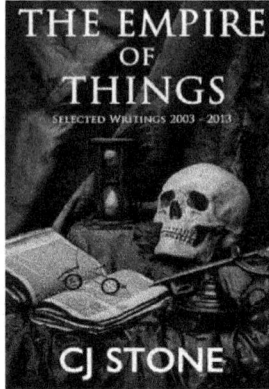

Politics, paganism and ... Vlad the Impaler. Selected stories from CJ Stone from 2003 to the present. Meet Ivor Coles, a British Tommy killed in action in September 1915, lost, and then found again. Visit Mothers Club in Erdington, the best psyche delic music club in the UK in the '60s. Celebrate Robin Hood's Day and find out what a huckle duckle is. Travel to Stonehenge at the Summer Solstice and carouse with the hippies. Find out what a Ranter is, and why CJ Stone thinks that he's one. Take LSD with Dr Lilly, the psychedelic scientist. Meet a headless soldier or the ghost of Elvis Presley in Gabalfa, Cardiff. Journey to Whitstable, to New York, to Malta and to Transylvania, and to many other places, real and imagined, polit ical and spiritual, transcendent and mundane. As The Independent says, Chris is "The best guide to the underground since Charon ferried dead souls across the Styx."

This is is the first in the highly acclaimed vampire novels of the late Mick Farren. Victor Renquist, a surprisingly urbane and likable leader of a colony of vampires which has existed for centuries in New York is faced with both admin istrative and emotional prob lems. And when you are a vampire, administration is not a thing which one takes lightly.

"The person, be it gentleman or lady, who has not pleasure in a good novel, must be intolerably stupid."

Jane Austen

Darklost

mick farren

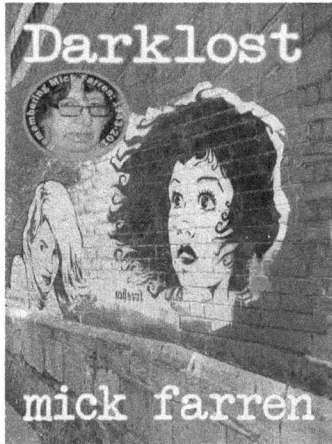

Los Angeles City of Angels, city of dreams. But sometimes the dreams become nightmares. Having fled New York, Victor Renquist and his small group of Nosferatu are striving to re establish their colony. They have become a deeper, darker part of the city's nightlife. And Hollywood's glitterati are hot on the scent of a new thrill, one that outshines all others immortality. But someone, somewhere, is med dling with even darker powers, powers that even the Nosferatu fear. Someone is attempting to summon the entity of ancient evil known as Cthulhu. And Ren quist must overcome dissent in his own colony, solve the riddle of the Darklost (a being brought part way along the Nosferatu path and then abandoned) and combat powerful enemies to save the world of humans!

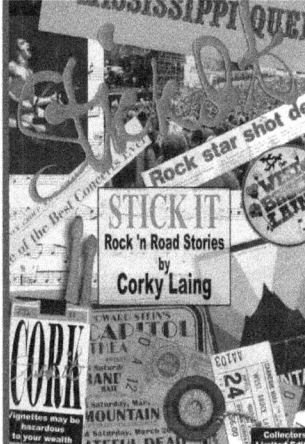

STICK IT
Rock 'n Road Stories by **Corky Laing**

Canadian born Corky Laing is probably best known as the drummer with Mountain. Corky joined the band shortly after Mountain played at the famous Woodstock Festival, although he did receive a gold disc for sales of the soundtrack album after over dubbing drums on Ten Years After's performance. Whilst with Mountain Corky Laing recorded three studio albums with them before the band split. Follow ing the split Corky, along with Mountain gui tarist Leslie West, formed a rock three piece with former Cream bassist Jack Bruce. West, Bruce and Laing recorded two studio albums and a live album before West and Laing re formed Mountain, along with Felix Pappalardi. Since 1974 Corky and Leslie have led Mountain through various line ups and recordings, and continue to record and perform today at numer ous concerts across the world. In addition to his work with Mountain, Corky Laing has recorded one solo album and formed the band Cork with former Spin Doctors guitarist Eric Shenkman, and recorded a further two studio albums with the band, which has also featured former Jimi Hendrix bassist Noel Redding. The stories are told in an incredibly frank, engaging and amusing manner, and will appeal also to those people who may not necessarily be fans of

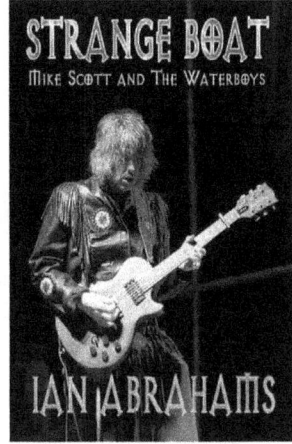

STRANGE BOAT
MIKE SCOTT AND THE WATERBOYS

IAN ABRAHAMS

To me there's no difference between Mike Scott and The Waterboys; they both mean the same thing. They mean myself and whoever are my current travel ling musical companions." Mike Scott Strange Boat charts the twisting and meandering journey of Mike Scott, describing the literary and spiritual references that inform his songwriting and explor ing the multitude of locations and cultures in which The Waterboys have assembled and reflected in their recordings. From his early forays into the music scene in Scotland at the end of the 1970s, to his creation of a 'Big Music' that peaked with the hit single 'The Whole of the Moon' and onto the Irish adventure which spawned the classic Fisher man's Blues, his constantly restless creativity has led him through a myriad of changes. With his revolving cast of troubadours at his side, he's created some of the most era defining records of the 1980s, reeled and jigged across the Celtic heartlands, reinvented himself as an electric rocker in New York, and sought out personal renewal in the spiritual calm of Findhorn's Scot tish highland retreat. Mike Scott's life has been a tale of continual musical exploration entwined with an ever evolving spirituality. "An intriguing portrait of a modern musician" (Record Collector).

"A room without books is like a body without a soul."
Marcus Tullius Cicero

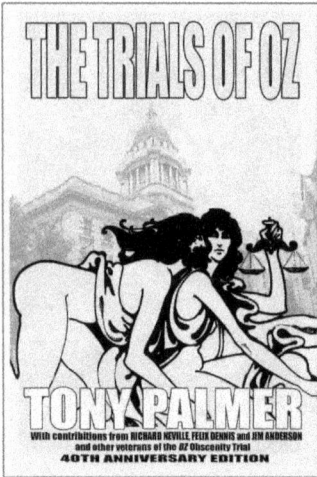

THE TRIALS OF OZ

TONY PALMER

With contributions from RICHARD NEVILLE, FELIX DENNIS and JIM ANDERSON
and other veterans of the OZ Obscenity Trial

40TH ANNIVERSARY EDITION

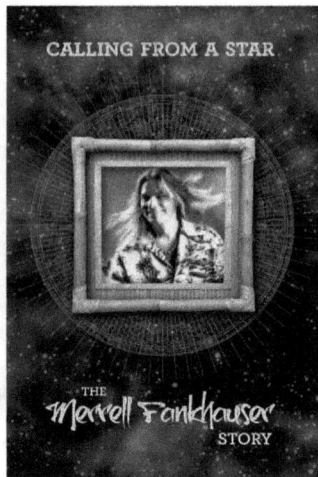

CALLING FROM A STAR

THE *Merrell Fankhauser* STORY

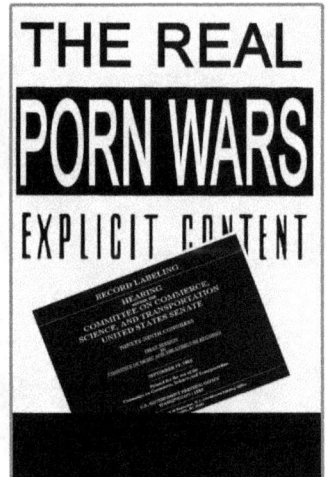

THE REAL PORN WARS

EXPLICIT CONTENT

The OZ trial was the longest obscenity trial in history. It was also one of the worst reported. With minor exceptions, the Press chose to rewrite what had occurred, presumably to fit in with what seemed to them the acceptable prejudices of the times. Perhaps this was inevitable. The proceedings dragged on for nearly six weeks in the hot summer of 1971 when there were, no doubt, a great many other events more worthy of attention. Against the background of murder in Ulster, for example, the OZ affair probably fades into its proper insignificance. Even so, after the trial, when some newspapers realised that maybe something important had happened, it became more and more apparent that what was essential was for anyone who wished to be able to read what had actually been said. Trial and judgment by a badly informed press became the order of the day. This 40th Anniversary edition includes new material by all three of the original defendants, the prosecuting barrister, one of the OZ schoolkids, and even the daughters of the judge. There are also many illustrations including unseen material from Felix Dennis' own collection...

Merrell Fankhauser has led one of the most diverse and interesting careers in music. He was born in Louisville, Kentucky, and moved to California when he was 13 years old. Merrell went on to become one of the innovators of surf music and psychedelic folk rock. His travels from Hollywood to his 15 year jungle experience on the island of Maui have been documented in numerous music books and magazines in the United States and Europe. Merrell has gained legendary international status throughout the field of rock music; his credits include over 250 songs published and released. He is a multi talented singer/songwriter and unique guitar player whose sound has delighted listeners for over 35 years. This extraordinary book tells a unique story of one of the founding fathers of surf rock, who went on to play in a succession of progressive and psychedelic bands and to meet some of the greatest names in the business, including Captain Beefheart, Randy California, The Beach Boys, Jan and Dean... and there is even a run in with the notorious Manson family.

On September 19, 1985, Frank Zappa testified before the United States Senate Commerce, Technology, and Transportation committee, attacking the Parents Music Resource Center or PMRC, a music organization co founded by Tipper Gore, wife of then senator Al Gore. The PMRC consisted of many wives of politicians, including the wives of five members of the committee, and was founded to address the issue of song lyrics with sexual or satanic content. Zappa saw their activities as on a path towards censorshipand called their proposal for voluntary labelling of records with explicit content "extortion" of the music industry. This is what happened.

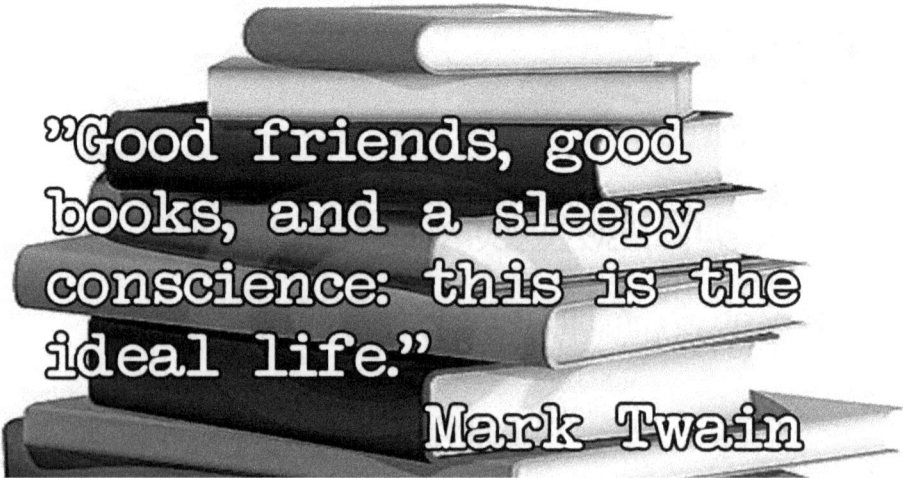

"Good friends, good books, and a sleepy conscience: this is the ideal life."
Mark Twain

THE TRIALS OF OZ

TONY PALMER

With contributions from RICHARD NEVILLE, FELIX DENNIS and JIM ANDERSON and other veterans of the OZ Obscenity Trial

40TH ANNIVERSARY EDITION

CALLING FROM A STAR

THE Merrell Fankhauser STORY

THE REAL PORN WARS

EXPLICIT CONTENT

RECORD LABELLING
HEARING
COMMITTEE ON COMMERCE,
SCIENCE AND TRANSPORTATION
UNITED STATES SENATE

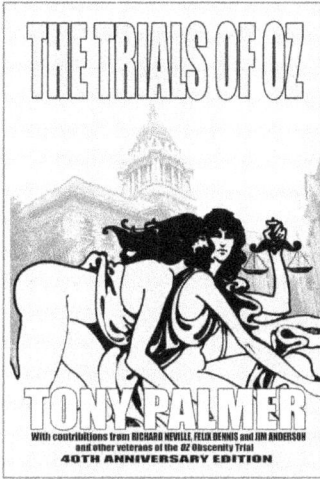

The OZ trial was the longest obscenity trial in history. It was also one of the worst reported. With minor exceptions, the Press chose to rewrite what had occurred, presumably to fit in with what seemed to them the acceptable prejudices of the times. Perhaps this was inevitable. The proceedings dragged on for nearly six weeks in the hot summer of 1971 when there were, no doubt, a great many other events more worthy of attention. Against the background of murder in Ulster, for example, the OZ affair probably fades into its proper insignifi cance. Even so, after the trial, when some newspapers realised that maybe something important had hap pened, it became more and more apparent that what was essential was for anyone who wished to be able to read what had actually been said. Trial and judgment by a badly informed press became the order of the day. This 40th Anniversary edition includes new material by all three of the original defendants, the prosecuting barrister, one of the OZ schoolkids, and even the daughters of the judge. There are also many illustrations including unseen material from Felix Dennis' own collection.

Merrell Fankhauser has led one of the most diverse and interesting careers in music. He was born in Louisville, Kentucky, and moved to California when he was 13 years old. Merrell went on to become one of the innovators of surf music and psychedelic folk rock. His travels from Hollywood to his 15 year jungle experience on the island of Maui have been documented in numerous music books and magazines in the United States and Europe. Merrell has gained legendary international status throughout the field of rock music; his credits include over 250 songs published and released. He is a multi talented singer/songwriter and unique guitar player whose sound has delighted listeners for over 35 years. This extraordi nary book tells a unique story of one of the founding fathers of surf rock, who went on to play in a succession of progressive and psychedelic bands and to meet some of the greatest names in the business, including Captain Beefheart, Randy California, The Beach Boys, Jan and Dean... and there is even a run in with the notorious Manson family.

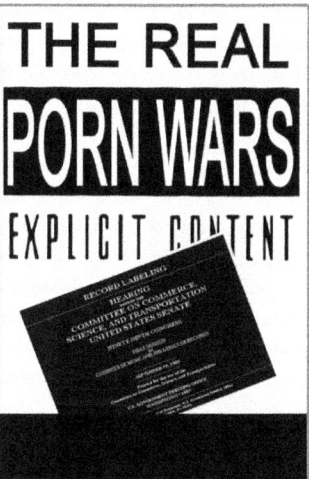

On September 19, 1985, Frank Zappa testified before the United States Senate Commerce, Technology, and Transportation committee, attacking the Parents Music Resource Center or PMRC, a music organization co founded by Tipper Gore, wife of then senator Al Gore. The PMRC consisted of many wives of politi cians, including the wives of five members of the committee, and was founded to address the issue of song lyrics with sexual or satanic content. Zappa saw their activities as on a path towards censor ship and called their proposal for voluntary labelling of records with explicit content "extor tion" of the music industry. This is what happened.

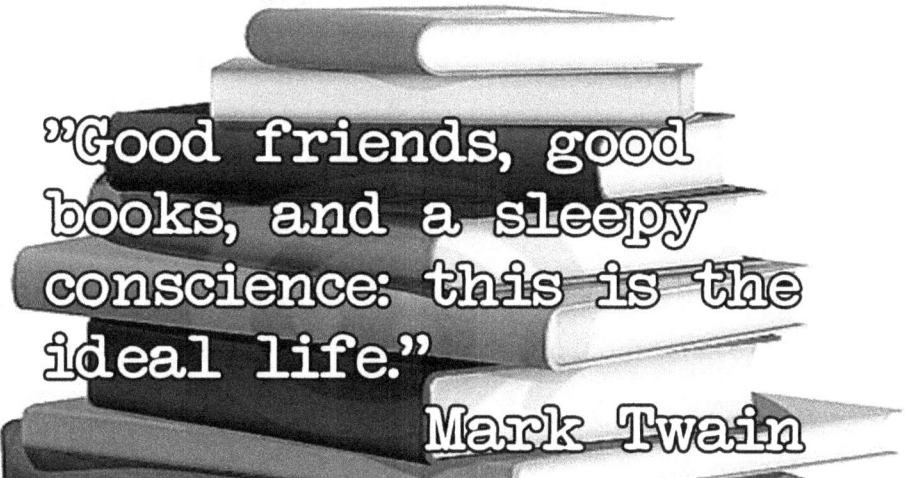

"Good friends, good books, and a sleepy conscience: this is the ideal life."
Mark Twain

.

www.ingramcontent.com/pod-product-compliance
Lightning Source LLC
Chambersburg PA
CBHW071946090426
42740CB00011B/1837